IMAGES
of America

MONTGOMERY
NEW YORK

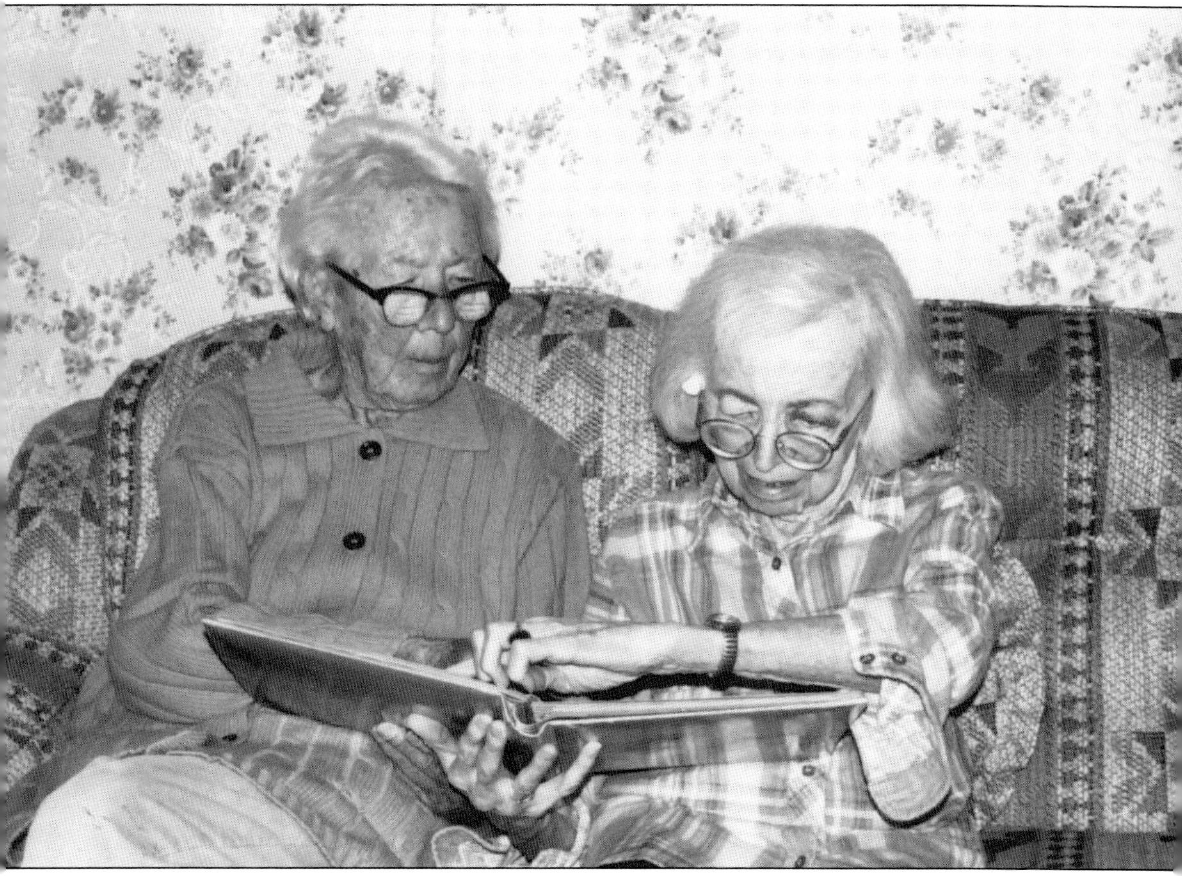

This book is dedicated to Lemma Crabtree and Gertrude Cahill, whose words of encouragement have been a constant source of strength for me. Both lifelong residents of the town of Montgomery, their help and guidance into our town's rich past has been nothing less than inspirational. I will always treasure their friendship and count my blessings that our paths have crossed in this life.

IMAGES
of America

MONTGOMERY
NEW YORK

Robert L. Williams

ARCADIA
PUBLISHING

ISBN 978-0-7385-0096-6

Published by Arcadia Publishing
Charleston, South Carolina

Printed in the United States of America

Library of Congress Catalog Card Number: 2008927343

For all general information contact Arcadia Publishing at:
Telephone 843-853-2070
Fax 843-853-0044
E-mail sales@arcadiapublishing.com
For customer service and orders:
Toll-Free 1-888-313-2665

Visit us on the Internet at www.arcadiapublishing.com

Contents

ACKNOWLEDGMENTS

The author wishes to express sincere appreciation to Louise Andrews, Olive Burnett, Lemma Crabtree, Mr. and Mrs. Roscoe Crist, Robert C. Eurich, Jonathan C. Hawkins, Marjorie Jones, Mr. and Mrs. Thomas Joyce, Agnes Karsten, Monty and Nancy Mathias, the Mead family, Marcus Millspaugh, Alfred Olsen, Ruth Overhiser, Roberta Petzold, Sam Phelps, Ruth Porto, John Roebuck, David Scott, Susan Vanderburgh, Mr. and Mrs. Joseph Weight, Mr. and Mrs. Robert Tweddle, and Mr. and Mrs. Charles Wille for the use of their irreplaceable old photographs. The Historical Society of Walden and the Wallkill Valley, as well as the Maybrook Railroad Historical Society and the First Reformed Church of Walden, allowed the use of their photographic material, which helped to further this endeavor. A sincere thank you goes to Bob Bush, Micky Millspaugh, Roberta Petzold, Ella Orndorff, and Charlie Wille, who edited the manuscript. Bonnie Williams delivered the photographs to Krauss Photo Service of Port Jervis, where they were carefully and professionally handled. The author's parents, Robert and Lucretia Williams, also provided support for this book. Last but by no means least, a debt of gratitude is owed to the many people who shared their memories of Montgomery's rich past. Without their encouragement and support, this work would not have been possible.

INTRODUCTION

Change is a dominating force within today's Montgomery. It seems that scarcely a week goes by without a new building springing up in what was once pastoral farmland or venerable old homes undergoing vast renovations or even removal. As the town progresses into the new millennium, its greatest challenge will be to provide a place in the future for our irreplaceable landmarks of the past and to properly conserve and appreciate those that survive. This photographic history is intended to be an overview of the town's rich and proud heritage. It will show where Montgomery has been, what it still has that makes it unique, and some of what it has lost along the way.

Settled early in the 18th century, Montgomery's first pioneers carved their farmsteads from a vast wilderness. It is almost impossible to conceive how different and difficult life was for them in an area that had no improvements whatsoever. They endured what today would be considered insurmountable odds. Yet, for generations, they survived and consistently improved the quality of life in the town. Some of their sturdy dwellings still stand as silent testimonials to their time and monuments to their builders. Montgomery is blessed in having many of its landmarks, tangible links to an honorable past.

Through the years, the town's forefathers established churches, schools, and service organizations that helped shape the Montgomery of today. When called upon to defend the country's liberty and freedom, Montgomery residents served honorably, and some made the supreme sacrifice by giving their lives.

Change came slowly at first, primarily because of the primitive roadways throughout the interior region. The first significant improvement in transportation occurred in the beginning of the 1800s, when a group of promoters financed and constructed the Newburgh and Cochecton Turnpike. Known today as Route 17K, the road was the first of three turnpikes that stimulated growth in the region. The Newburgh and Cochecton allowed early pioneers easy access to the markets of Newburgh and to other towns up and down the Hudson River.

Shortly after the Civil War, a rail line was built from Goshen to the village of Montgomery. It was later extended to Walden, the industrial hub of the town, and north to Kingston. With the completion of the rail line, Montgomery began to awaken from its long and peaceful slumber as an isolated community. City dwellers flocked to the region in search of fresh air and relaxation. They often boarded with local farmers who opened their homes to supplement their income. In the 1880s, another rail line was constructed through the southeastern portion of the town, which brought significant development into what later became the village of Maybrook.

As the town developed, its three villages and crossroads hamlets thrived. Mills, general stores, and blacksmith shops opened to support the agricultural base. The village of Montgomery, which was not formally incorporated until 1810, had the deepest roots of the three hamlets, going back to the mid-1700s. It was initially called Wards Bridge after James Ward, who established a mill on the east side of the Wallkill River and then constructed a bridge to make his mill accessible to patrons on the west side. By the end of the 1800s, Montgomery had fallen behind the town's other two villages in terms of development. As a result, it retained a great deal of integrity with much of its historic architecture, dating from the Federal, Greek Revival, and Victorian eras.

The villages of Walden and Maybrook also were settled in the 18th century, but both developed differently from Montgomery. By the late 19th and early 20th centuries, industry and transportation had transformed them into thriving communities.

In 1812, Jacob Treadwell Walden, a prosperous New York City shipping merchant, visited the area and fully recognized the manufacturing potential of the high falls. He purchased the Erwin stone house, along with surrounding properties on North Montgomery Street, and made it his home. He and others encouraged manufacturers to move to the area. By the late 1800s, Walden had become a prosperous manufacturing and trading center, home to large companies such as the New York Knife Works, the Walden Knife Works, Rider-Ericcson (succeeded by Spence Engineering), and Wooster Manufacturing. As the 20th century progressed, these businesses (with the exception of Spence) declined and then vanished.

Maybrook was primarily comprised of farmsteads through much of the 19th century. This changed when a rail line was established through the community in the 1880s. Shortly after the turn of the century, Maybrook became host to one of the largest rail terminals in the East. The terminal disappeared in the 1970s and eventually was replaced, in part, by Yellow Freight, one of the largest trucking companies in the U.S.

In recent years, Montgomery has undergone unprecedented growth. Four-lane superhighways crisscross the region, opening the town's boundaries to the outside world and bringing in new people and new industry. As we pave the way to the future, we must not forget the contributions and sacrifices made by earlier residents who strove hard to make this a better place to live. Today's residents must preserve for future generations the essence of what makes Montgomery special: its surviving landmarks and the surroundings in which they stand. Many of these sites, along with some of those that have been lost, are revealed in the chapters ahead.

One

EARLY ROOTS

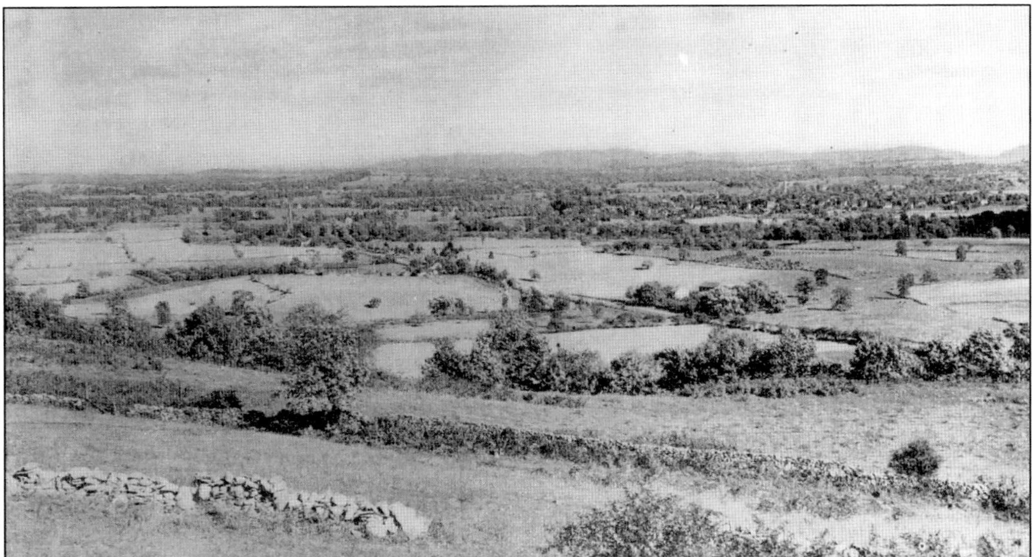

One cannot begin to imagine the time and energy needed to create the cultural landscape shown in the above photograph, *c.* 1906. When the town was first settled in the early 18th century, a view from the Comfort Hills would have revealed a heavily forested terrain. As settlers moved in, they created roadways, cleared fields, and planted crops by hand. They often enclosed their fields with stone walls to contain livestock and define property lines. Many of these walls have survived and add to the character of the area.

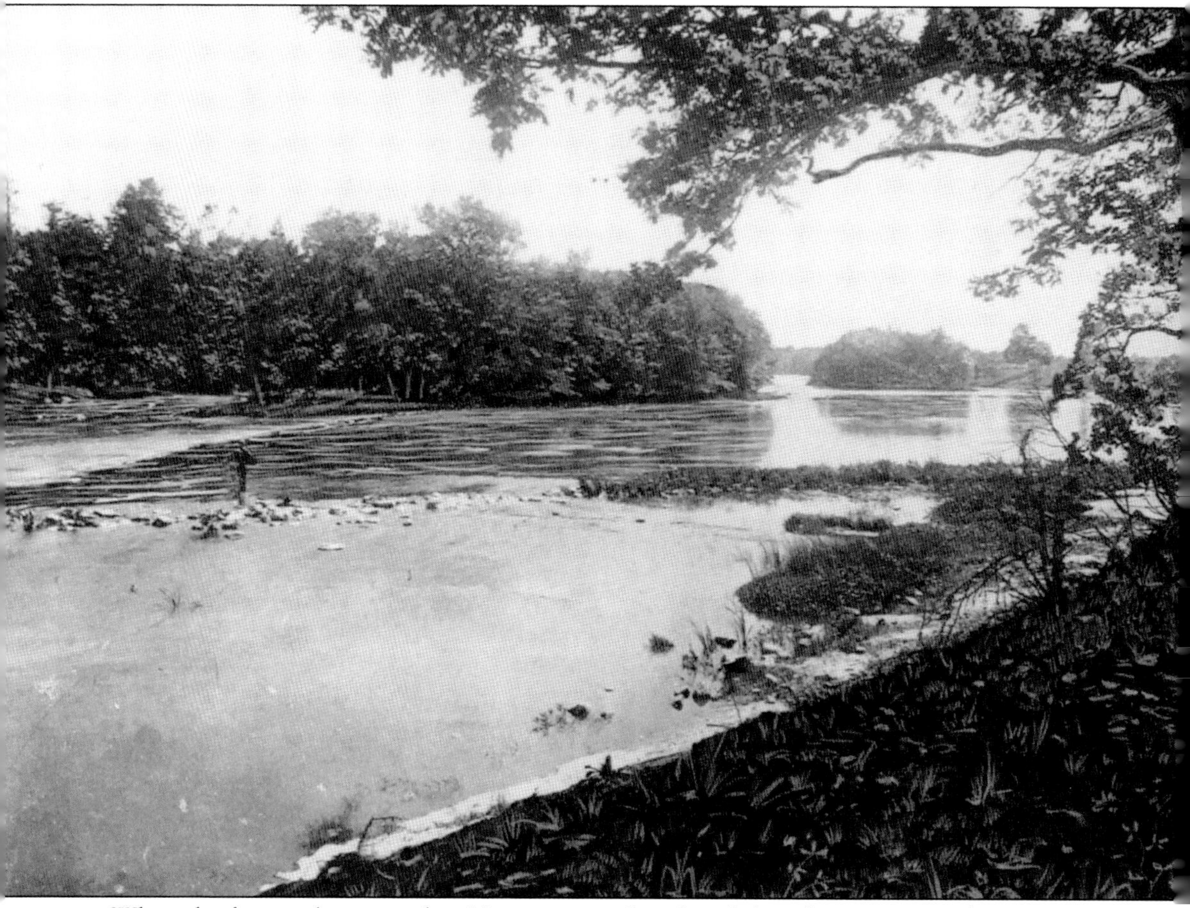

When the first settlers moved to Montgomery, they found that they were not alone. Historical records indicate that *c.* 1727, when Johannes Miller settled on a hilltop off what is today Canning Road, Native-American shelters stood nearby. What is believed to be the last of such settlements in town was located on the Mould Farm on Albany Post Road, near Hill Avenue. This settlement vanished in 1775, when the Native Americans moved to more remote regions. Today, the town contains a wealth of archaeological sites that, when professionally excavated, provide valuable information about the lives of these original residents. Many artifacts have been found over the years along the Wallkill River and offer silent testimony of their existence. This photograph, taken in the 1890s, shows the Twin Islands of the Wallkill, near the village of Walden.

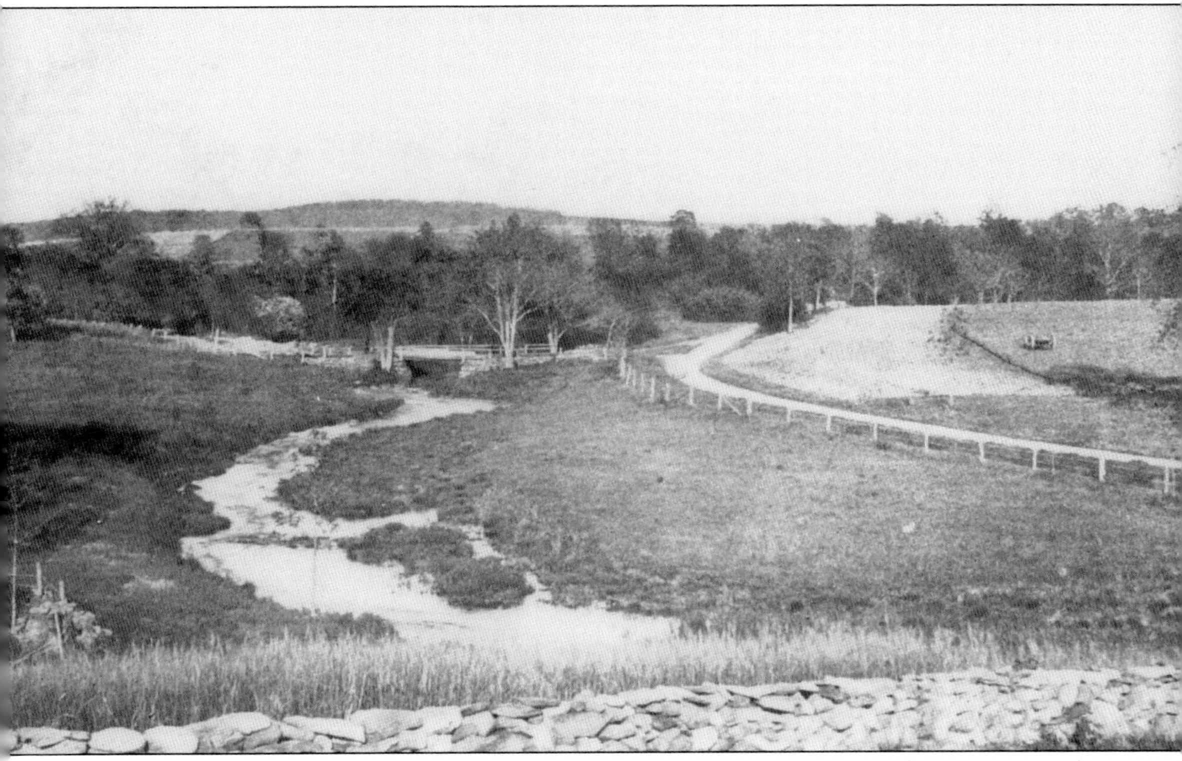

Settlement was slow, but by 1810, the town had a population of 4,710—less than a quarter of what it is today. Initially a part of the precinct of Shawangunk, the town became part of the precinct of Wallkill in 1743. Twenty-nine years later, it became part of the precinct of Hanover. After the Revolution, the precinct was renamed Montgomery in honor of patriot Richard Montgomery, who died at the Battle of Quebec in 1775. This view, *c.* 1900, shows Browns Road to the right and Hart Lane, which crosses Tin Brook, in the center. The 18th-century Haines homestead once stood in this area.

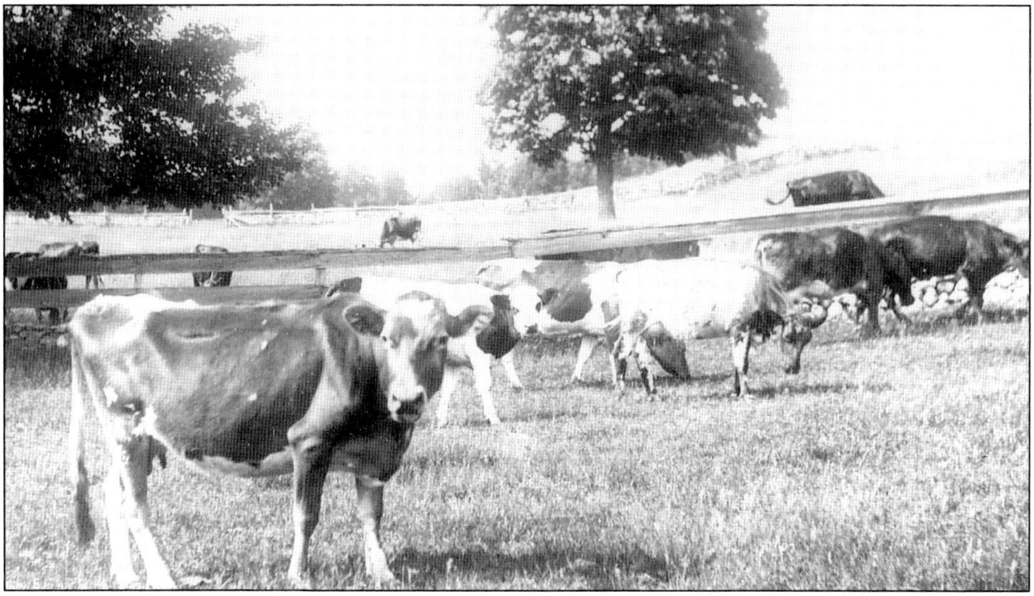

The first farmsteads were small and provided a meager living for their occupants. With the passing of time, fields were enlarged, and new crops were introduced. Many early farms had a cow or two, but not until the latter part of the 19th century, with the advent of the railroad, did dairy farming become popular. This picture, *c.* 1900, shows Dutchess and her herd at the Suydam Farm on Bailey Road. Several large dairies still operate in the town today.

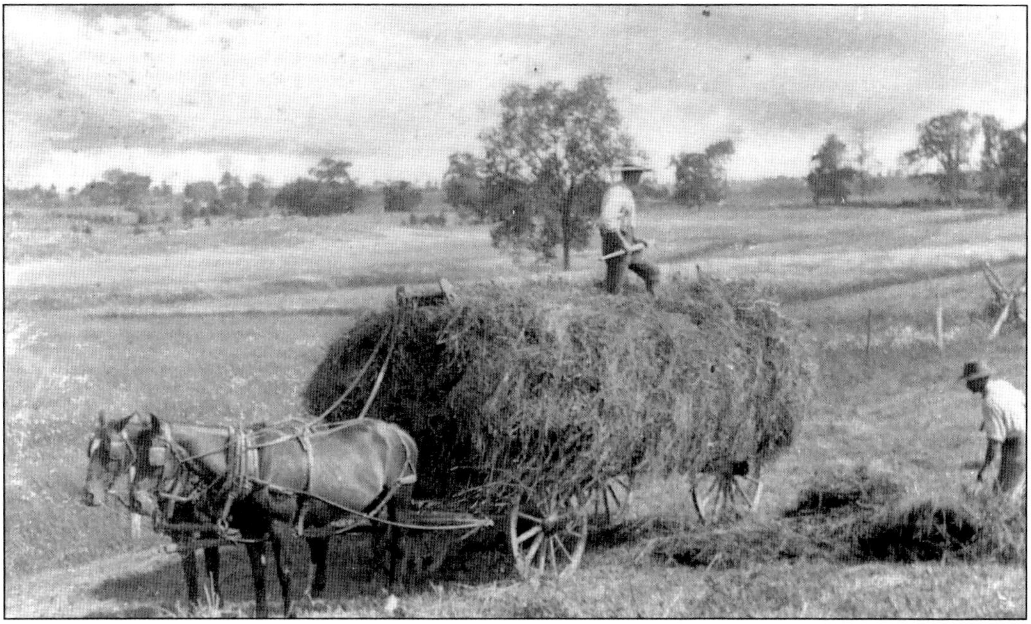

Farming was a rigorous occupation that required an enormous amount of energy and know-how. The normal workday, in both the planting and harvesting seasons, extended from before dawn to after dusk. For years, a good portion of farm labor was performed without the benefit of machinery. This view, *c.* 1900, shows hay being loaded at the Rowe Farm on Dunn Lane. After it was gathered from the fields, the hay was brought to the barn, where it was stored for winter feed.

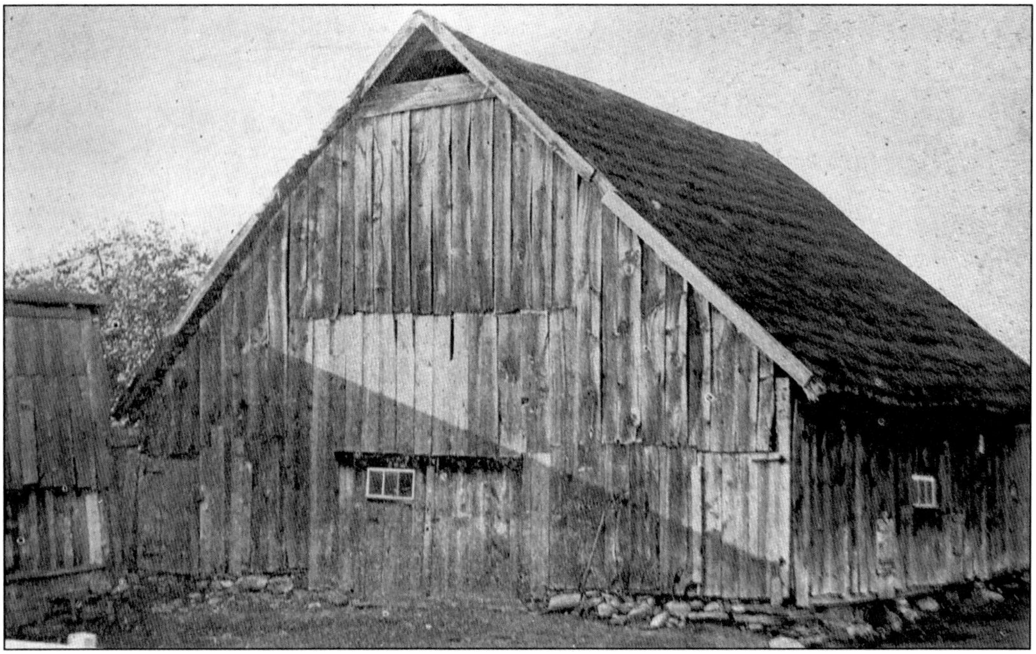

The first barns were small and differed in shape according to the ethnic background of the builder. This rare Dutch barn, with its thatched roof, was located on the Rowe Farm, now the property of Ralph Dunn, a descendant of the original owners. Dating to the 18th century, the barn was removed in 1897. Outbuildings are a vital component of any historical homesite.

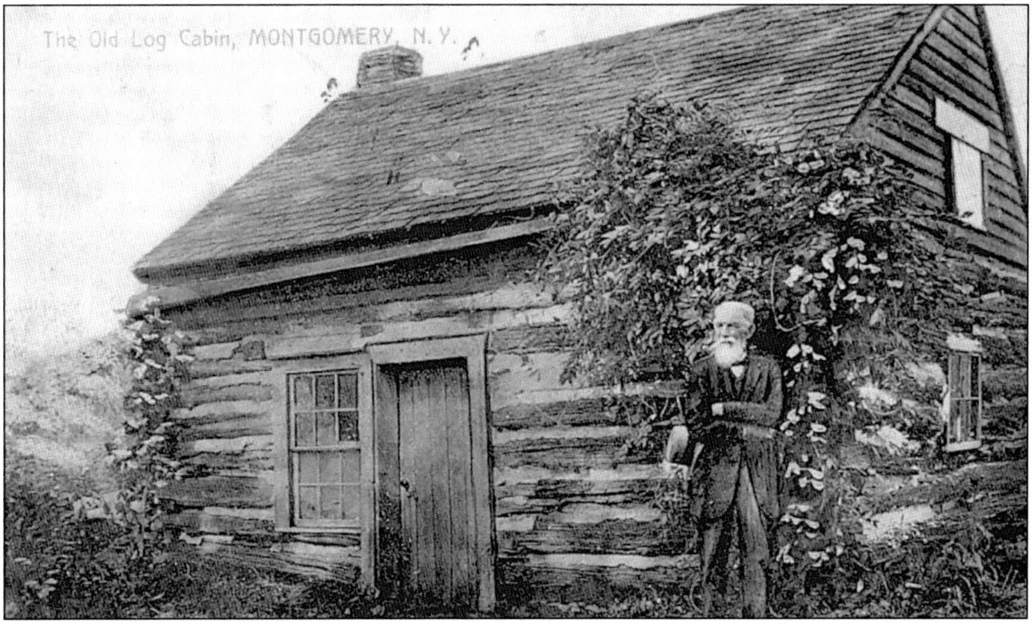

Many of the first pioneers built primitive log cabins. Generally no larger than a room or two, the cabins contained a large hearth for cooking and heating. Living conditions were cramped, but as families prospered, they built newer and more spacious dwellings. This view dates from about 1900, although the location of this cabin remains undetermined. Unfortunately, no pioneer log cabins remain in town.

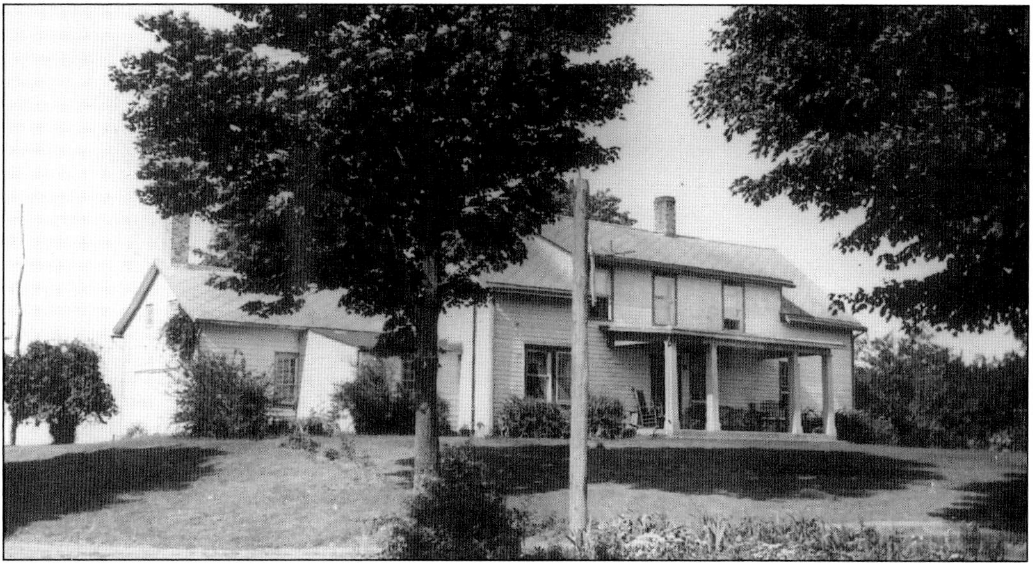

At the end of a tree-shaded lane off of Searsville Road is this farmhouse, dating from the mid-18th century. Known as the Nehemiah Andrews Farm, the name of the original builder has been lost with time. Nineteenth-century maps label it as the Sears Farm. The house has undergone much remodeling but still shows its antiquity in the huge overhead beams on the first floor and in the Dutch doors. In recent years, Montgomery has lost four of its 18th-century buildings.

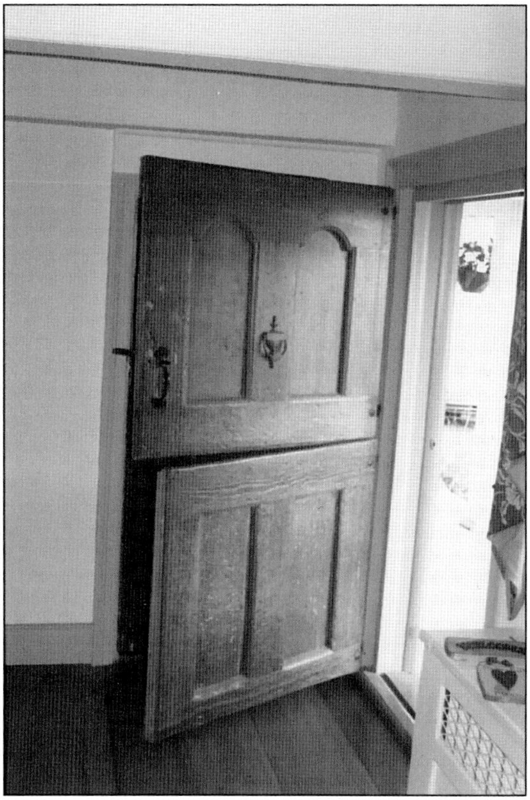

Dutch doors only survive in a handful of early homes around the town of Montgomery. The function of the Dutch door was to allow fresh air into the house by opening the top half and to keep young children in and animals out by leaving the bottom half closed. This view shows one of the three doors at the Nehemiah Andrews farmhouse. Two of these doors contain arched top panels, and all have the hand-forged Germanic-style strap hinges.

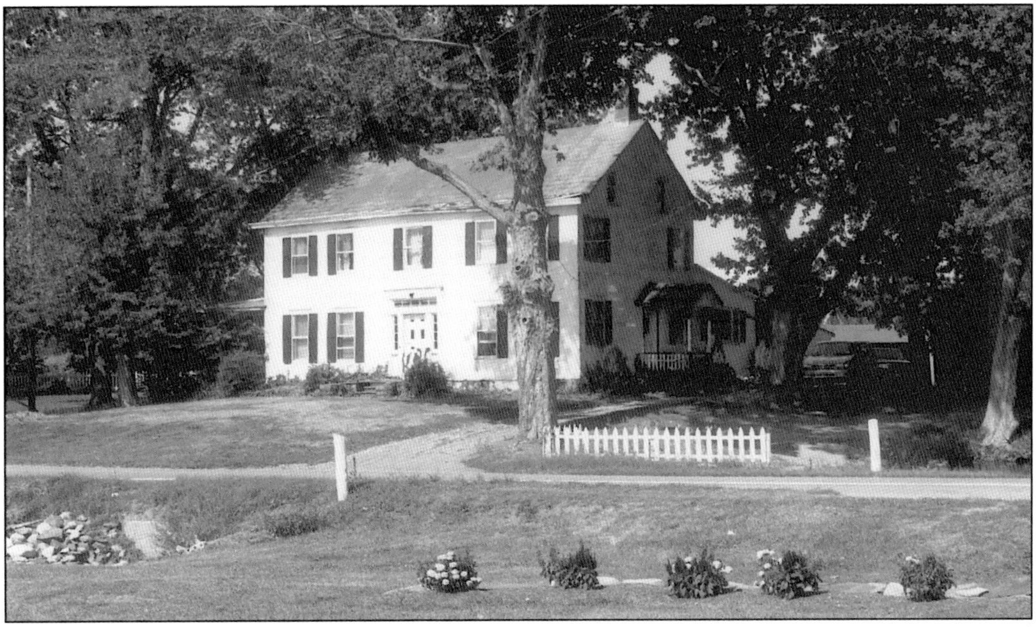

The Brach farmhouse is located on River Road, between the villages of Montgomery and Walden. The building's Greek-Revival features point to the 1830s, but the foundation is much older. The Brach Farm is today one of the largest and most productive in the town, and it provides a pastoral setting along much of River Road.

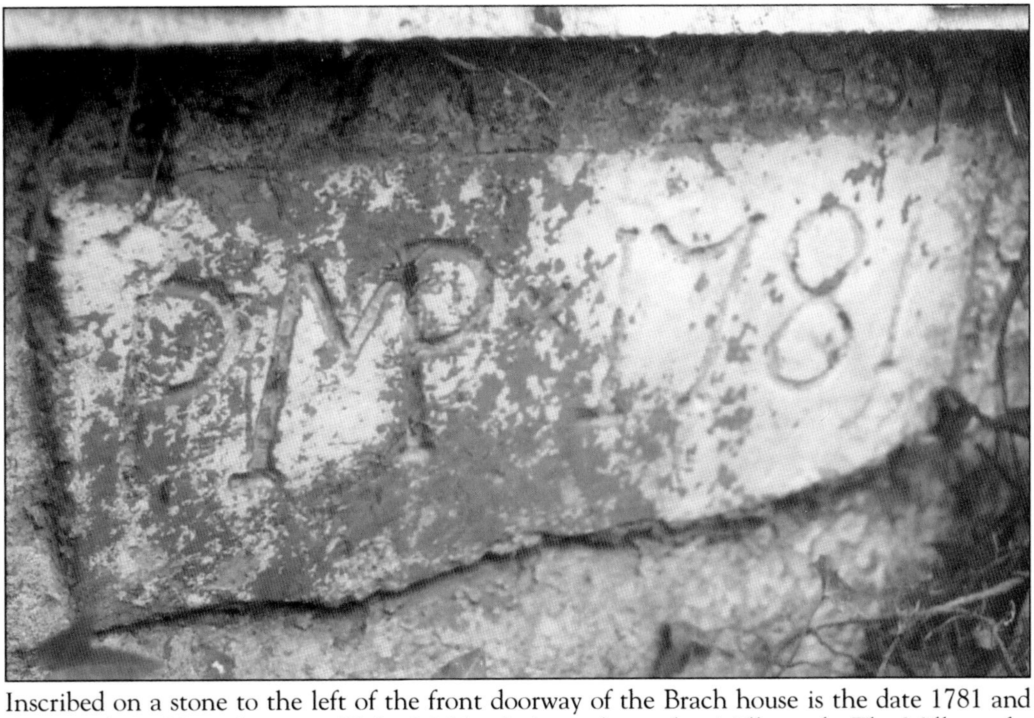

Inscribed on a stone to the left of the front doorway of the Brach house is the date 1781 and the initials P.M.P., referring to Philip Melsbach, later changed to Millspaugh. The Millspaughs were among the earliest families of the town. They initially settled on the nearby Hawkins Farm. Both properties remained in the family for over a century.

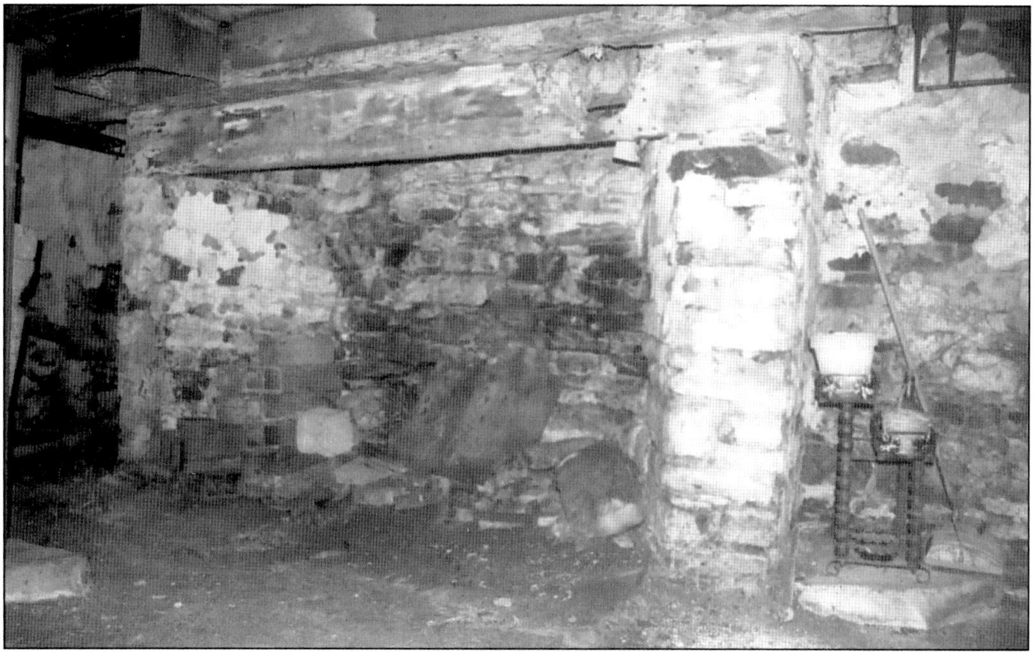

This huge hearth is located in the Brach basement and is a fascinating relic of a bygone era. One cannot help but wonder how many meals were prepared here and how different life must have been for the early pioneers. A preliminary examination indicated that this house was completely rebuilt in the 1830s.

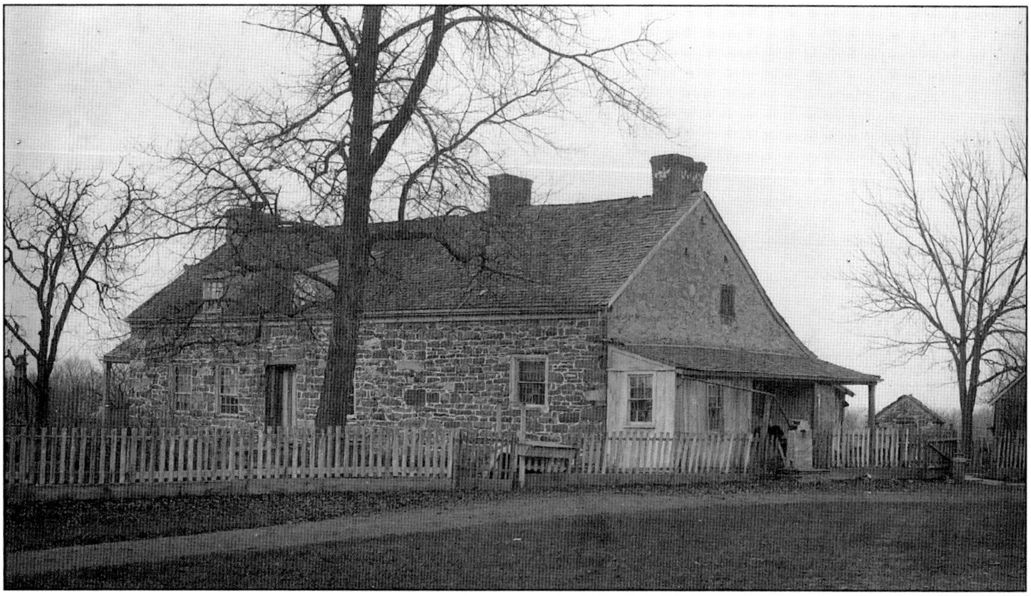

John McNeal was among a small group of Scots-Irish pioneers who settled around the Goodwill Church. Research indicates that McNeal built the original portion of the Van Keuren homestead. Some 30 years later, Henry Van Keuren enlarged the homestead. In 1900, it was extensively updated, bringing it to its present appearance. Recently, developers bought the rolling fields that surround the house and border Goodwill Road with the intention of building there. This will forever change the placid agricultural setting.

Two

GATHERING PLACES

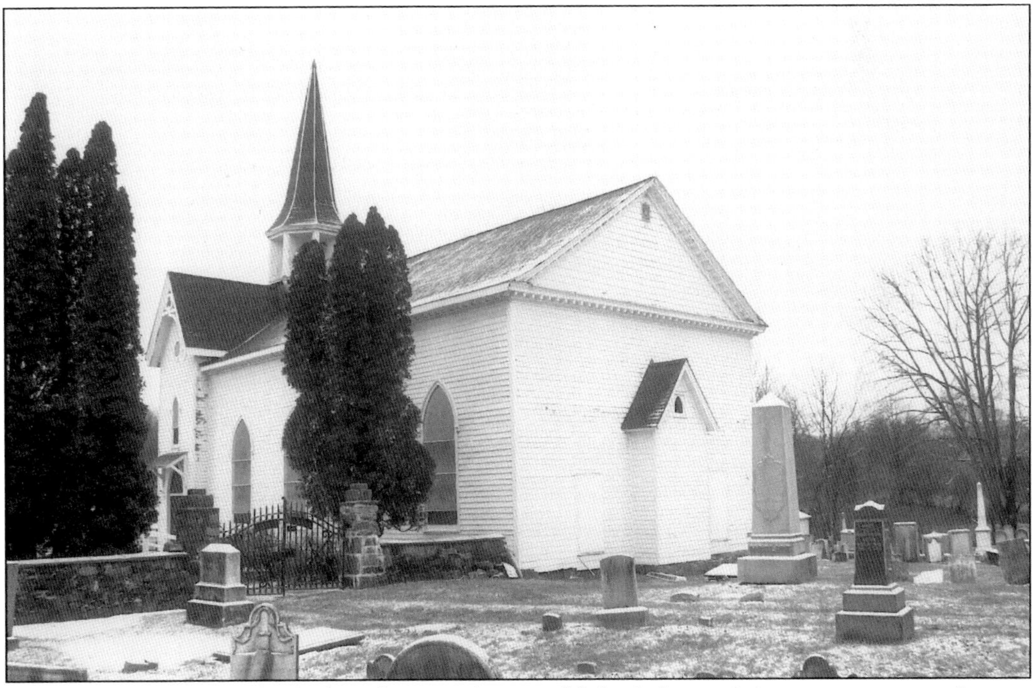

Soon after the settlers built their homes, they established their religious institutions. Among the first in Montgomery was the Goodwill Church, originally known as the Wallkill Meeting. It was organized in the 1720s by a group of Scots-Irish pioneers who had established themselves in the area. The rear portion of the present edifice was constructed in 1765 to replace an earlier building. Over a century later, in 1871, the church underwent an extensive remodeling, which included new windows and a new front block with a tower. In recent years, the neighborhood around the Goodwill Church has undergone vast changes, with office buildings and warehouses replacing what was farmland. In an abandoned field to the rear of the cemetery, under the huge limbs of an old sycamore, lie the magnificent ruins of an early parsonage, dating from 1756. The future of this archeological treasure remains uncertain.

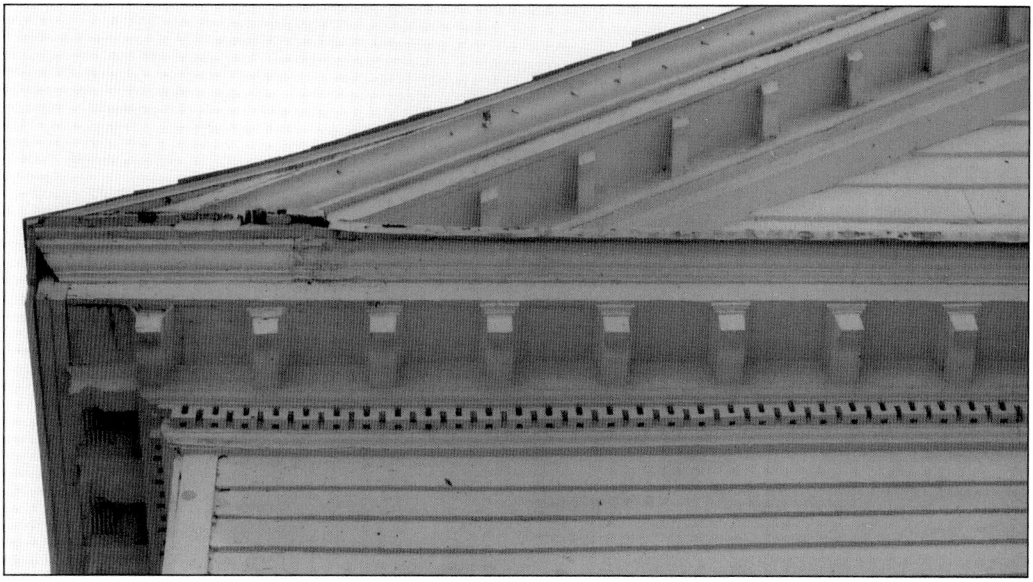

One of the most outstanding 18th-century features of the Goodwill Church is its Georgian-era cornice. Like the rear of the edifice, the front facade of the original building undoubtedly contained a pediment with one or two windows and two entryways below. The cornice design is nearly identical with that of nearby Brick House, which also dates from the 1760s. An entry in Alexander Clinton's diary, dated 1767, refers to the church, noting that "the carpenter had 120 [pounds] for enclosing the house and flooring it and making the sashes and window frames."

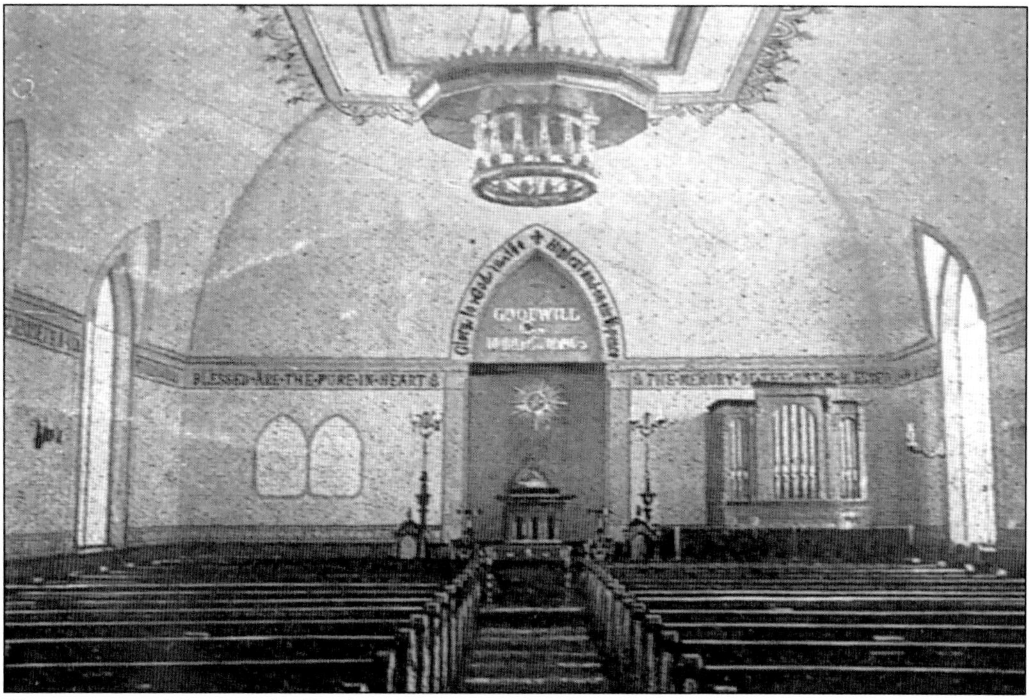

The interior of the Goodwill Church was completely refurbished in 1871 and today contains some of its Victorian-era detailing. This view dates from the 1890s. Note the kerosene lamp chandelier and the curved ceilings.

The congregation of the Brick Reformed Church was organized in 1732. Tradition holds that the first building was constructed of logs and entered from the outside by a ladder so that the group, when assembled, was protected against attacks by Native Americans. This crude structure was replaced *c.* 1760 with a more formal frame building with a belfry and spire. The first Brick Church was built in 1803. It was replaced by the present edifice in 1858 at a cost of $12,541.

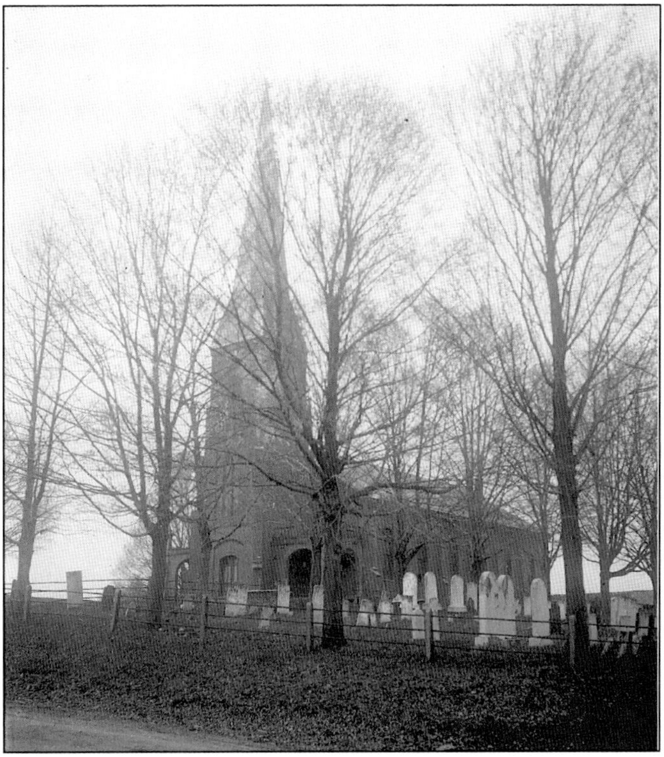

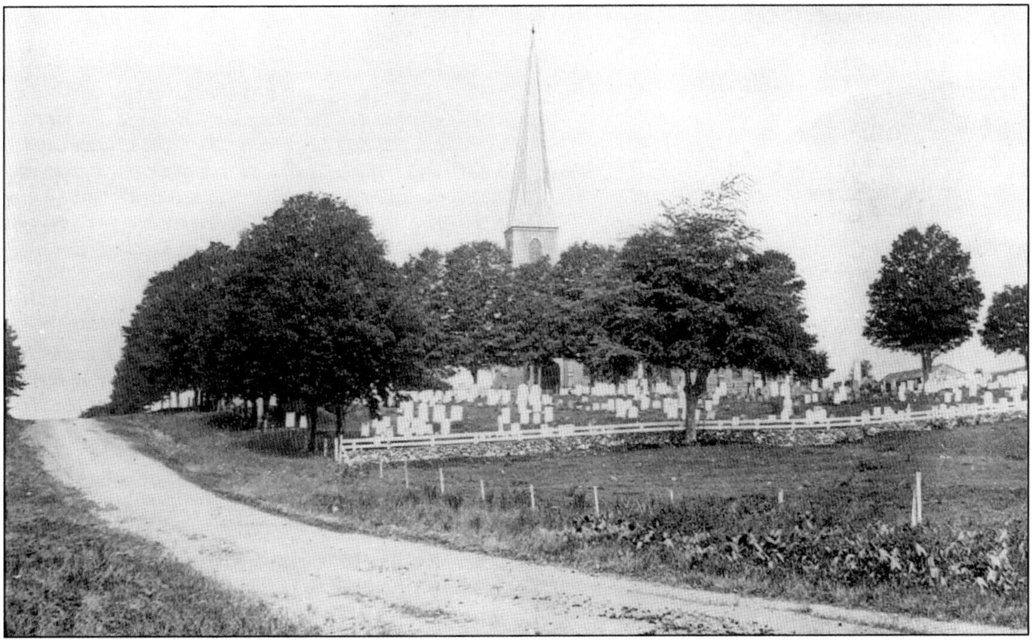

The cemetery adjacent to the Brick Church is one of the oldest and most fascinating in the town of Montgomery. Dating to the mid-18th century and containing many primitive markers, the burial ground was used until shortly after the Civil War, when the newer cemetery farther west on Route 17K was established. A significant link to the town's heritage, it is deserving of inclusion on the National Register of Historic Places.

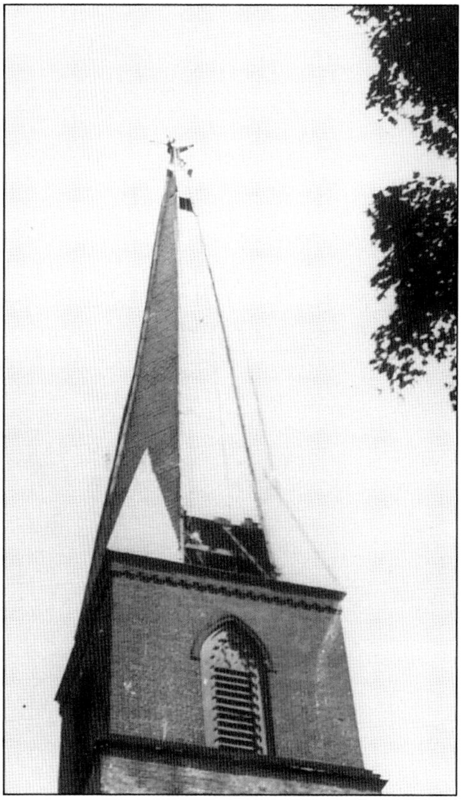

Although initially designed to include a spire, the large steeple on the Brick Church was not constructed until 1880 at a cost of $1,400. In 1925, it was removed for $700 as it had become dilapidated and dangerous. These photographs show the steeplejack, dismantling the steeple in one photo and up close in the other. The large weather vane on the peak of the spire is now preserved inside the church, along with an old bell from the church's earlier building.

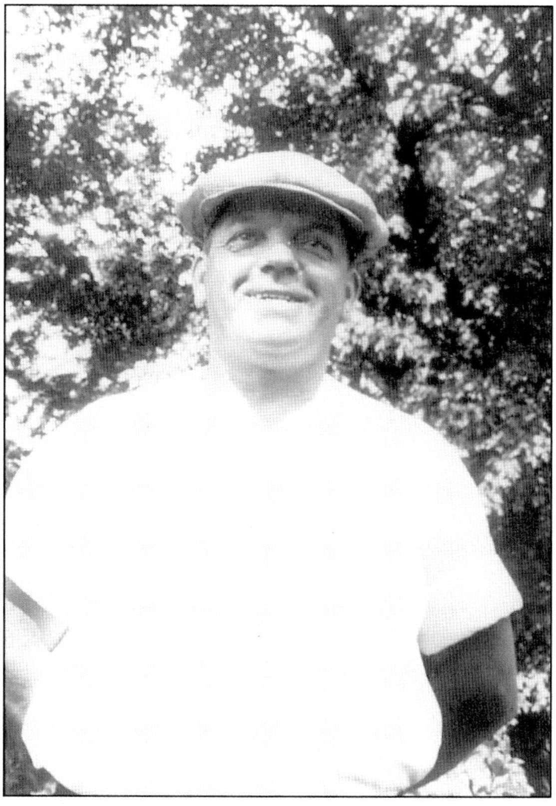

St. Andrew's Episcopal Church of Walden was established early in the 18th century at the crossroads in northeast Montgomery that today bears its name. The first building was constructed of logs and contained a fireplace. Later in the 1700s, as more settlers trickled into the area, a new church was built. In 1826, the congregation moved to the village of Walden. The present Episcopal church, a brick, Gothic Revival-style structure, was built in 1871 to replace a frame church.

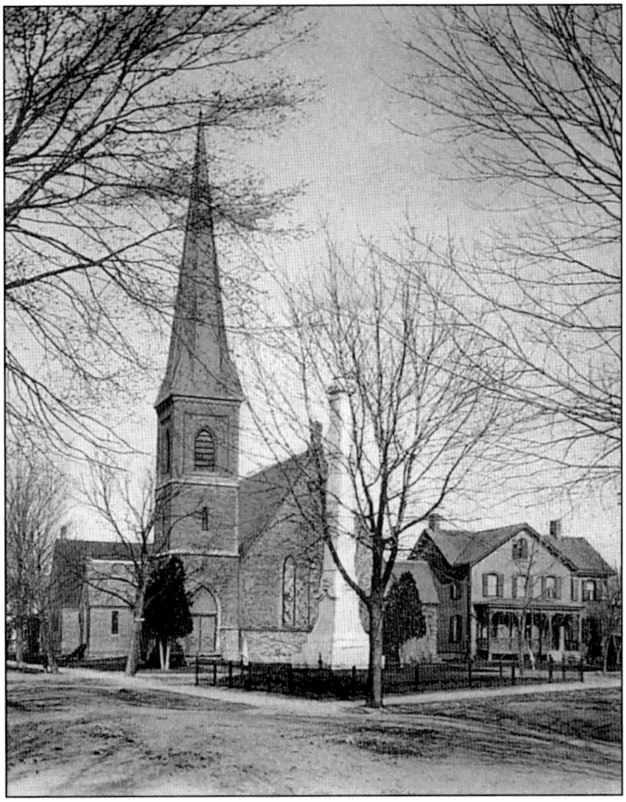

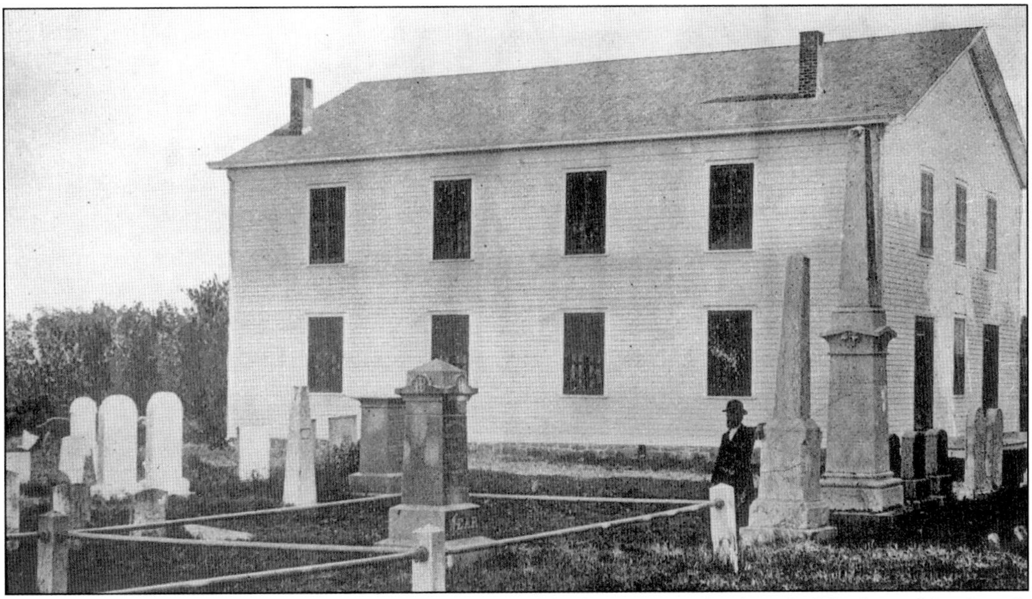

On Coldenham Road, near the village of Coldenham, stands the Coldenham-Newburgh Reformed Presbyterian Church. It was built in 1838 to replace an earlier edifice dating from 1799, four years after the organization of the congregation. Tradition holds that Alexander McLeod, an early pastor, refused to serve the congregation until the members freed their slaves. His request must have been granted, because he served at the church for a number of years.

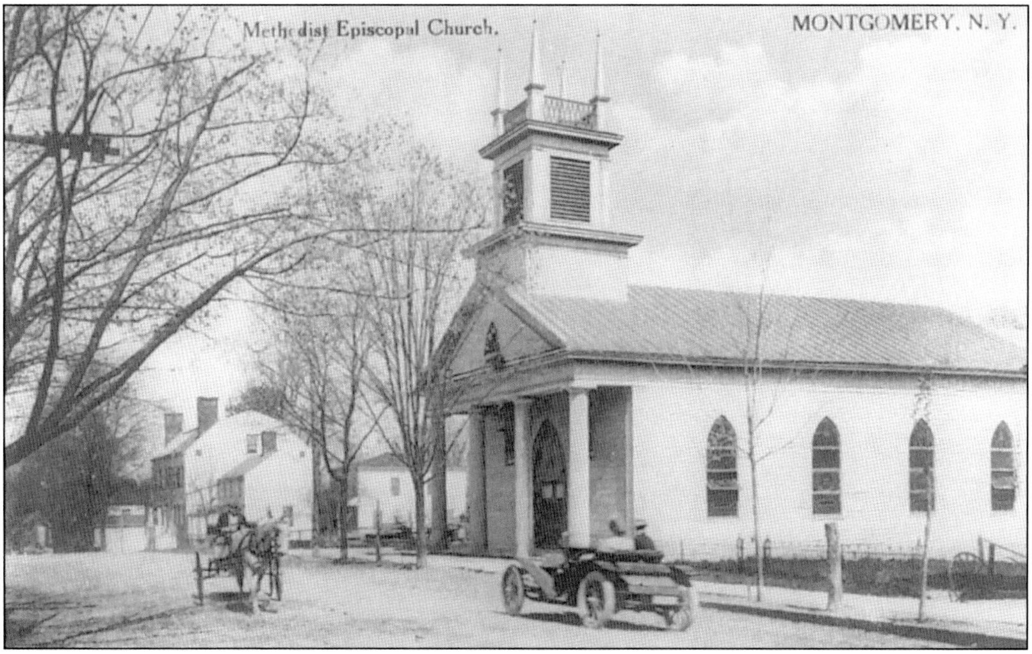

The large building on the east corner of Clinton Street and Wallkill Avenue in the village of Montgomery served as the Methodist church. Early histories reveal that the first edifice was constructed in 1829. The current building appears to be of a later vintage and was probably built about 1840. It was updated around the turn of the 20th century. The Methodist congregation has long since disbanded, and today the building has been renamed Wesley Hall. It currently serves as a center for Montgomery's senior citizens.

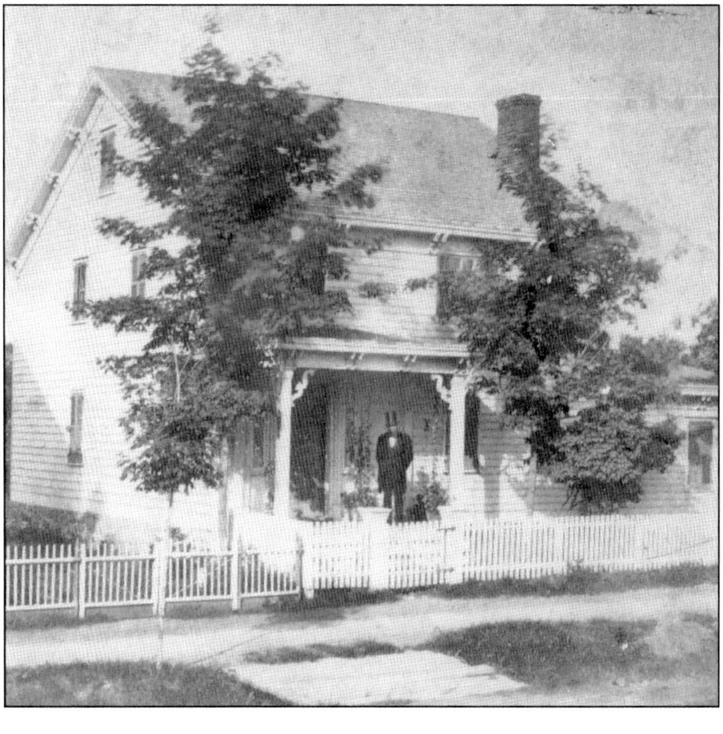

East of Wesley Hall stands the former Methodist parsonage, built in the fall of 1833. This photograph, taken by local photographer G.B. Barnes, shows the building as it appeared in the 1870s, shortly after it had acquired some Victorian-era detailing. Today the parsonage is a private residence.

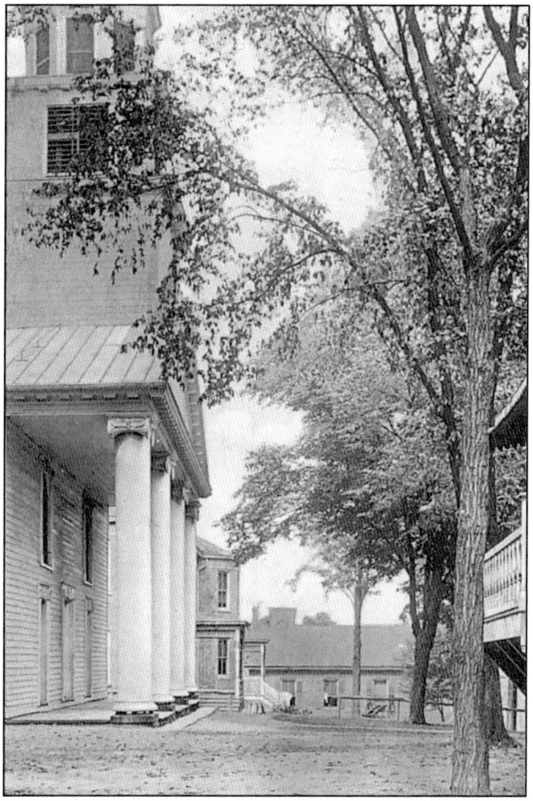

Diagonally opposite Wesley Hall is the First Presbyterian Church, a magnificent example of vernacular Greek Revival architecture. The cornerstone bears the date of July 19, 1831. A large rear wing was added late in the 19th century. These postcard views, *c.* 1900, show the adjacent bandstand (barely visible at the far right in the photograph at right), which for many years offered entertainment.

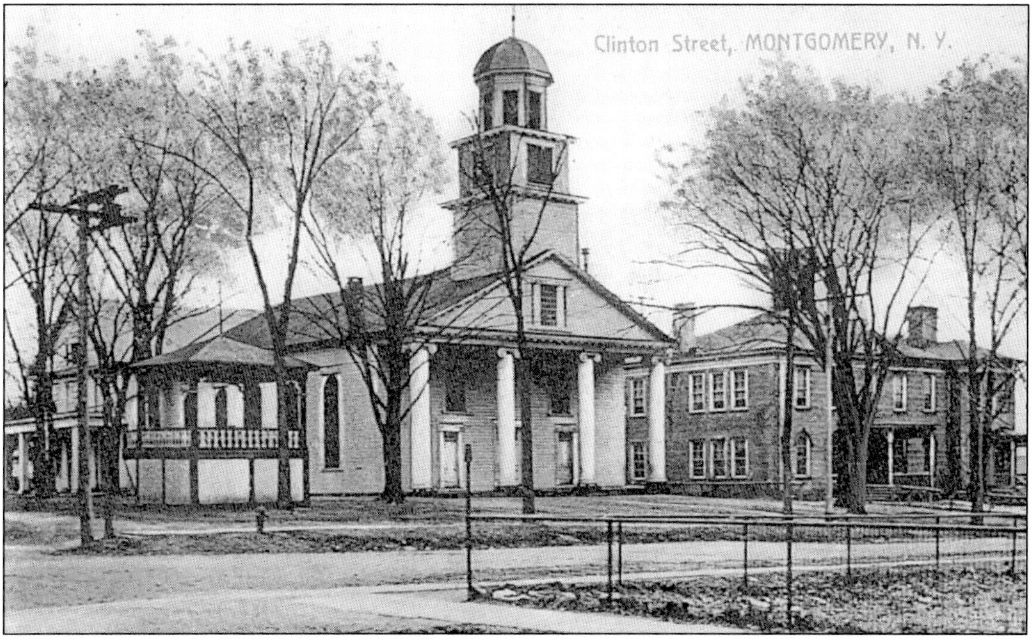

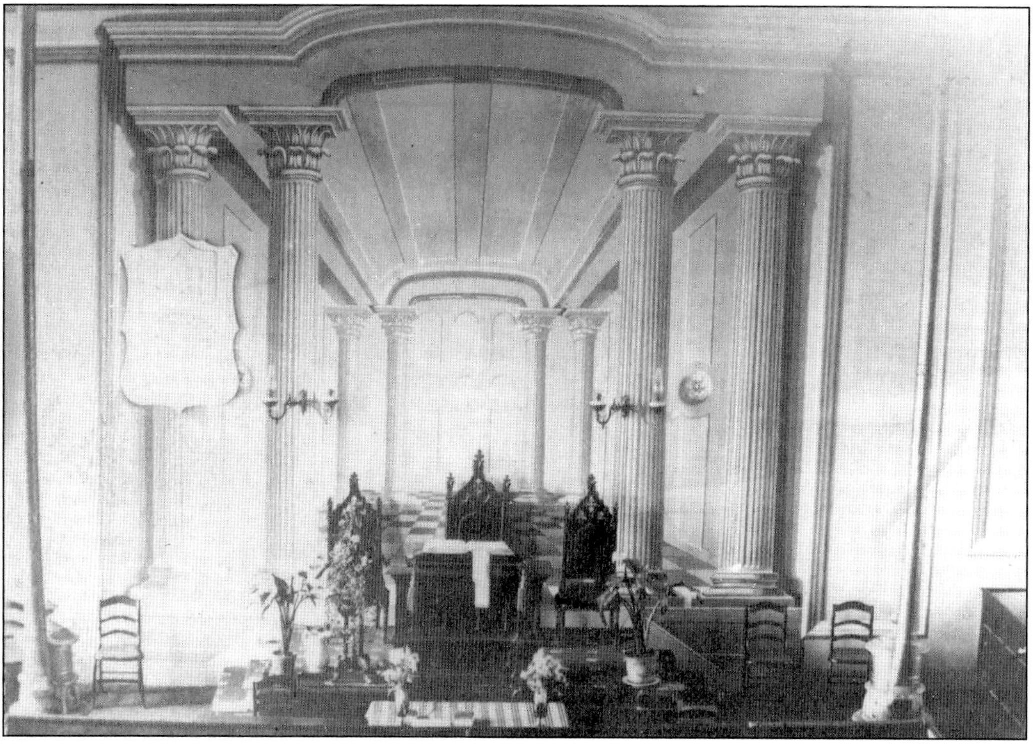

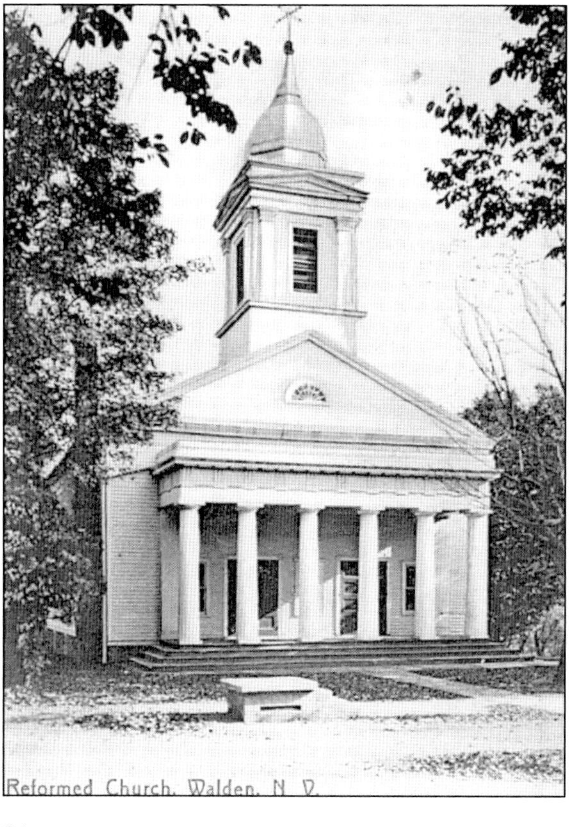

The interior of the Montgomery Presbyterian Church contained beautiful painted finishes on the walls and ceiling. This technique, known as trompe l'oeil, uses paint on flat wall surfaces to create the illusion of three-dimensional architectural details. Note the illusion of a hallway behind the pulpit. This G.B. Barnes photograph dates from the 1870s.

High on a hill in the village of Walden is the First Reformed Church. Built from 1835 to 1838 at a cost of $12,000, the church was dedicated by the Rev. Thomas Dewitt, D.D., of New York City. Shortly thereafter, a parsonage was constructed adjacent to the church. It was enlarged and updated during the Victorian era with a mansard roof and new windows. This view of the church dates from *c.* 1900.

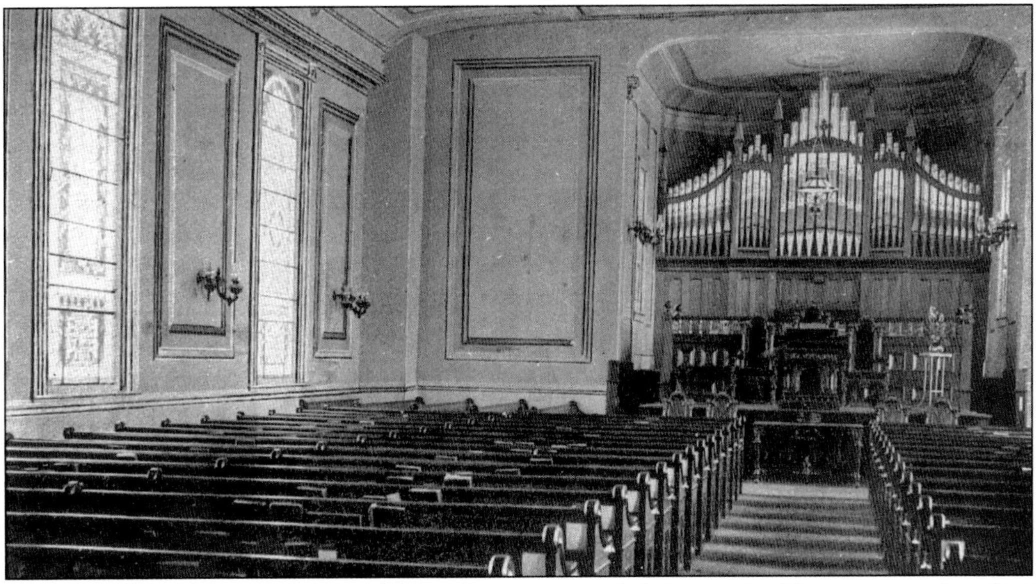

The interior of the First Reformed Church was remodeled during the Victorian era. Installed were stained-glass windows, new pews, a new pulpit, and a new pipe organ to replace the small melodeon. Note the painted finishes on the walls and ceiling, similar to those in the Montgomery Presbyterian Church. A tablet in the church foundation states that the edifice was enlarged in 1886 and 1896. This photograph dates from that decade.

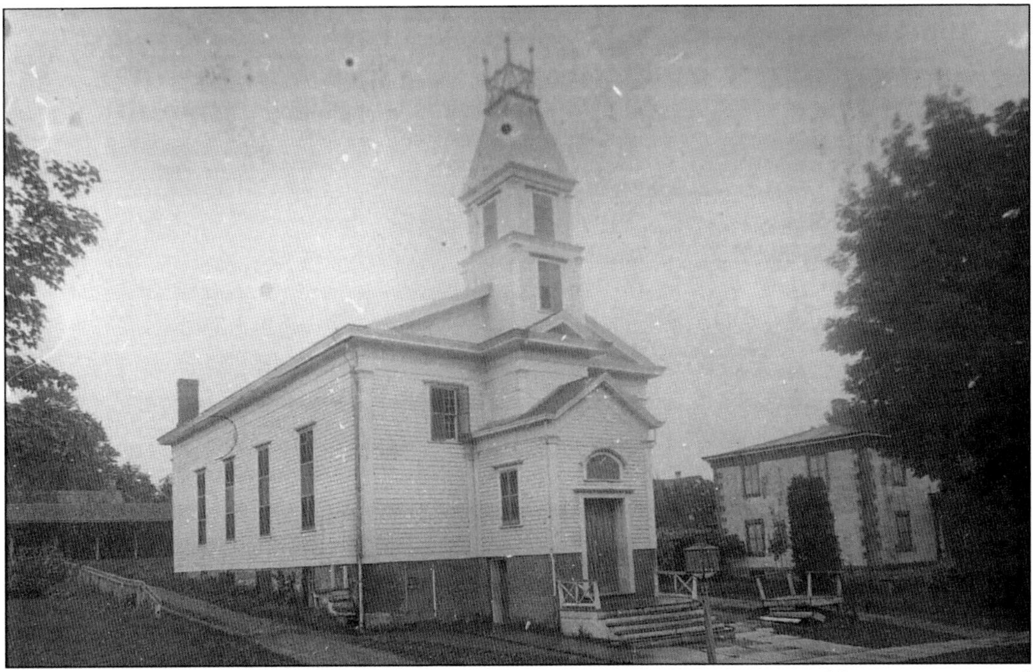

Dating to the 1830s, this beautiful church stood on West Main Street in Walden. It was created as a result of a division of the Reformed Presbyterian Church in Coldenham. Known as Beattie's Church (William Beattie had the building erected chiefly at his own expense.), it remained a Presbyterian church for about six years. In 1850, the Methodist Episcopal Society of Walden purchased the church. The Methodists' present brick building was built in 1893.

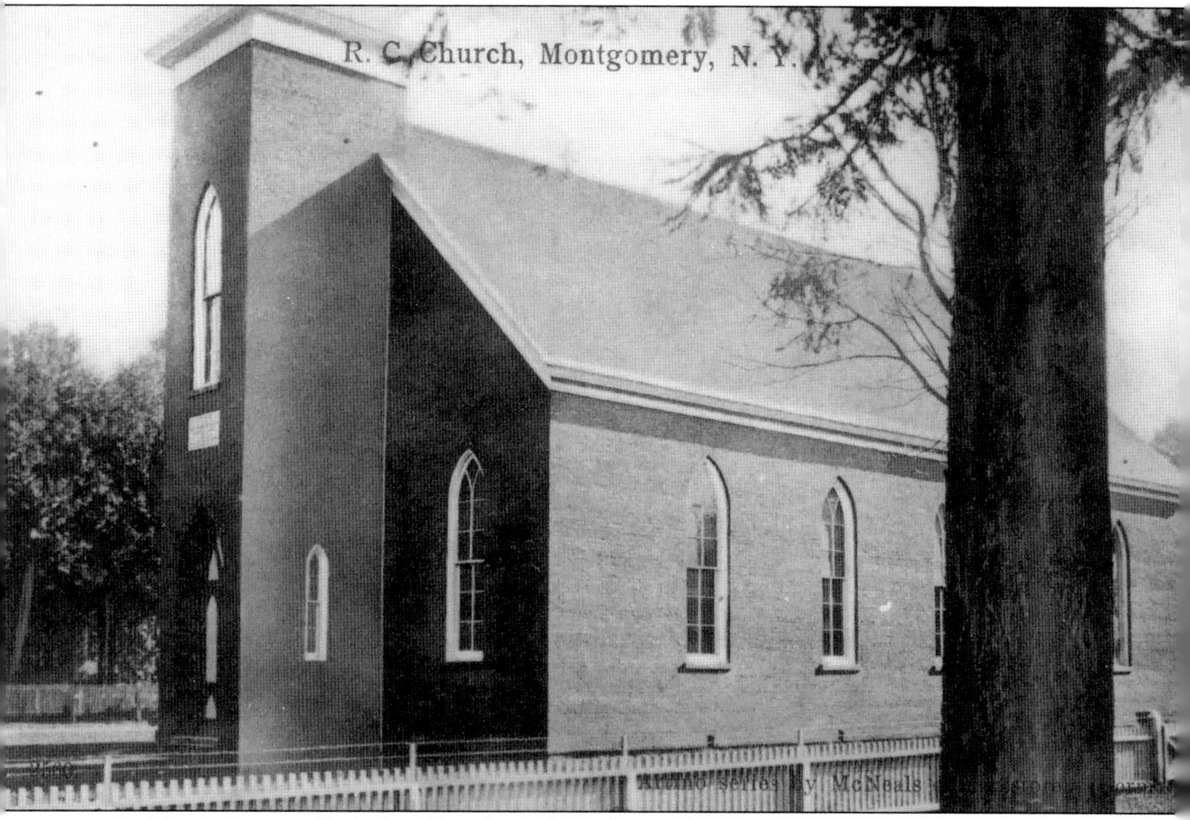

St. Mary's Roman Catholic Church in the village of Montgomery traces its roots to the late 1700s. Historians record that some of the first Masses were held at the residence of Dr. Joseph Whalen, which stood on the corner of Albany Post Road and Route 17K. By 1864, the Rev. Hugh O'Hare arrived in the village to organize a parish. Four years later, a handsome brick church was built on Union Street. Patterned in the ornate slate roof was the wording "Sancta Maria." This view dates from 1905. A tower and stained-glass windows were added to the church *c.* 1913.

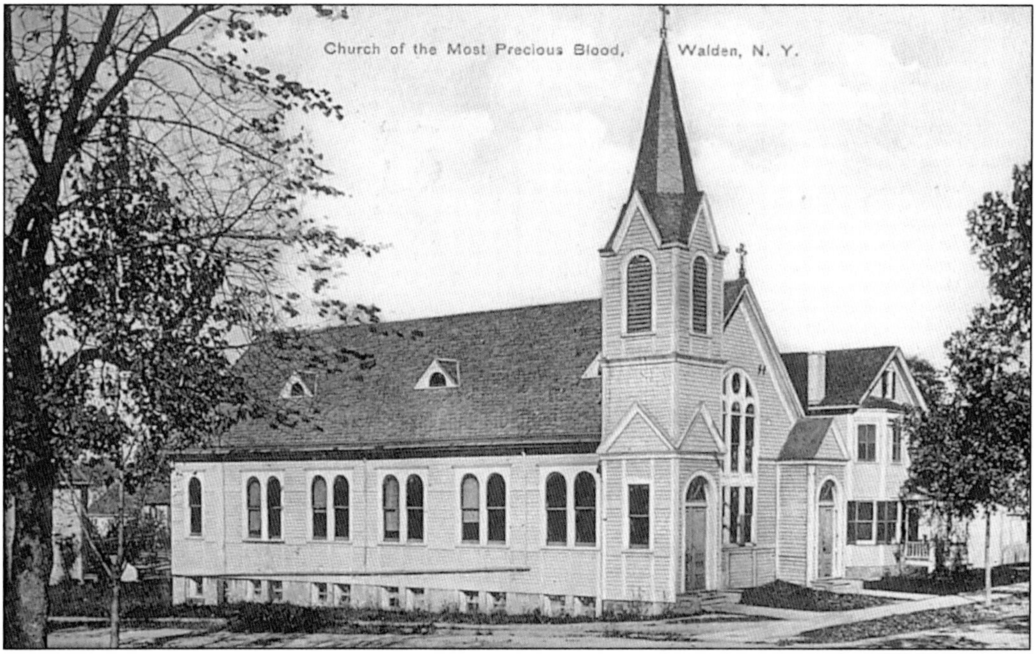

Walden's Church of the Most Precious Blood, located on Walnut Street, was established in 1887. Until the church edifice was completed in the mid-1890s, Masses were held in Lustig's and Condon's Halls. In 1952, this Victorian building was torn down and replaced with the present brick building.

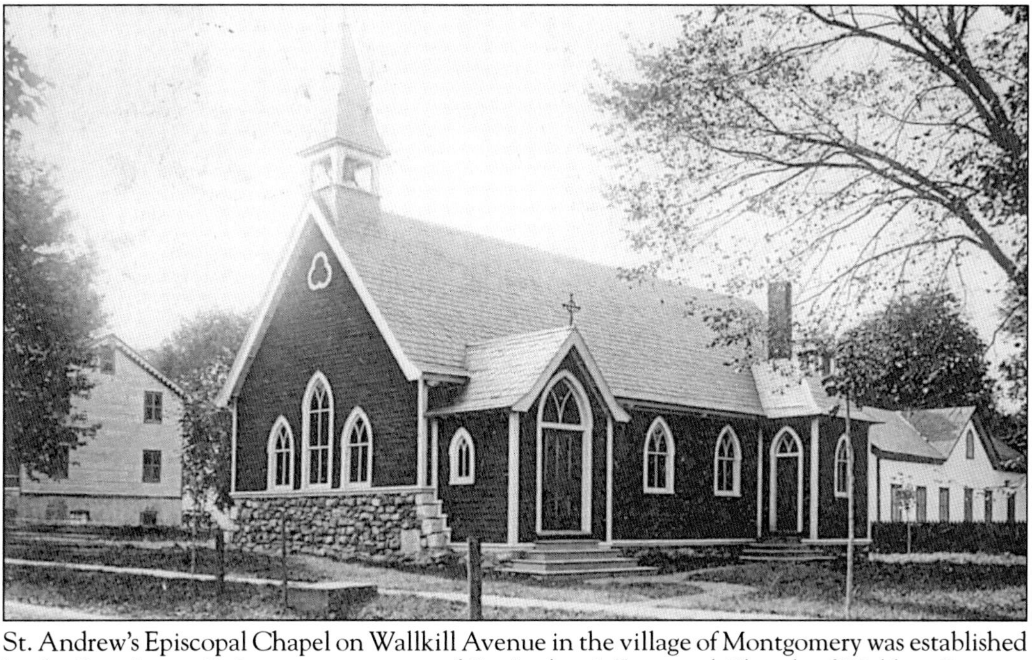

St. Andrew's Episcopal Chapel on Wallkill Avenue in the village of Montgomery was established by the Rev. James G. Lewis as a mission of St. Andrew's Episcopal Church of Walden. Services were first held in a building on Charles Street. The cornerstone of the present building was laid in 1903. St. Andrew's remained a mission until 1955, when it became a self-sustaining church. The parish hall was added in the summer of 1950.

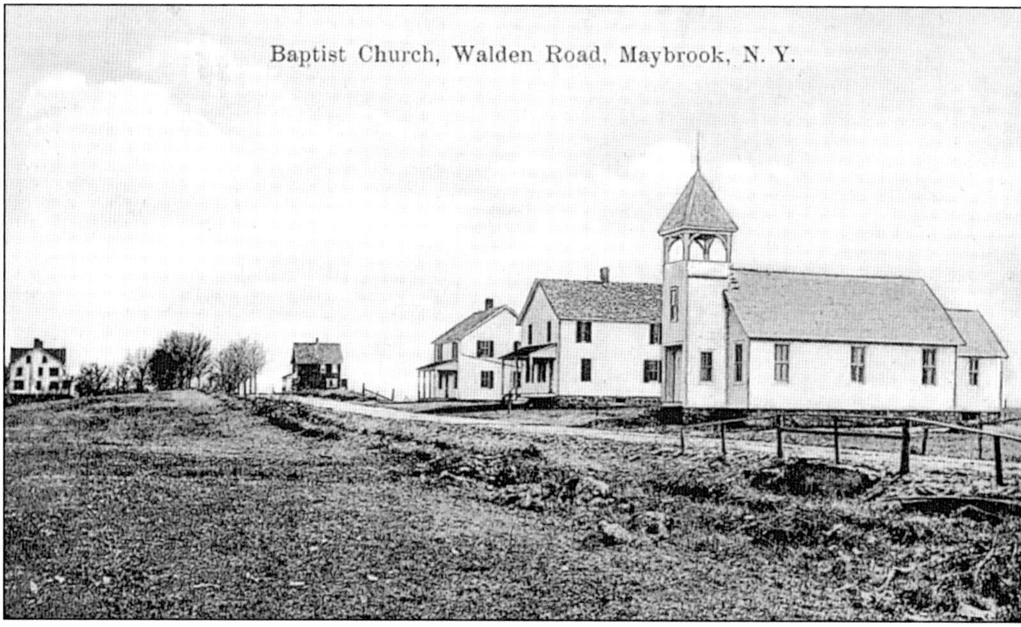

When the Peoples' Baptist Church of Maybrook was built on Homestead Avenue in 1906, few homes stood in the vicinity. Today, the church appears much the way it did years ago; however, buildings have sprung up around it. The bell in the tower was a gift from George and John Morrison, prominent residents of the village.

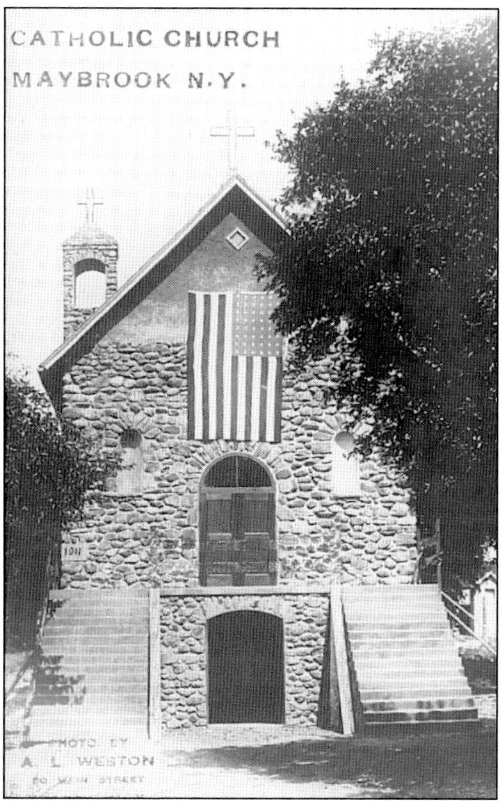

Soon after the organization of the Baptist church, a Catholic church was established in Maybrook, and the current Church of the Assumption was constructed in 1911. In 1924, the Methodist church was built on the corner of Broadway and Homestead Avenue and it is now an integral part of the community.

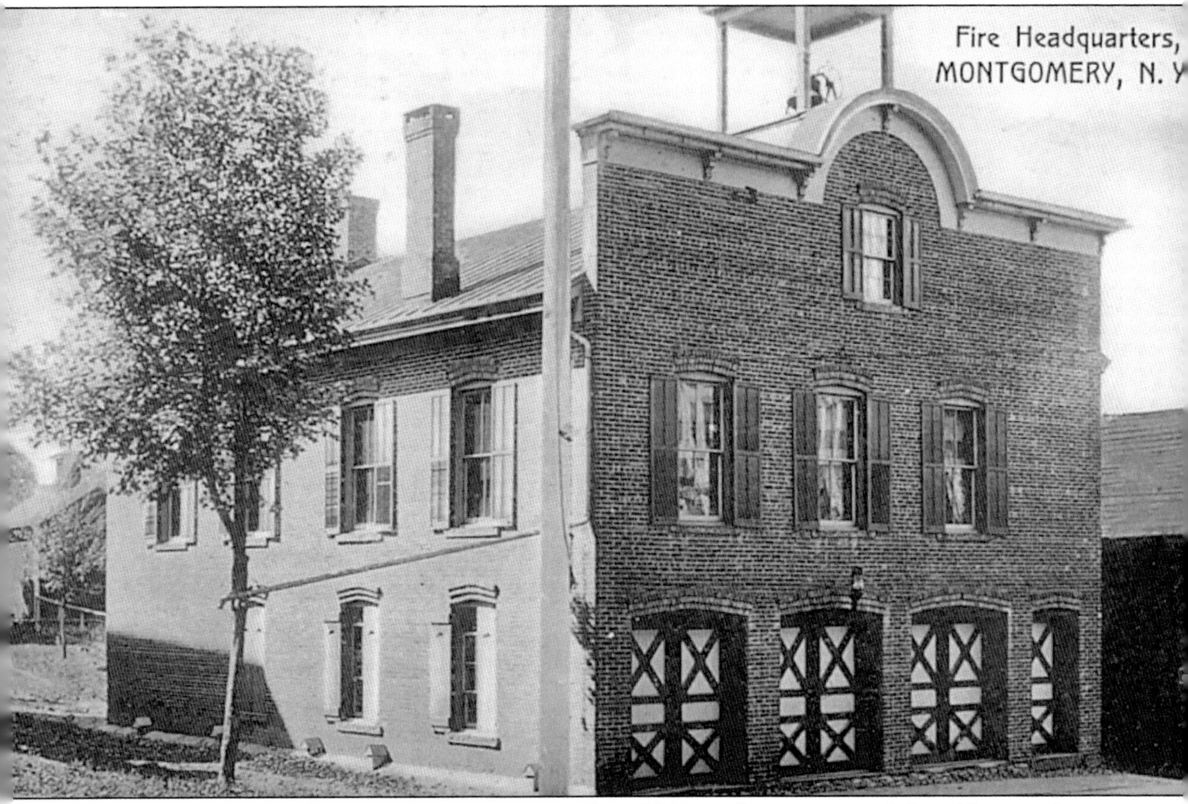

The Montgomery Fire Department was organized in 1810, making it one of the oldest in the area. The brick firehouse, shown in this *c.* 1905 picture, stood on Clinton Street, adjacent to the current post office. Built in the 1870s or 1880s, it replaced a wood-frame structure. In 1913, the adjacent horse sheds of the Palace Hotel caught fire. Flames spread to the firehouse, destroying it. The fire also spread to Montgomery Academy, which was left heavily damaged. Soon afterward, the firehouse was incorporated into the new village hall, which is now the Orange County Firemen's Museum.

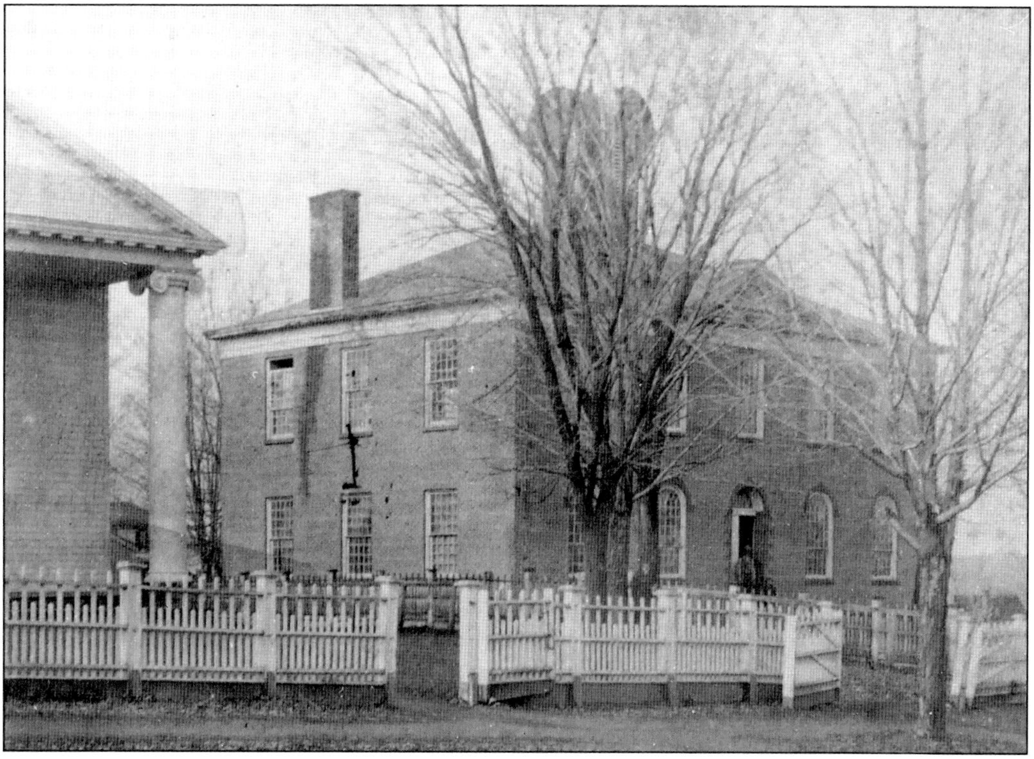

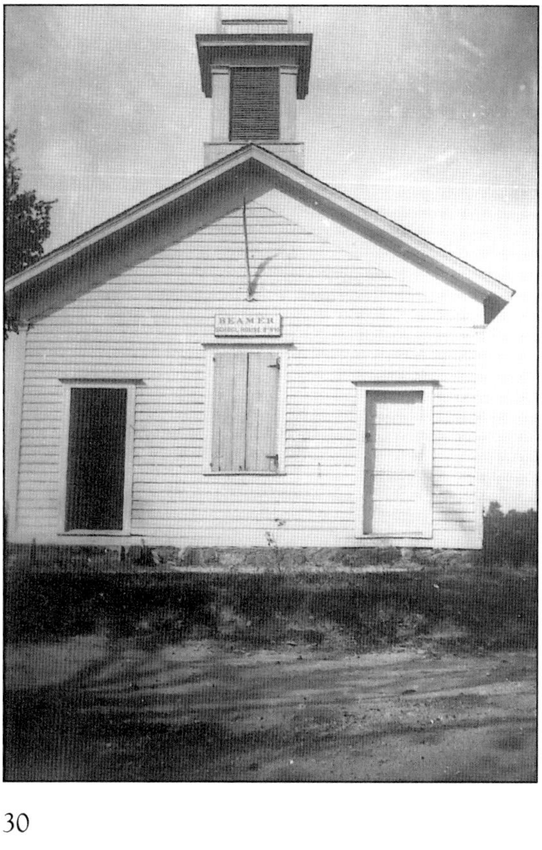

The former Montgomery Academy was one of the oldest public academies in the state. It was organized in 1787 and incorporated in 1791. The academy building was replaced in 1818 by the current Federal-style structure. This photograph dates from the 1870s. During the Victorian era, the building was updated several times before fire heavily damaged it in 1912. The academy was refurbished, and it serves today as a village hall, a reminder that old buildings can be successfully adapted for new purposes.

A 1908 historical account notes that Montgomery was divided into "thirteen school districts, and parts of districts." Of those, 12 had schoolhouses. One of these was the one-room Beamer Schoolhouse, located on a point created by the intersection of Beamer and Albany Post Roads. Standing since the mid-1800s, it serves today as a private residence, with the exterior schoolhouse appearance maintained.

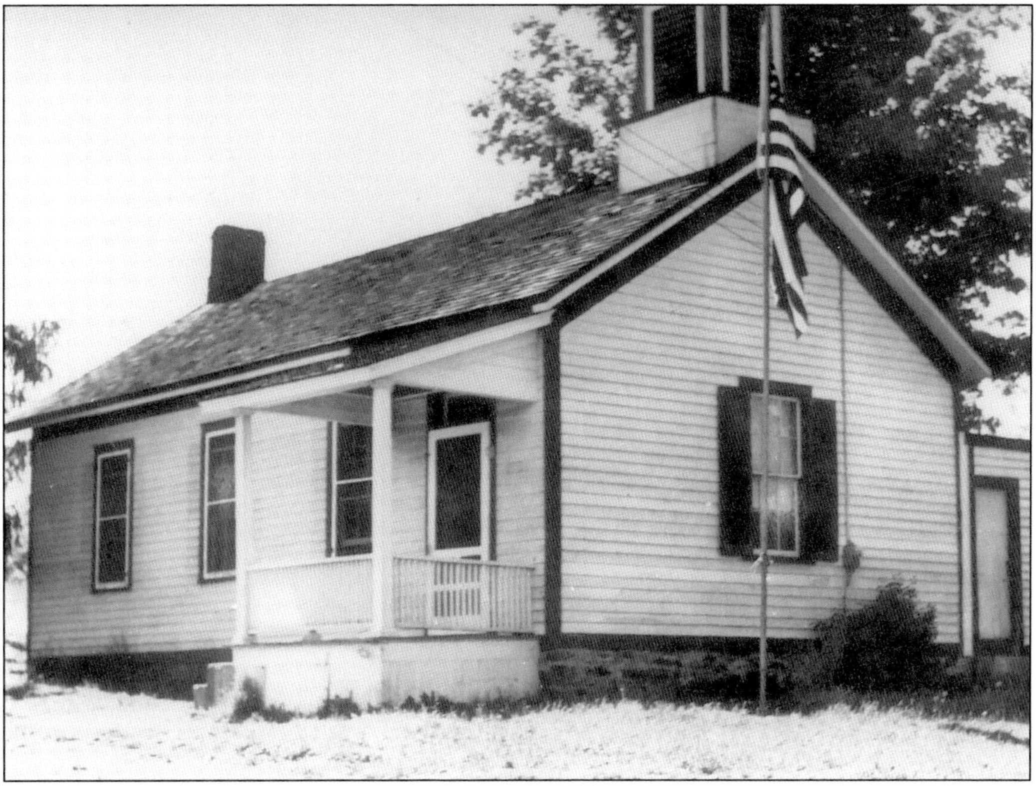

Another surviving schoolhouse, which also serves as a private residence, is the Kaisertown School on Kaisertown Road. Possibly built in the 1870s, it is believed to have replaced an earlier structure. The above photograph was taken in the 1930s and the one below, of students and their teacher saluting the flag, was taken in 1921. Montgomery's early settlers would have found it hard to believe that, in 1907, the value of the schoolhouses and sites totaled a staggering $42,450. One can only imagine what they would have thought of the value of today's schools.

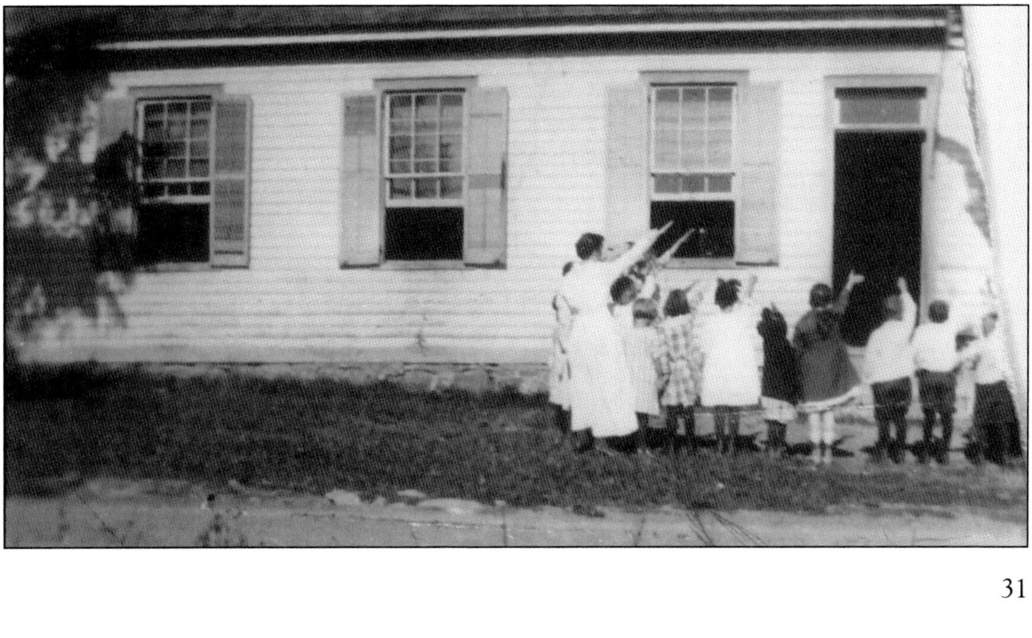

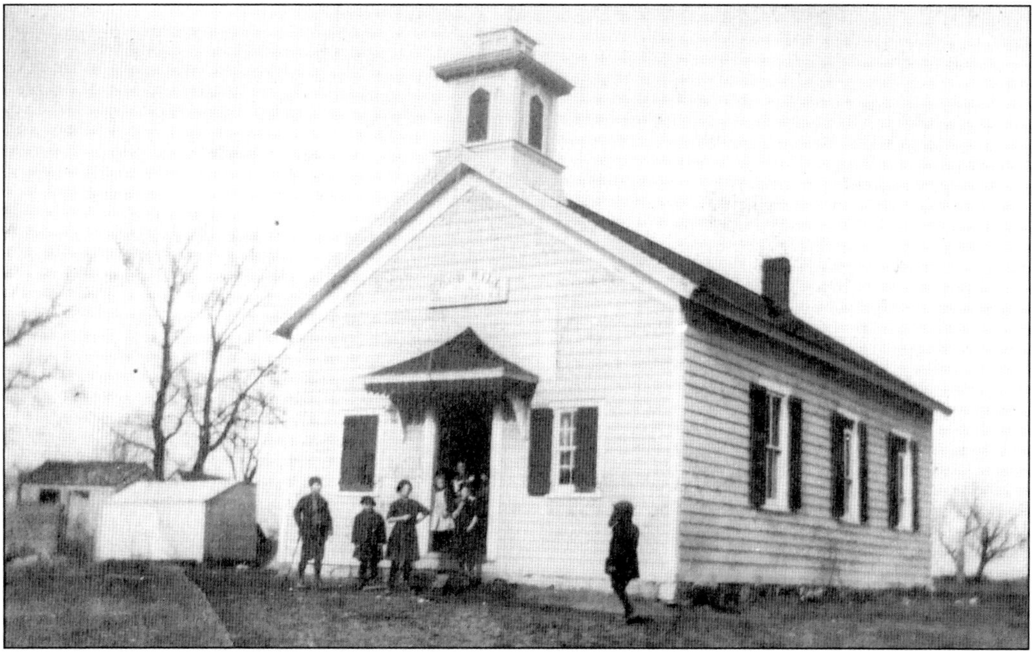

The Goodwill Schoolhouse was located on Route 208, adjacent to the old cemetery. It was included on the 1862 Montgomery Farm Map. This photograph dates from *c.* 1910. In later years, the building was moved, and today it serves as a portion of the Education Center of the Goodwill Church.

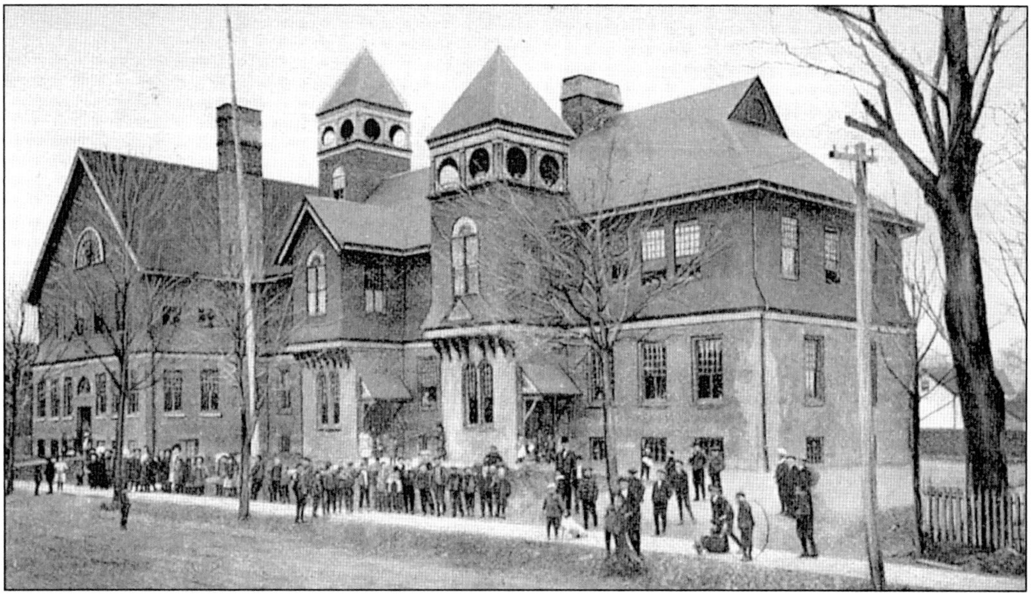

By the late 1800s, Walden had a wide array of manufacturing concerns, making it the largest village in the town of Montgomery. This school on Orchard Street was built in 1888 and replaced an earlier structure. In 1899 a large wing was added to the right portion of the above building. The present school was built in the 1920s on the same site. It included the 1899 wing of the school until 1961, when the old section was taken down.

Three

TRAVEL

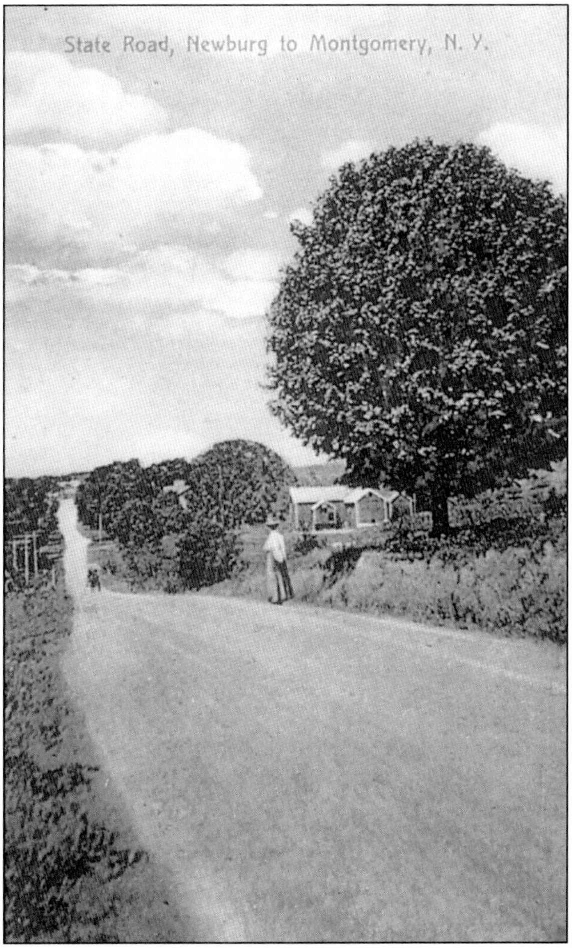

Prior to the 19th century, many roadways throughout the region were nothing more than unimproved paths. As settlers trickled into the area, the demand for improved roads increased. Early in the 19th century, turnpikes were constructed throughout the country. Three of them were built in Montgomery: the Newburgh and Cochecton Turnpike, now Route 17K; the Newburgh and Ellenville Turnpike, now Route 52; and the Minisink and Montgomery Turnpike, now Route 211. Private investors formed turnpike companies, hoping to gain a return on their investment from the tollgates. Residents who resented the tolls used side roads, or shunpikes, to avoid the tollgates. Consequently, few turnpikes proved profitable to investors. However, the contribution made to the development of the area was significant. This 1905 view of Route 17K was taken at the village of Montgomery line. The Patchett homestead stands in the background. Constructed in the early 1800s, this venerable brick building once served as a tavern. Today, it is in a state of disrepair.

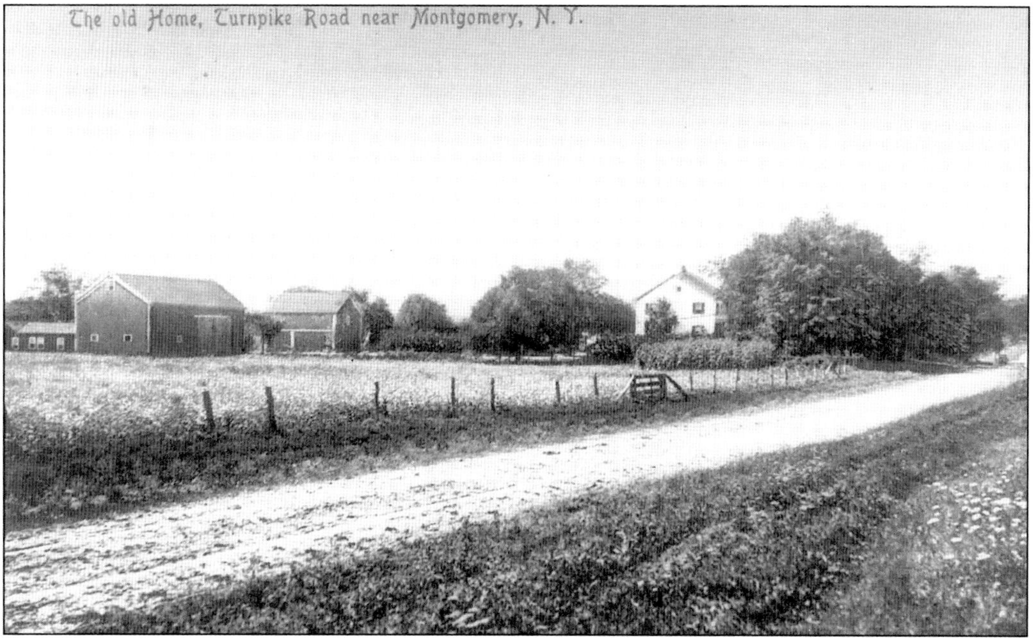

Turnpikes generally were built upon existing, unimproved roadways, which tended to meander. The new turnpikes were made straighter, wider, and more direct than the old roads. This postcard, *c.* 1905, shows Route 17K, west of the Brick Church. Note the straightness of the highway. The old farmhouse, built *c.* 1870, still stands. Mueller's 1903 *Atlas of Orange County* identifies the house as the residence of A.D. Burnett.

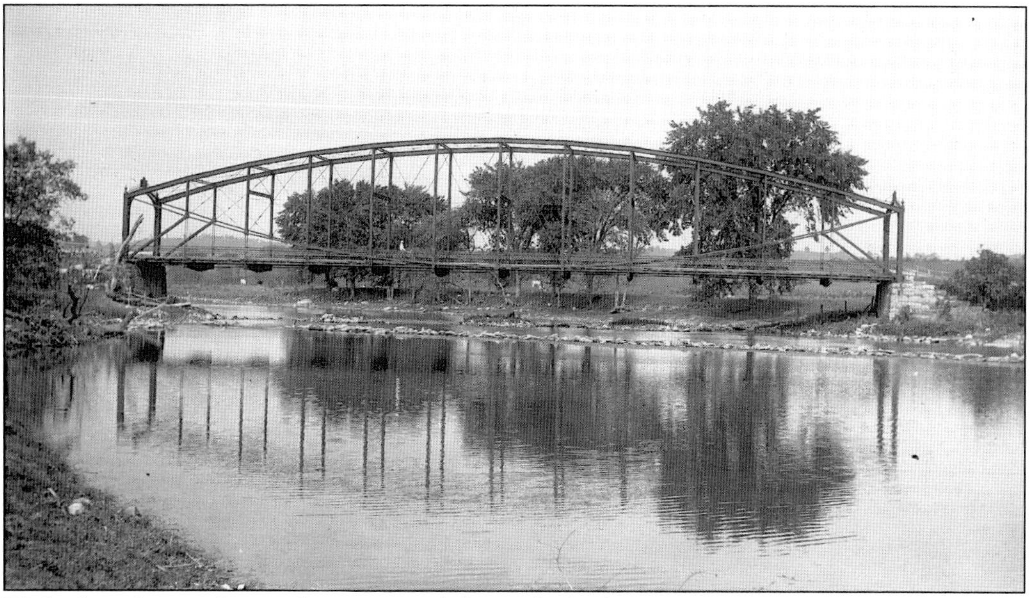

With the advent of turnpikes, many of the early fording spots were replaced with bridges. Bodine's Bridge, on Route 211 at the Orange County Airport, is one example. The original bridge was a wooden structure. This Victorian-era span, constructed late in the 19th century, was replaced some years ago by the present bridge.

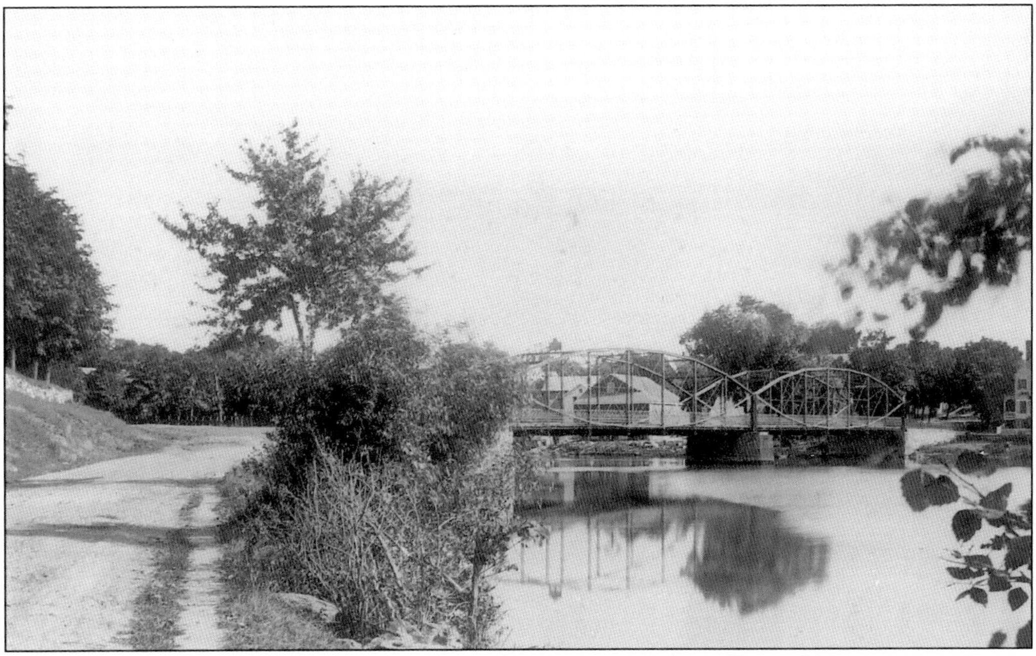

One of the first bridges to be constructed in the area was in the village of Montgomery. It predated the establishment of the Newburgh & Cochecton Turnpike and was built by James Ward in the mid-18th century so that patrons could gain access to his mill. This photograph, *c.* 1890, shows the Berlin Iron Bridge, built in 1887 to replace a wooden bridge. The Berlin Bridge became the subject of many postcard views of the village.

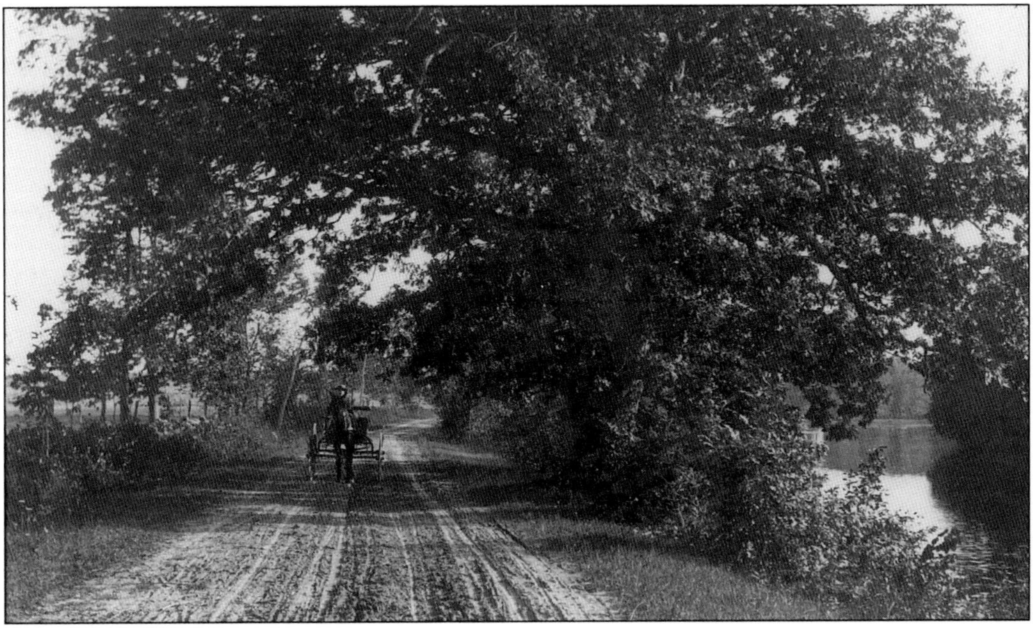

For years, the only forms of wheeled transportation were stage, carriage, or wagon. Many people simply walked or rode horseback. This view, *c.* 1890, shows a carriage and rider traveling along River Road toward the village of Montgomery.

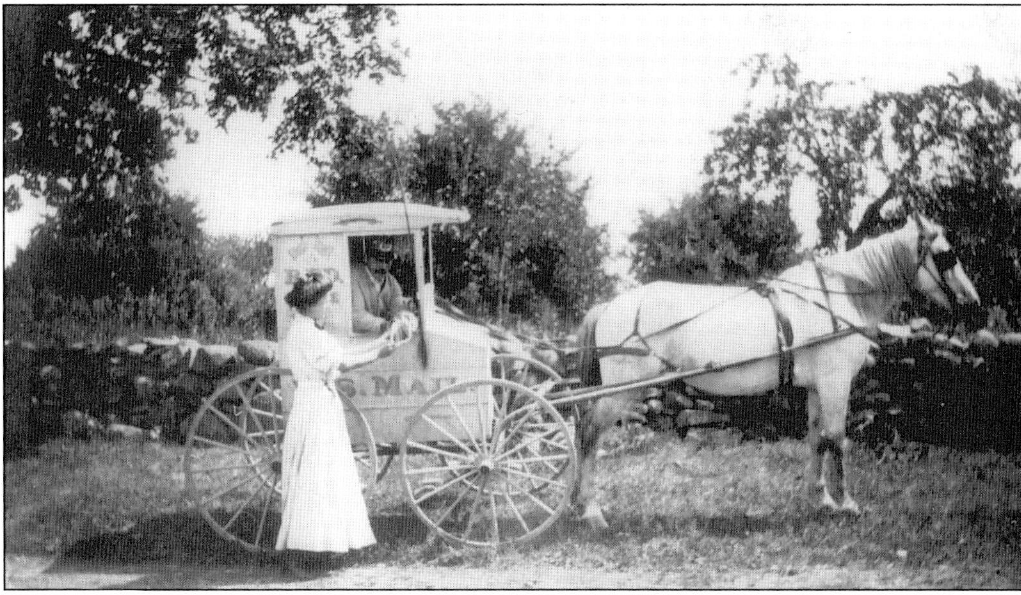

The horse-drawn delivery wagon, the forerunner of today's vans, was a common sight at the turn of the 20th century. The above view, c. 1908, shows a postman delivering mail at the Hawkins farmstead on Maple Avenue. The lower view, c. 1940, shows Frank Crist, then in his 80s, in his delivery wagon at the Crist Farm on Berea Road.

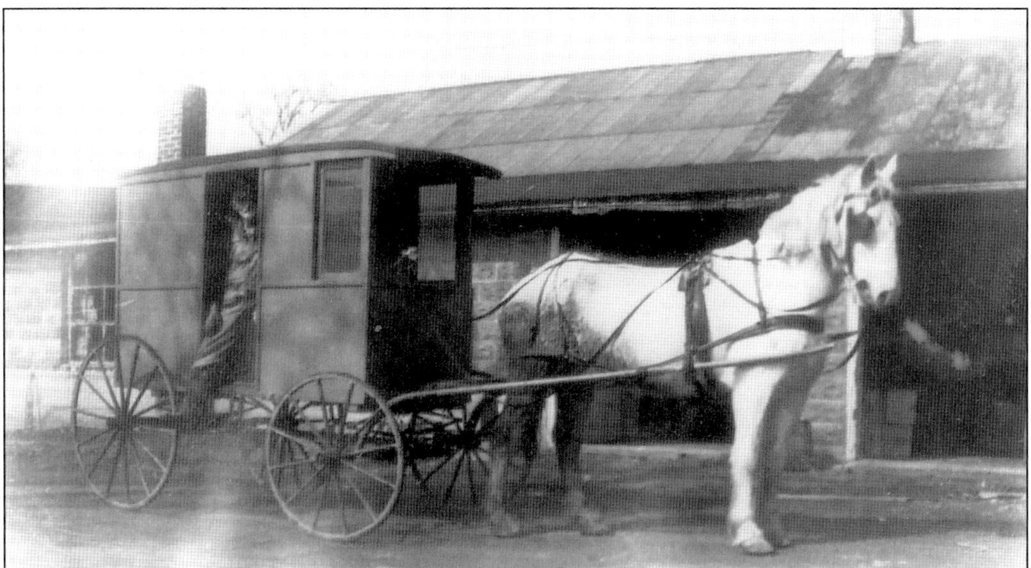

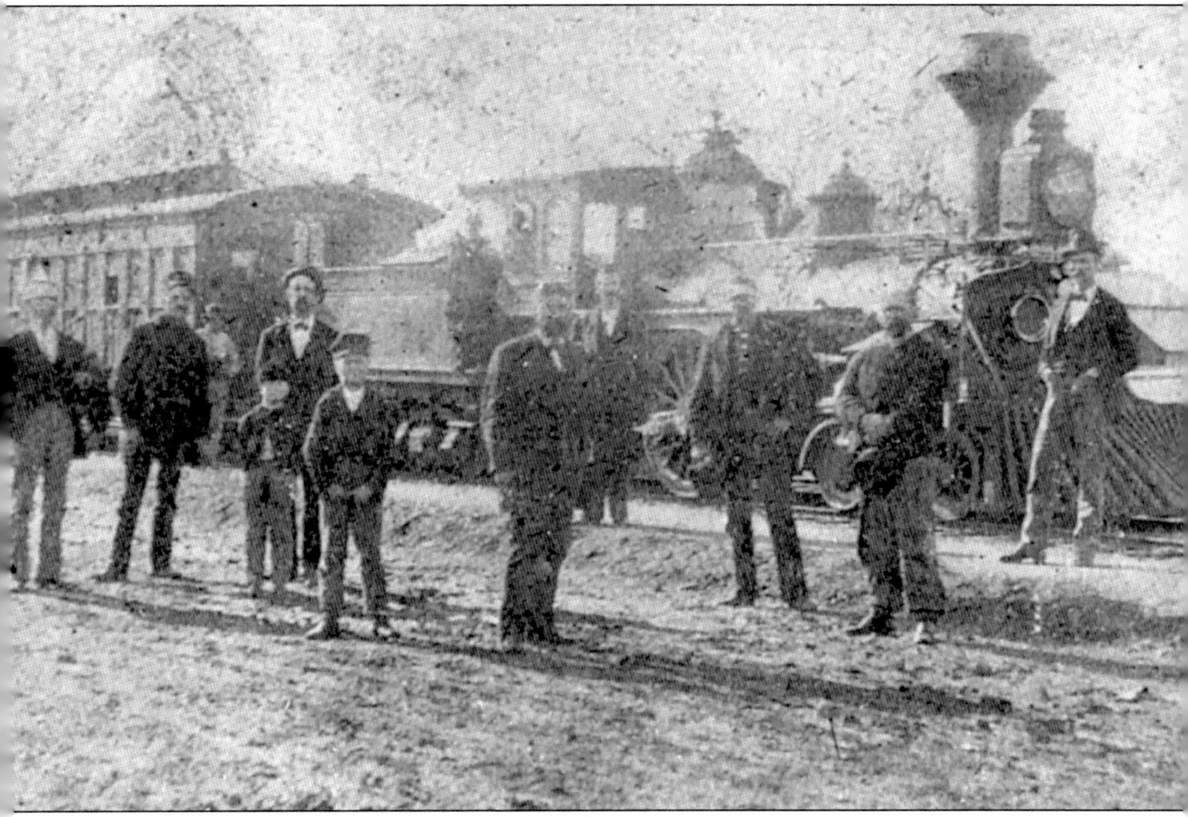

After the creation of turnpikes, the railway was the next major improvement in transportation. A rail line connecting Goshen with the village of Montgomery was constructed soon after the Civil War. The line was soon extended through Walden to Kingston, on the Hudson River. Some of the workers who built the line eventually made Montgomery their permanent residence. Chauncey Brooks was one of them. The Wallkill Valley quickly became a summer destination for city dwellers. Many local residents who had spare rooms supplemented their income by taking in boarders. The new line also provided rapid transportation for large quantities of products to and from the area. This G.B. Barnes photograph, *c.* 1870, shows one of the first locomotives in the area and is believed to have been taken in the village of Montgomery.

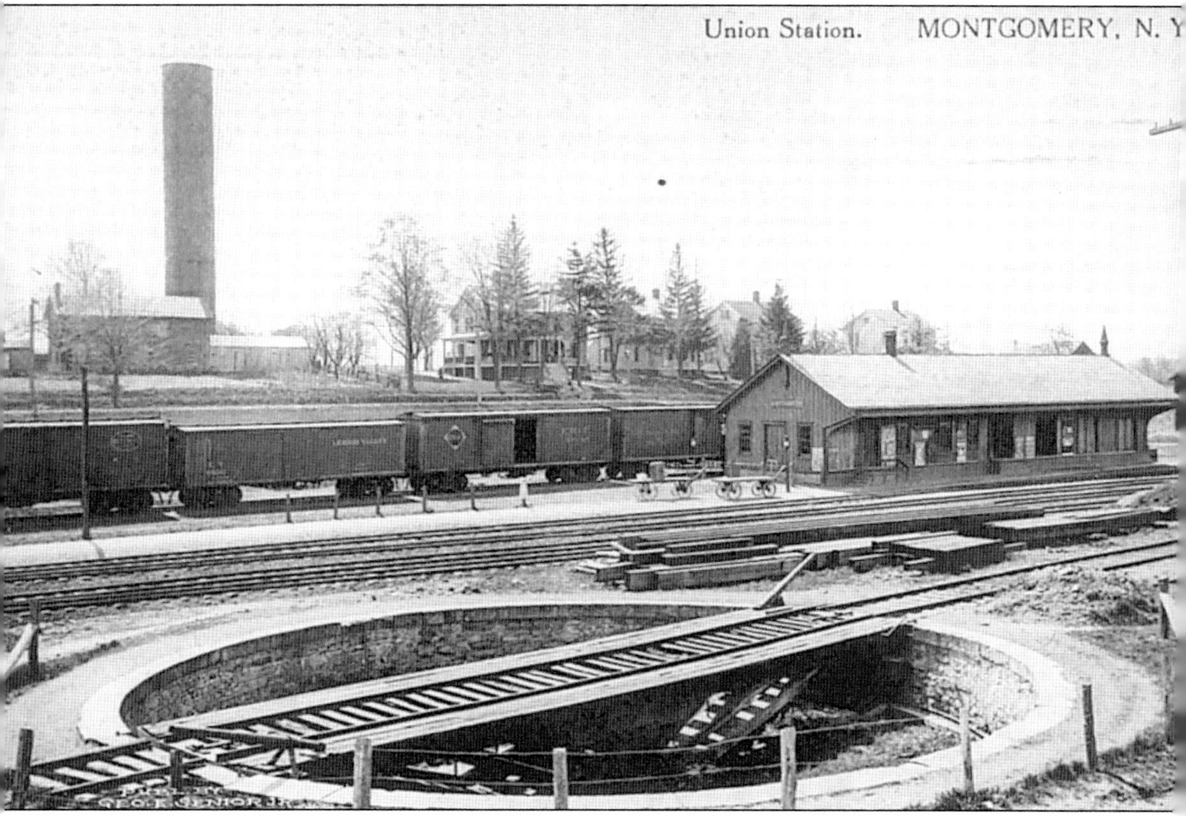

The Montgomery station was probably built in the 1870s and stood on property now occupied by Rowley Lumber. A turntable for locomotives was located nearby. Both the station and the turntable are gone. Among a small collection of railway documents recently discovered were agent's stubs for 25-trip family tickets between Montgomery and New York, issued to Ephraim Koffman of Searsville Road and William Crabtree of Factory Street. The fares cost $27.50 per ticket, or $1.10 per trip. The village standpipe is visible in the background of this *c.* 1900 postcard view.

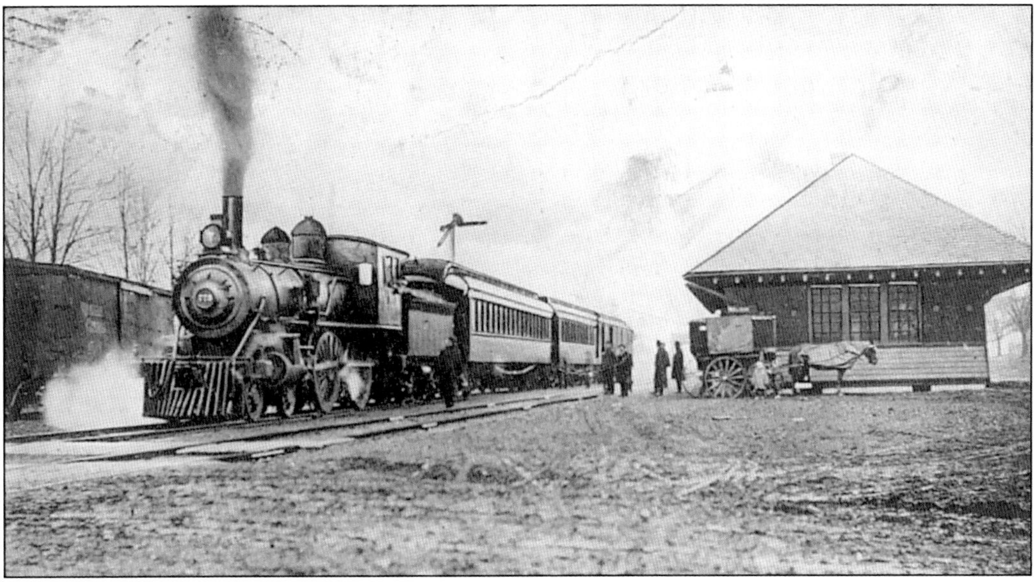

This *c*. 1905 view shows the Walden station, located between Railroad and Hepper Streets. The station, dating from around the turn of the 20th century, replaced an older building. After years of service, the station was moved to Wooster Grove, where it serves today as a recreation hall. The tracks still lie between Railroad and Hepper Streets, a subtle reminder of a once important transportation link.

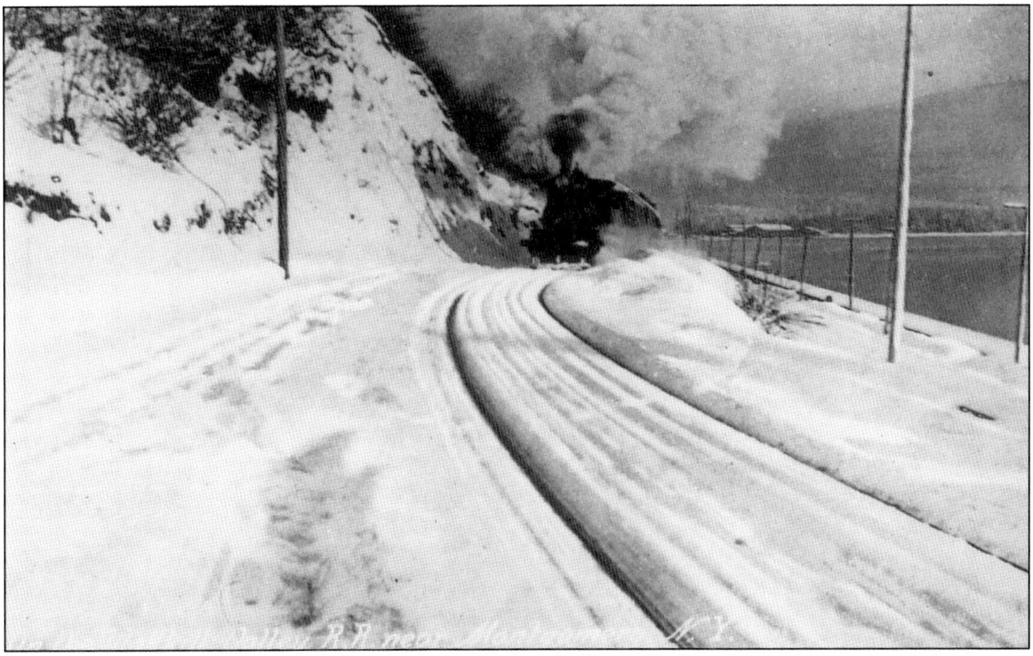

Late in the 1880s, a new rail line was constructed through the eastern portion of the town, parallel to the Wallkill Valley Railroad. Known as the Hudson Valley Connecting Railroad, it extended from the newly built bridge at Poughkeepsie to Orange Junction, which was renamed Maybrook. This line will be detailed in the following chapter.

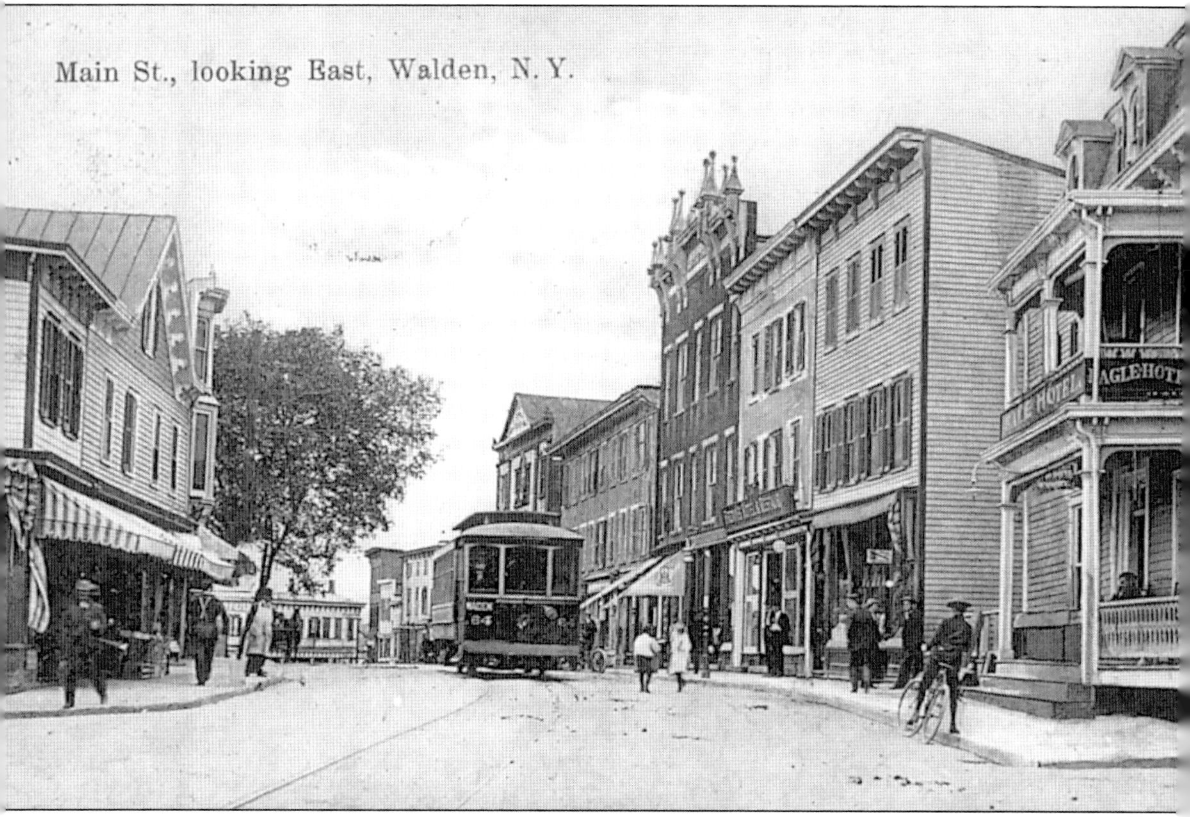

In the 1890s, an electric rail line, or trolley, was built to connect the village of Walden with Orange Lake, a popular recreation spot, and the city of Newburgh. At this time, Walden was truly the commercial hub of the town. Streets bustled with activity, and residents enjoyed the benefits of up-to-date living. The days of the trolley ended long ago, after cars and buses took over the roads.

This c. 1907 view of Walden's Main Street was taken looking east from the corner of Walnut Street. The pleasing Victorian streetscape changed over the years as important landmarks were replaced with modern structures. Changes continue today; recent plans called for the replacement of the Wooster building, which dated from the late Victorian era.

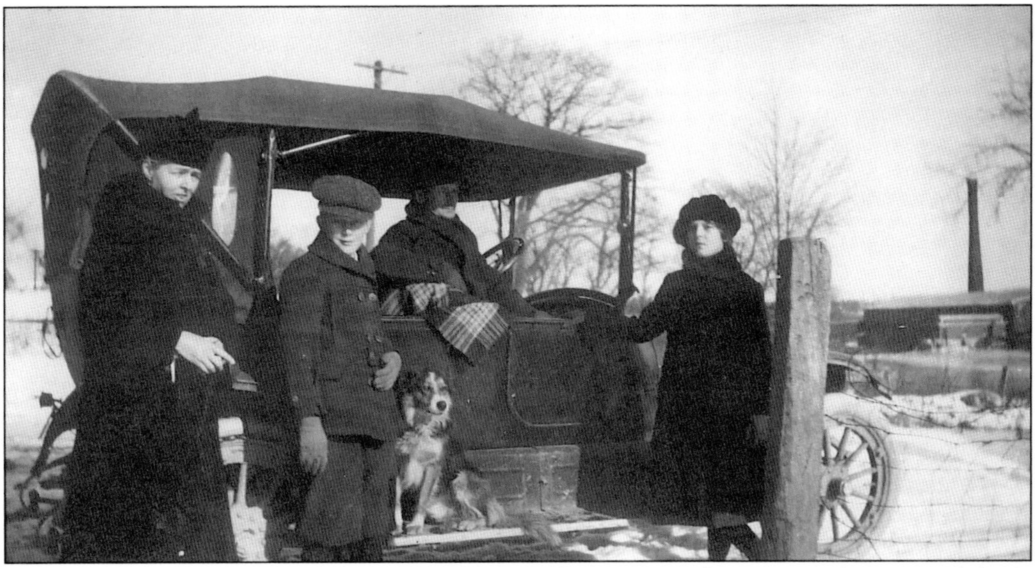

The mode of transportation that brought about the greatest change was the automobile. It bridged long distances and brought people and places closer together. The first autos were expensive and, thus, were considered to be the toys of the wealthy. However, with time, technology improved, and automobiles became available to the masses. This January 1921 photograph shows a Ford that belonged to the Sloan family, who lived on River Road, nearly opposite the Crabtree Mill.

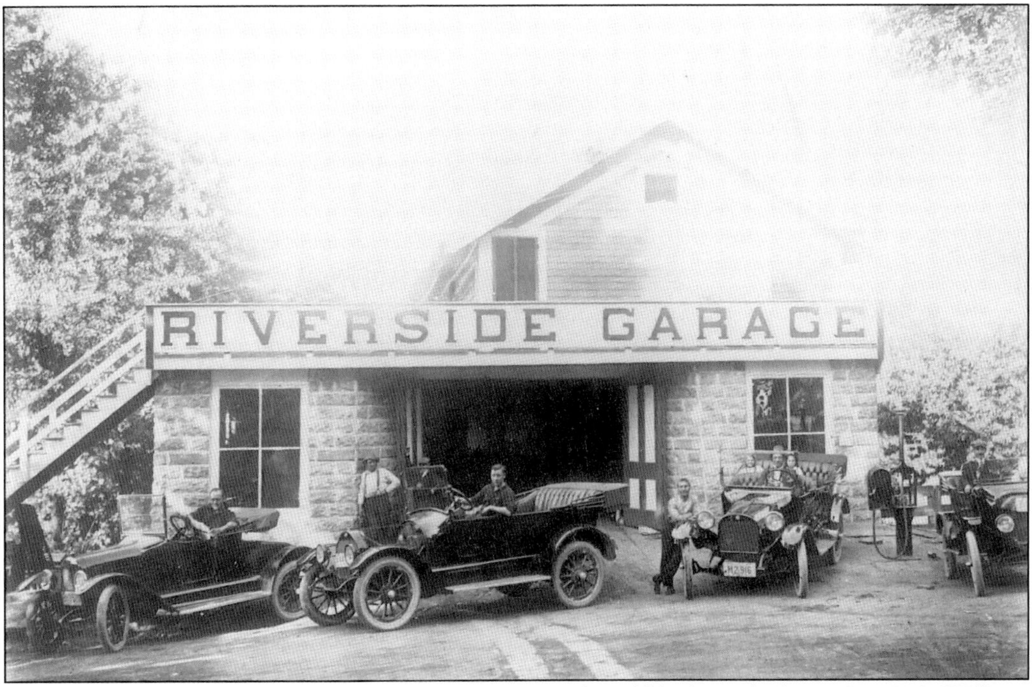

After automobiles became commonplace, garages replaced blacksmith shops. In 1912, William A. Hall established the Riverside Garage in a Greek Revival-era building on Ward Street, across from Union Street. In earlier years, the building served as Comfort's Hardware Store. Not long ago, it was renovated to its original form.

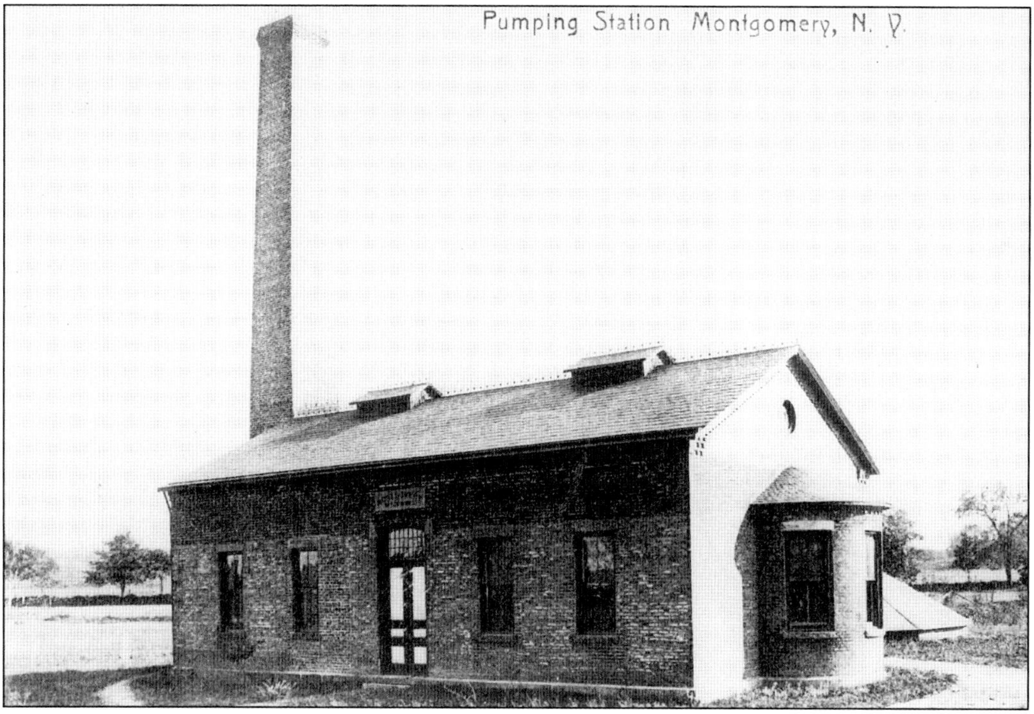

As transportation improved throughout the area, Montgomery became more accessible to the outside world and experienced a construction boom. By the 1890s, a public water system became a necessity. The pumping station on Ward Street was built in 1895, and a standpipe was constructed on the crest of the hill east of Prospect Street.

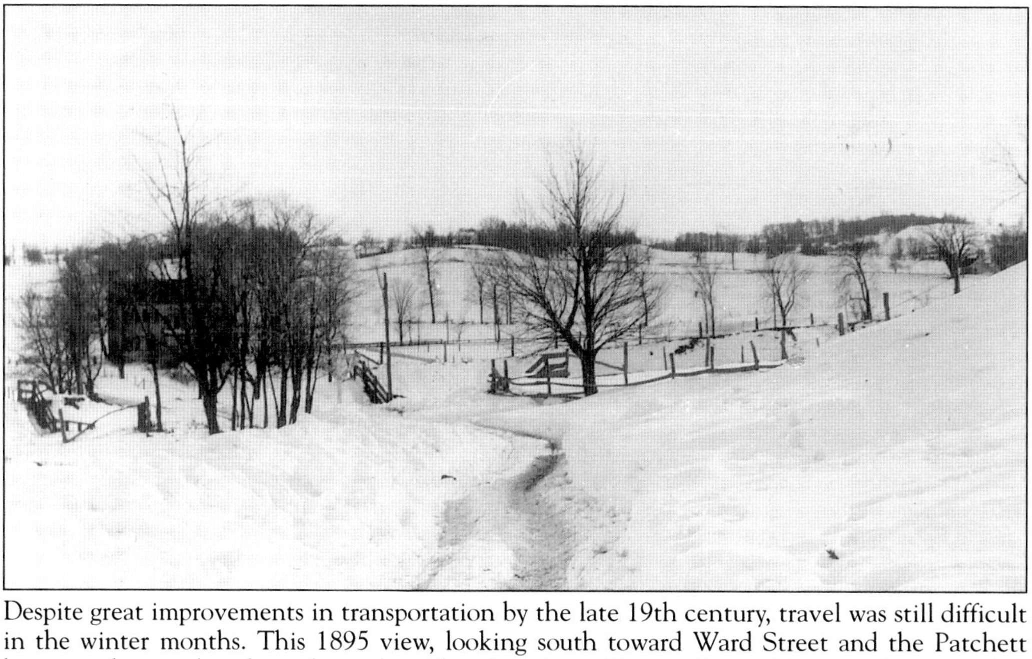

Despite great improvements in transportation by the late 19th century, travel was still difficult in the winter months. This 1895 view, looking south toward Ward Street and the Patchett homestead, was taken from above the railroad tracks on Factory Street. Note the footprints left in the snow by workers going to and from Crabtree's mill.

Four

LIVELIHOOD

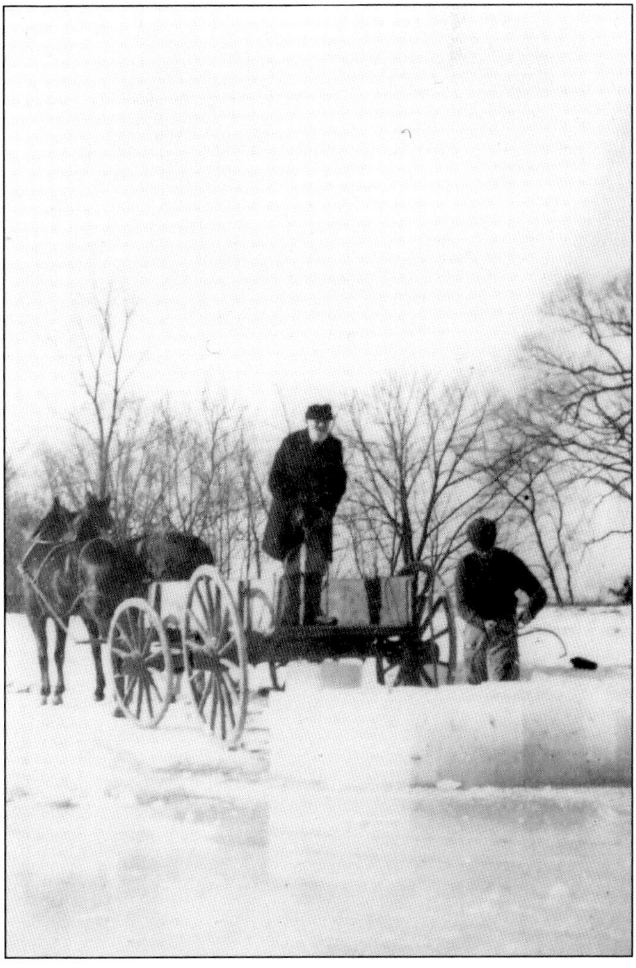

For years, farming was the dominating occupation in Montgomery. During the winter months, however, the local populace involved themselves in other necessary activities. After a good freezing period, it was not uncommon to see men harvesting ice, which was taken in blocks to icehouses for use during the warmer months. In this *c.* 1910 photograph, Mr. Brown and Jim are cutting ice on the Wallkill River for the Crabtree family. In some villages, the ever popular iceman went from door to door peddling ice from a horse-drawn wagon. With the introduction of electricity, wooden household iceboxes were replaced by refrigerators, which eventually put icehouses out of business. One of the only surviving icehouses in the area is located on Factory Street in the village of Montgomery. Its foundation extends more than 10 feet into the ground, and ice was stored there year-round.

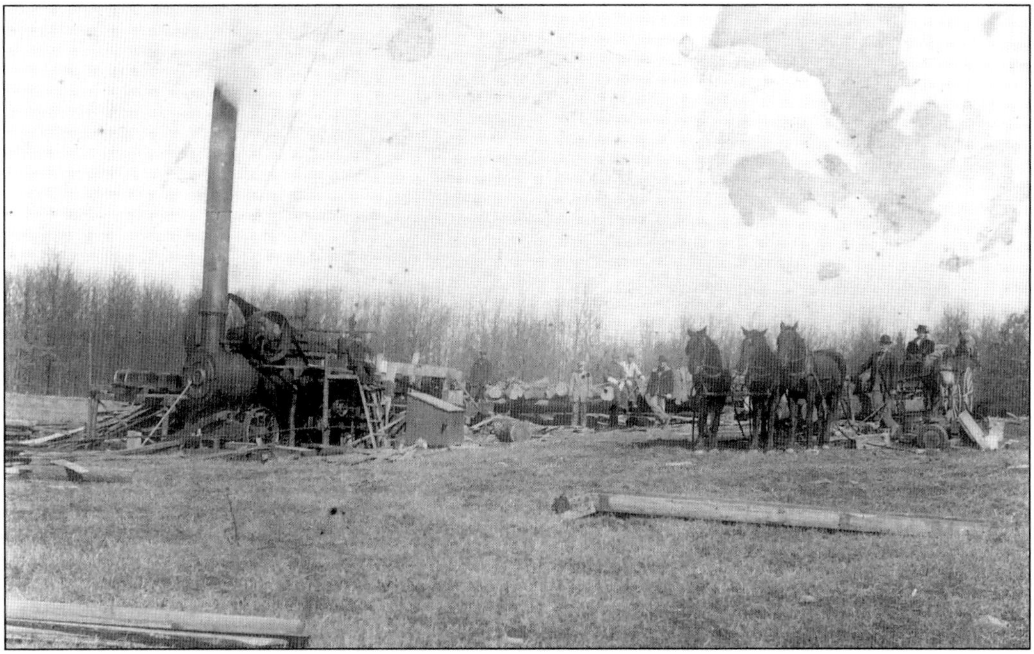

J.M. Hawkins of Peachcroft on River Road had a fairly sizable lumber operation in addition to his prosperous farm. The steam engine, with its many belts, powered a circular saw, which annually turned out hundreds of board feet of oak and pine lumber. This March 11, 1915 photograph shows J.M. Hawkins standing behind a team of horses.

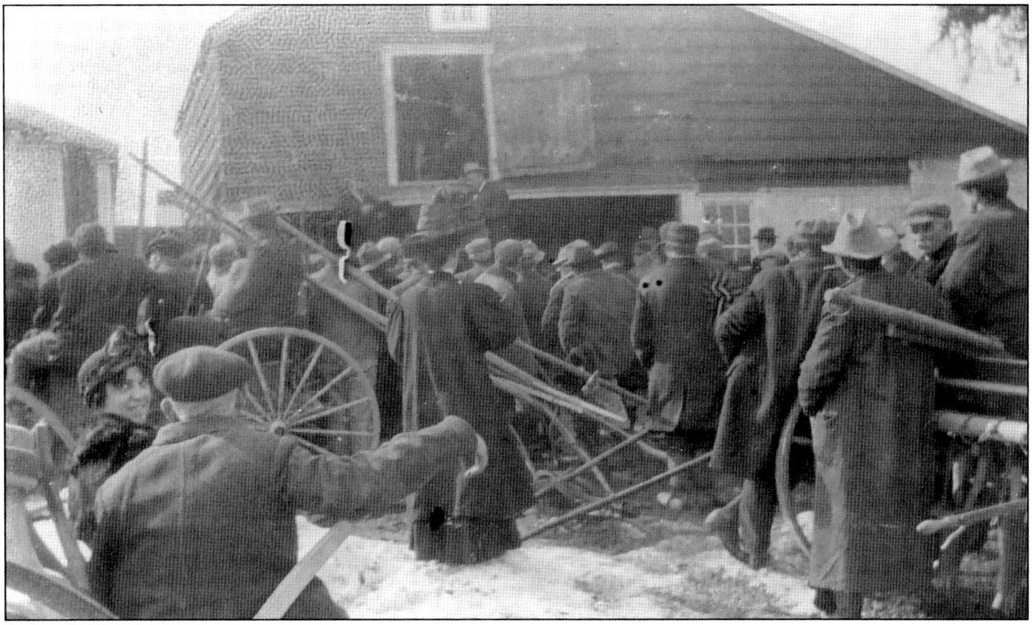

From earliest times up to the present, auctioning has been a common way of transferring real and personal property. Auctions serve not only as social gatherings, but also as entertainment. This auction was held in 1915 at the Bergen/Suydam Farm, located on the west side of Bailey Road. Years ago, a fire destroyed the old farmhouse; it has since been replaced, and one of the old barns still survives.

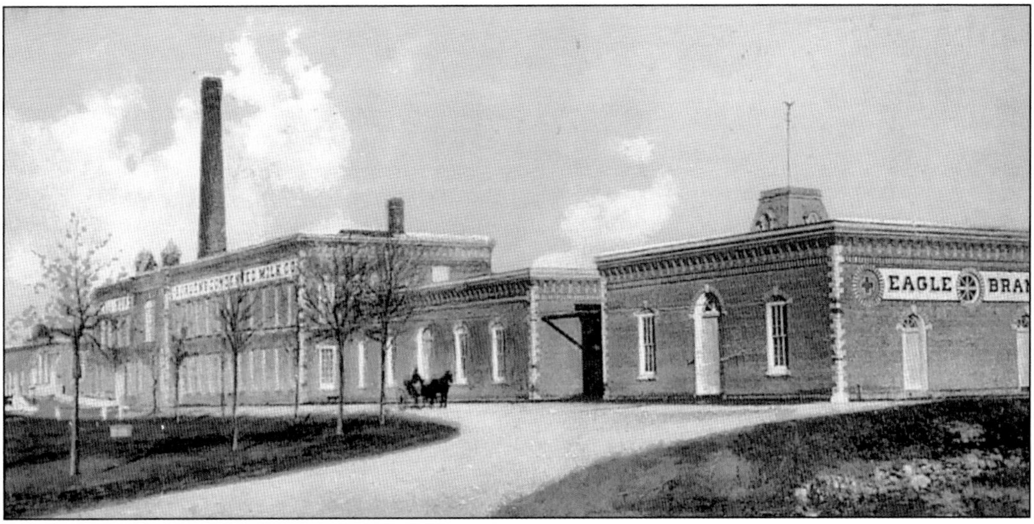

The Borden Condensery building on Route 52, between Walden and Wallkill, is an excellent example of industrial Victorian-era architecture. Built in the 1880s, it contains decorative brick and stone masonry. Despite neglect and a destructive fire, the building remains an important structure in Montgomery. During the years of operation, the condensery processed milk to improve its keeping qualities so that it could be shipped to distant locations.

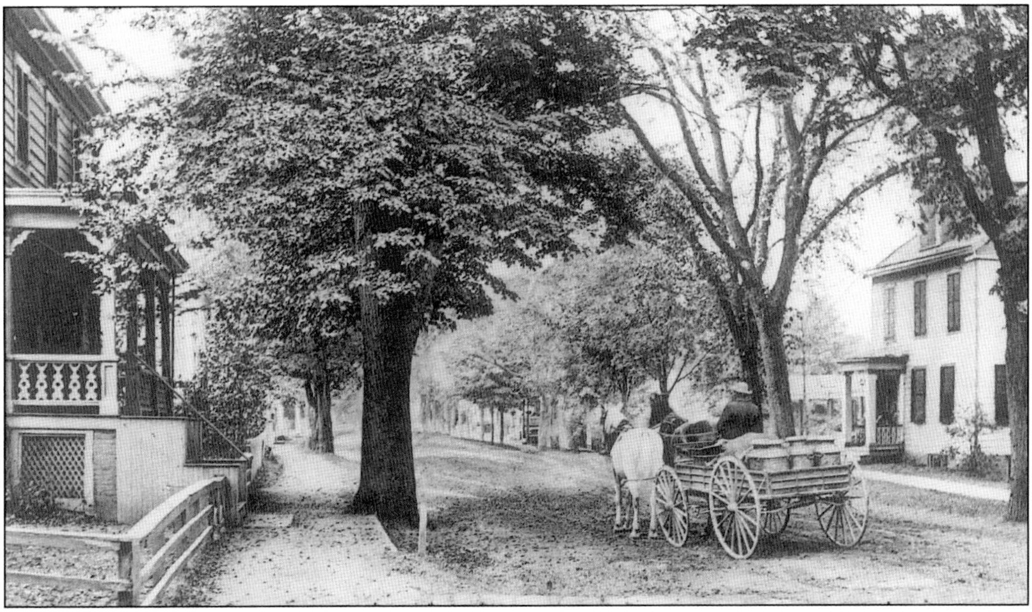

Dairy farming flourished during the late 1800s, after rail transportation linked the region to metropolitan areas. The Montgomery region was well suited to producing forage for dairy cattle. This postcard, *c.* 1900, shows a farmer transporting milk in front of the Eager house on Union Street at the corner of Mason Street in the village of Montgomery.

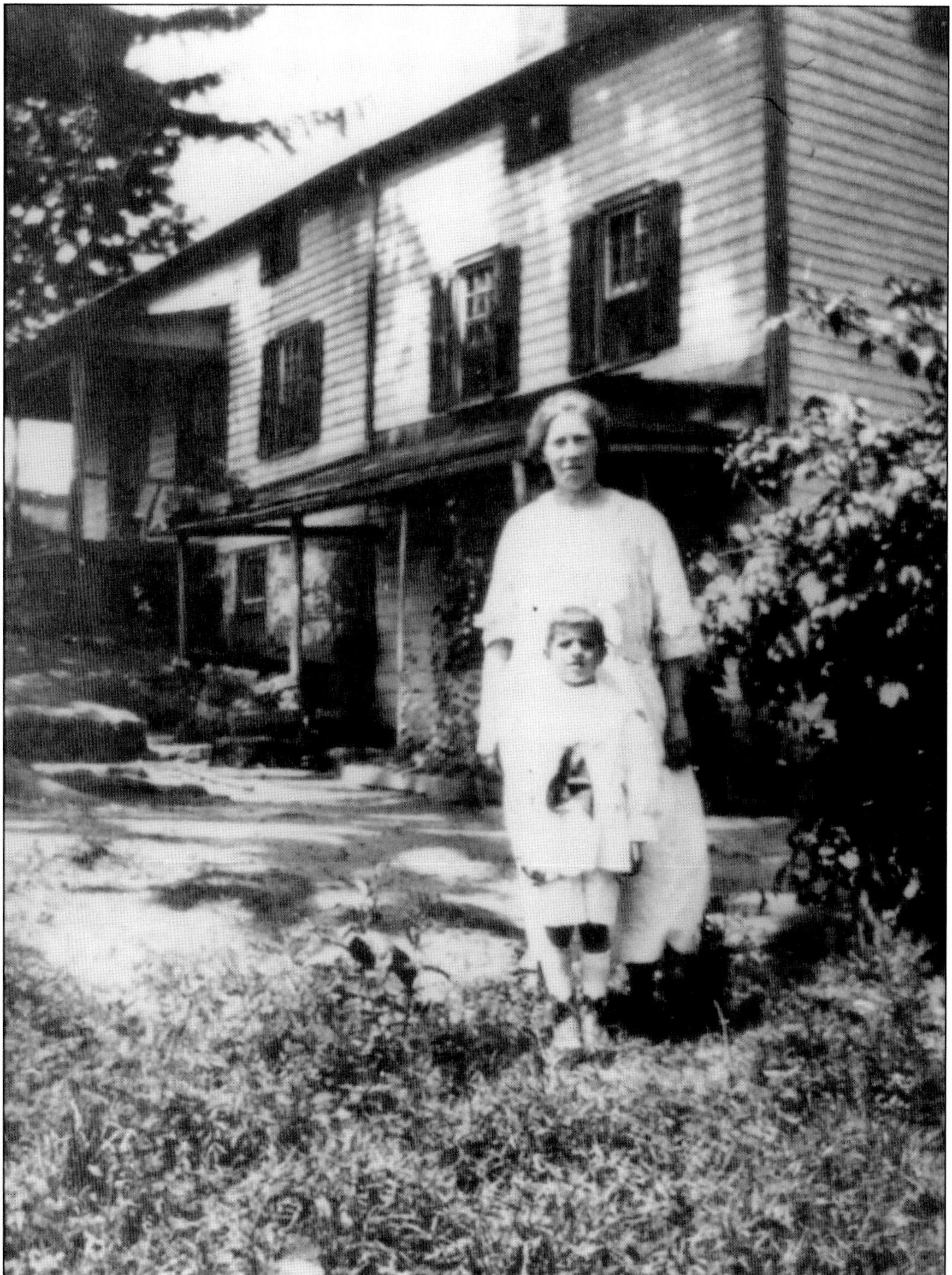

Many people struggled in order to survive. One of them was Grace Marks, shown in this photograph, *c.* 1914. She was a widow who supported her three children by hand-milking cows and sewing. She rented the Dickerson-Van Alst house (a late-18th-century home, listed on the National Register) on West Searsville Road. Even the day her elder son was laid out in a casket after his tragic death, Mrs. Marks walked up the road to the McKinney barn to milk the cows.

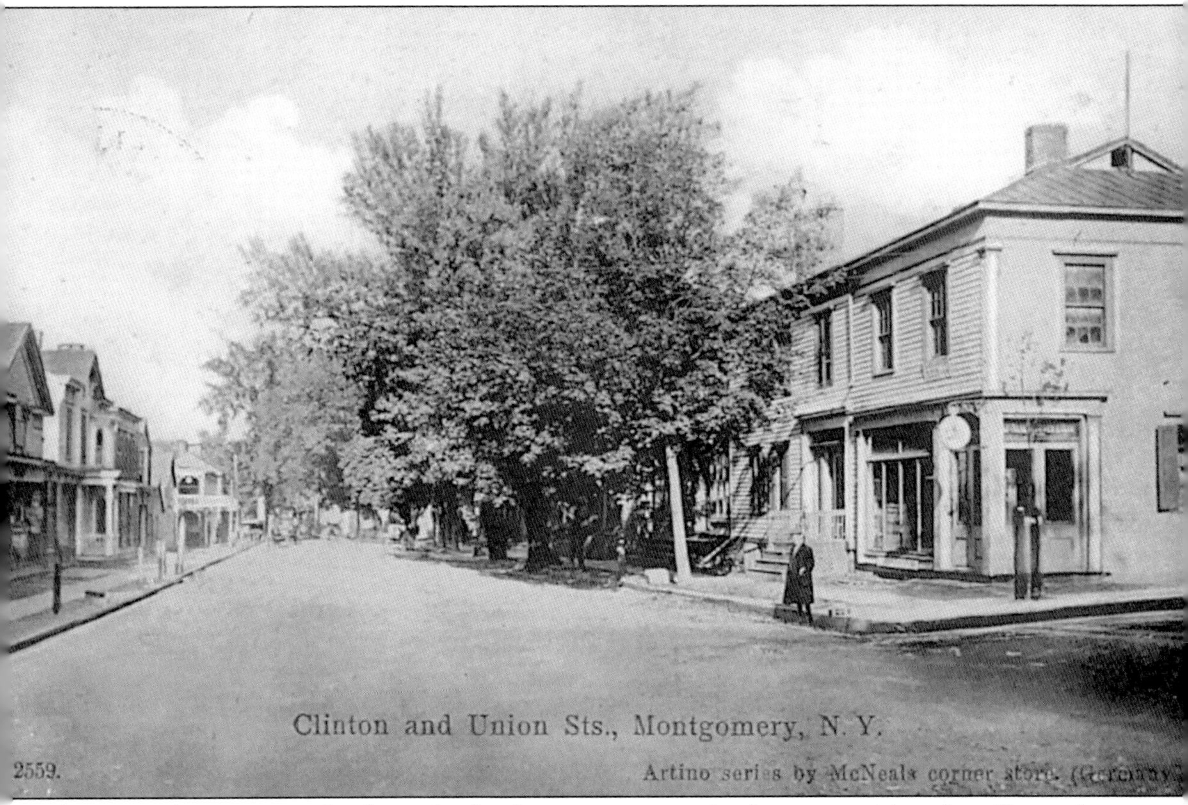

A group of promoters who formed a land company were the first to envision the village of Montgomery as it exists today. They acquired the old mill of James Ward and the adjoining 200 acres. Promoter James Clinton, who was a surveyor, prepared a plan and map of the village and included some new roads along with the existing ones. Throughout the 19th century, the village was a thriving center within the town. Today, it contains a wealth of architecture within its two National Register districts. This view, *c.* 1900, shows Clinton Street from the corner of Union Street. Many of these buildings still stand.

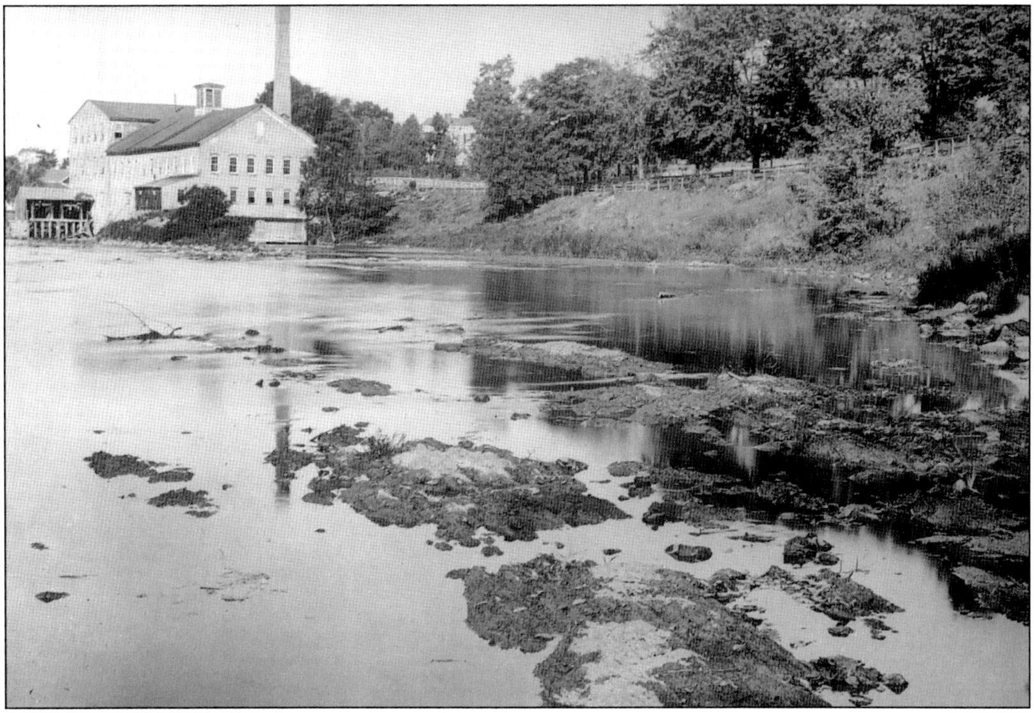

Mills were built along the Wallkill River early in the development of the town. In 1872, the Walker Brothers established the Montgomery Paper Mills on the north side of the Wallkill, opposite the village of Montgomery, for the production of manila and wrapping paper. Their establishment stood on the site of the 18th-century Crist Mill. Around 1900, the Walker Mill was destroyed by fire and never rebuilt. The above view dates from the 1890s, and the lower view from 1910.

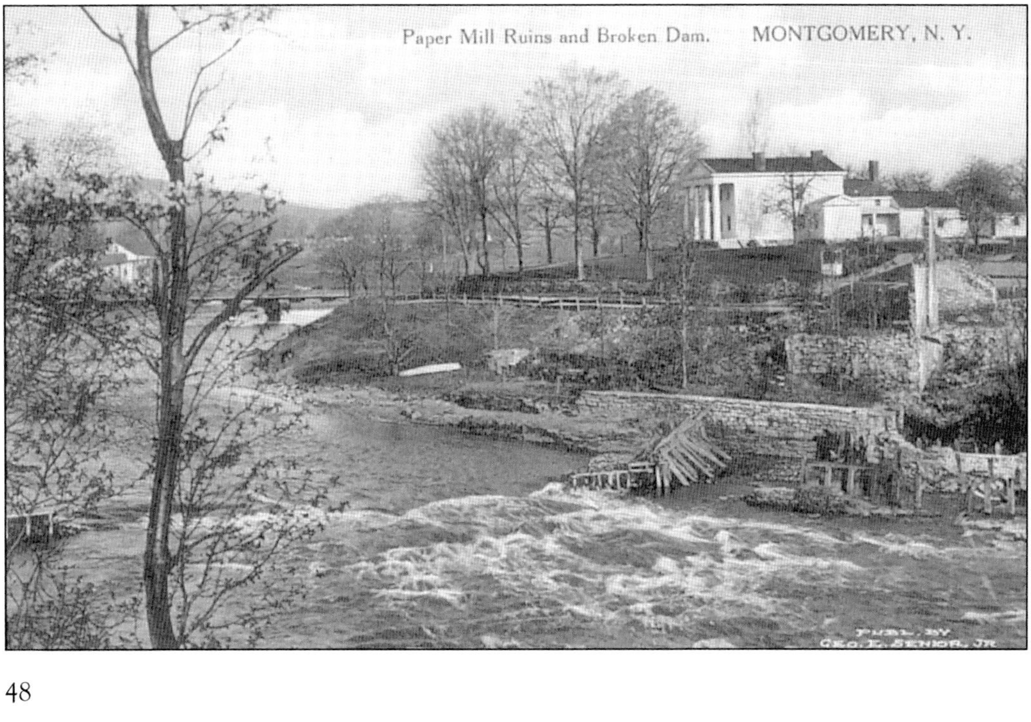

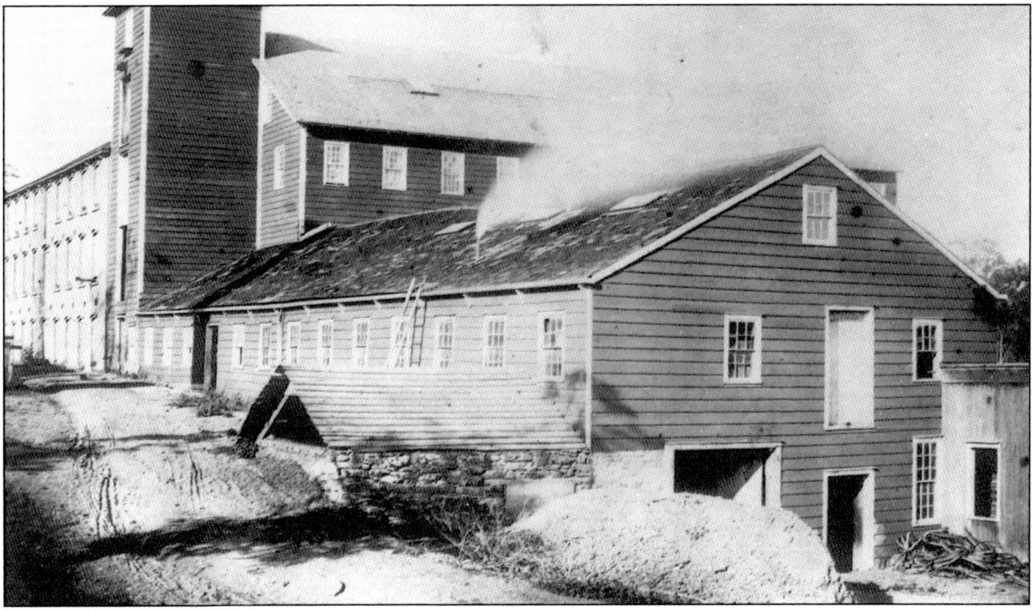

Farther north on the Wallkill River was the Montgomery Cotton Factory, constructed between 1813 and 1815. Because of an early failure, the factory never spun a pound of yarn nor wove a yard of cloth. In 1880, William Crabtree and Arthur Patchett bought the factory and produced worsted yarn. The building was destroyed by fire on Election Day of 1891 and was replaced with the original portion of the present building in 1892.

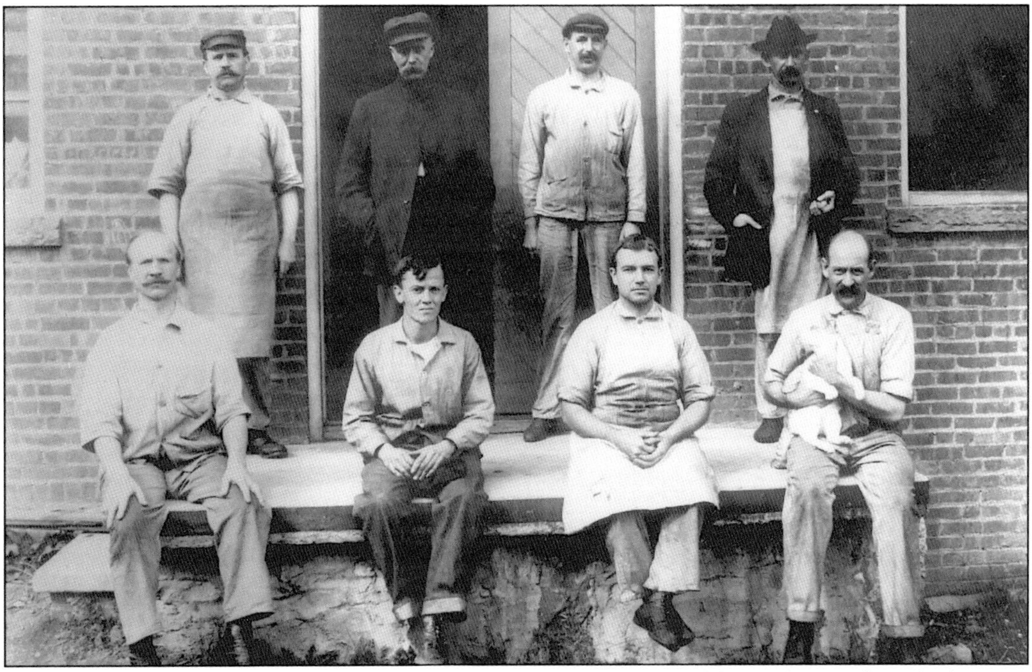

Crabtree and Patchett's mill produced worsted yarn that was sold to other mills, which wove it into cloth for suiting. In this photograph, c. 1918, workers pose at the side door of the mill. They are, from left to right, as follows: (front row) Fred Woodhead, Larry Gath, Wellington Sparks, and Joe Wade; (back row) George Clark, unidentified, unidentified, and Mr. Legg.

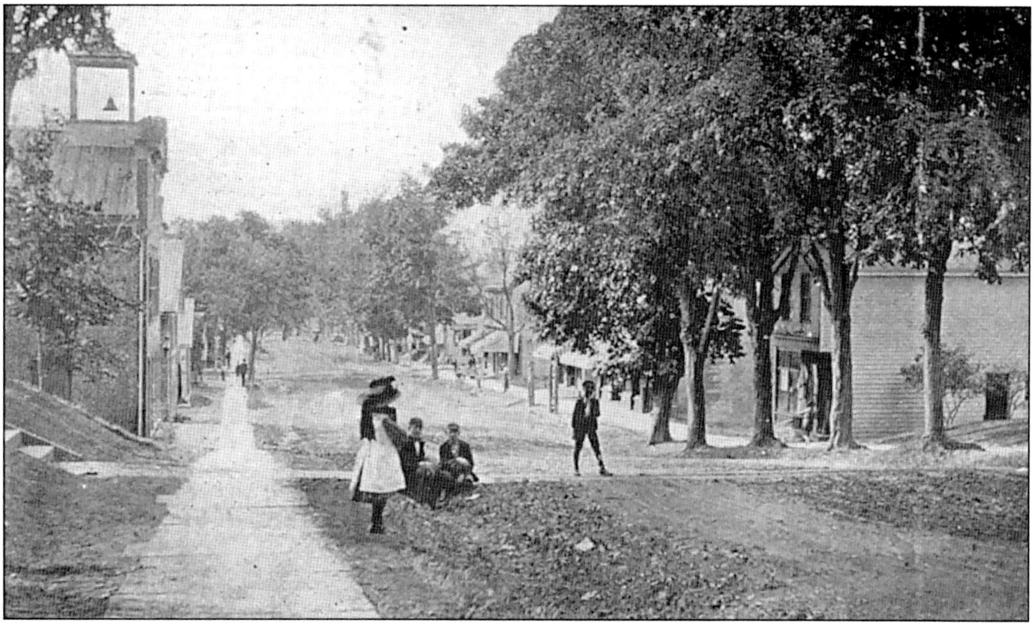

The village of Montgomery became a thriving community in the 19th century. This postcard, c. 1900, shows a view of Clinton Street looking west. The building on the left with a bell tower was the old firehouse, which was destroyed by fire in 1913. The store on the right, behind the trees, was Hanlon's Harness Shop, which today is the Village Sampler.

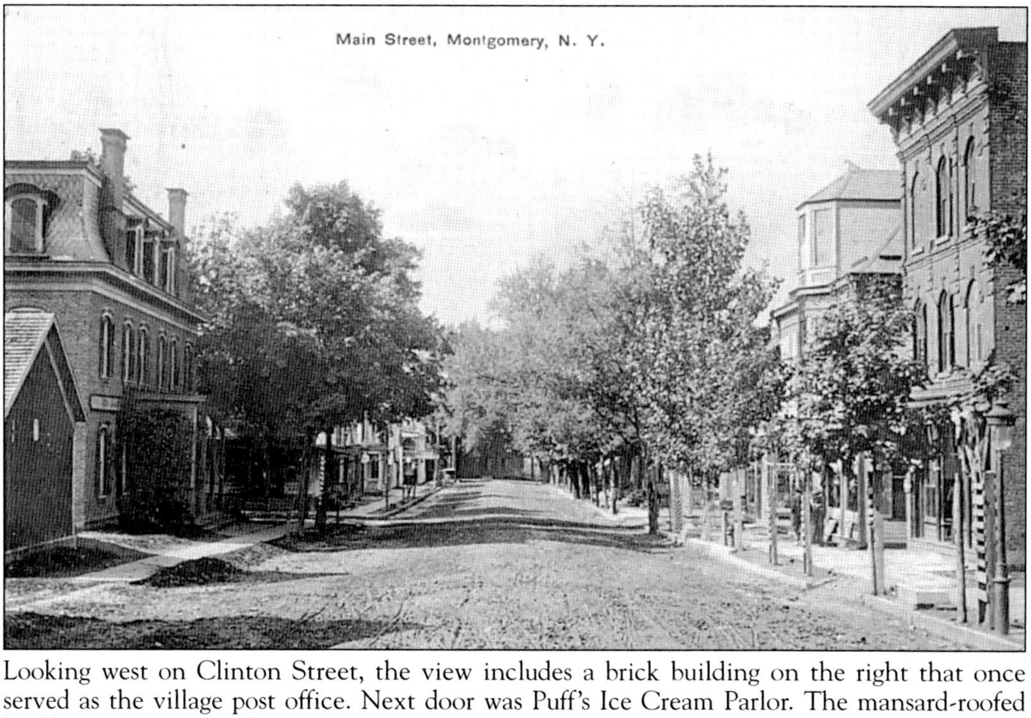

Looking west on Clinton Street, the view includes a brick building on the right that once served as the village post office. Next door was Puff's Ice Cream Parlor. The mansard-roofed building across the road was the Palace Hotel, which, sadly, was demolished some years ago.

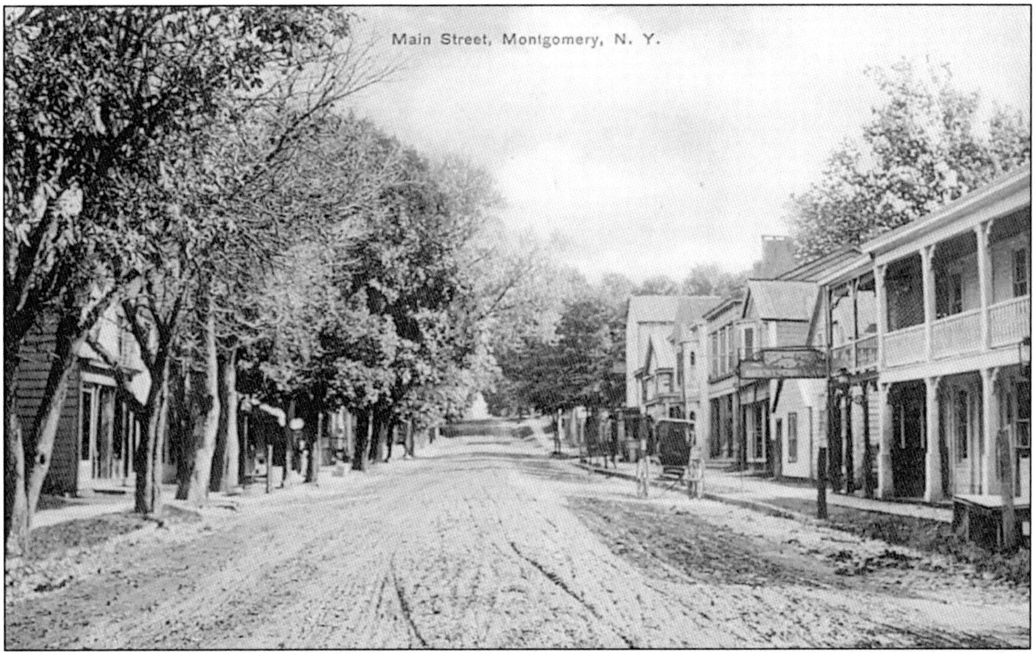

Clinton Street has always been the business center of the village. This postcard, *c.* 1900, presents the view looking east. The National Hotel is on the right. Diagonally opposite the hotel is a store building, which was recently rehabilitated. In 1840, a disastrous fire destroyed the west side of Clinton, extending from Union Street to a point opposite the hotel. This explains why the majority of the buildings in this section date to the Greek Revival era.

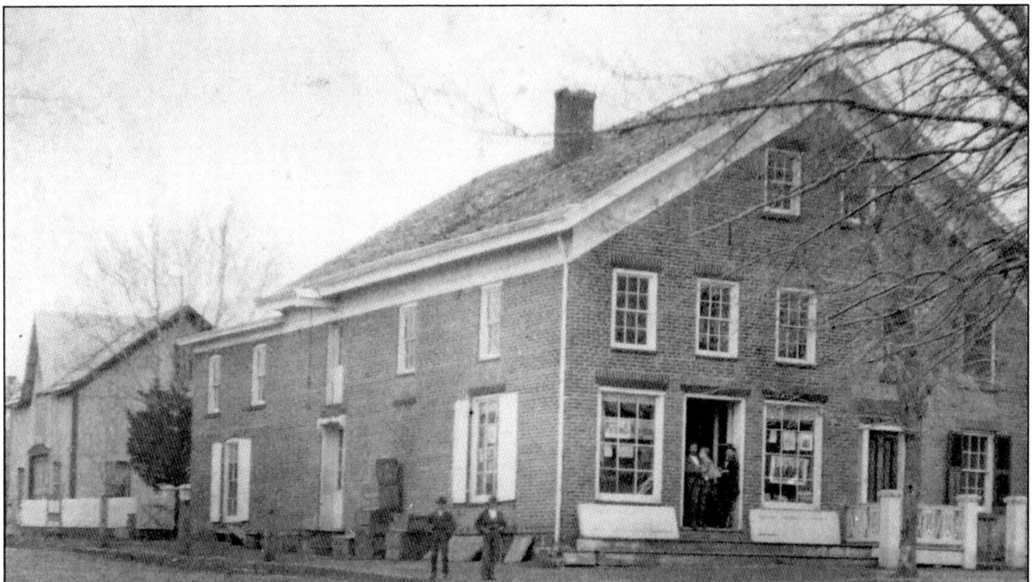

This brick structure was one of the earliest store buildings in the village. Located on the corner of Union and Ward Streets, it was occupied early on by the Seniors, who ran a dry goods business. The building has long since passed into history, and a vacant lot remains in its place. This G.B. Barnes photograph dates from the 1870s.

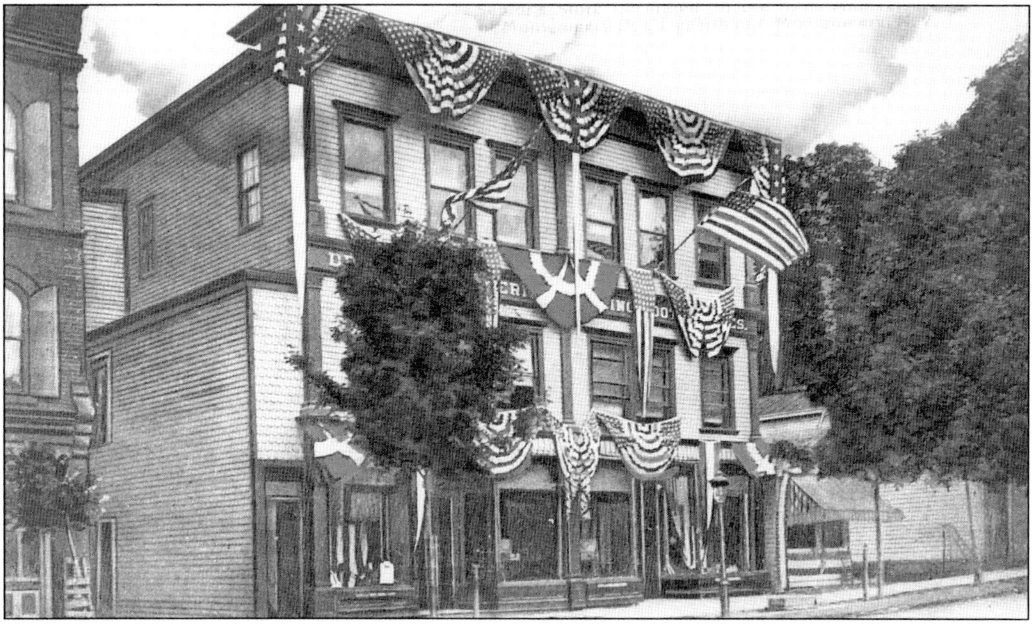

In the late 1800s, the Senior family built a large three-story building on Clinton Street. They opened a store on the first floor that became the business and social center of the village for many years. They stocked everything from clothes and shoes to hardware. Note the postcard rack hanging from the ceiling.

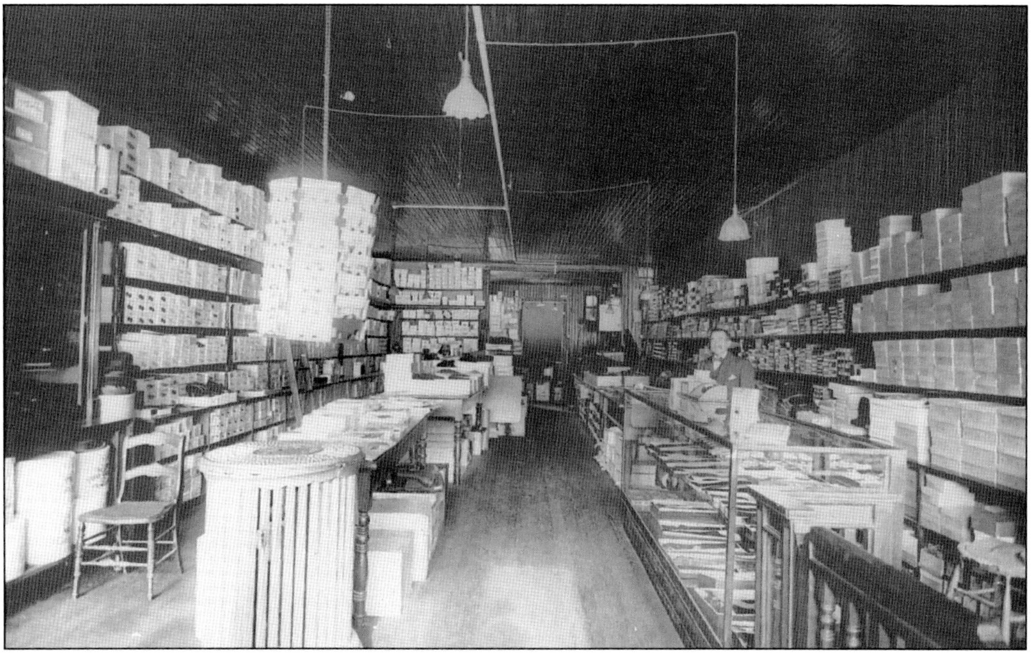

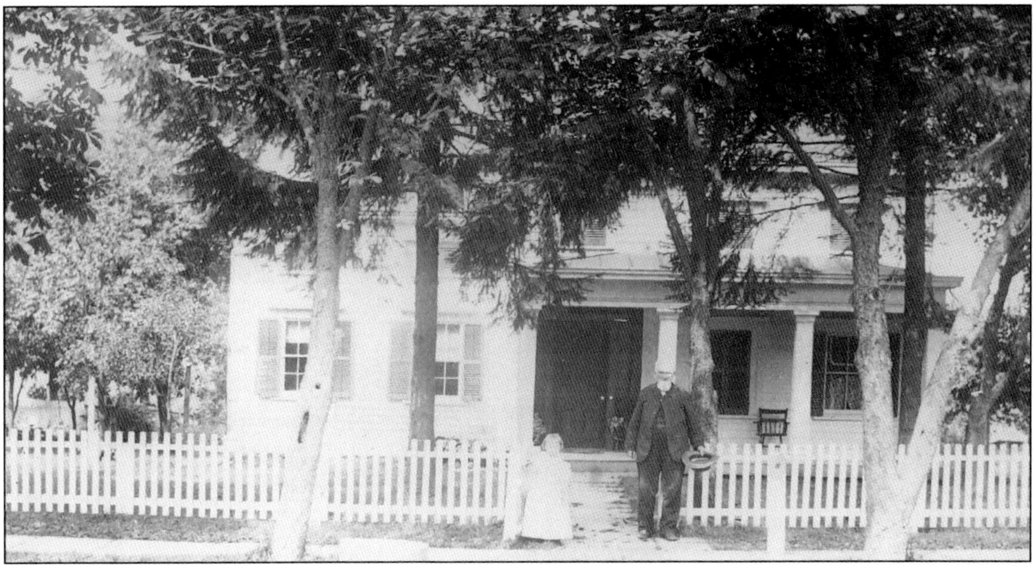

The Overhiser Funeral Home is one of the oldest continuing businesses in the town of Montgomery. The home, built *c.* 1840, also serves as the residence of Ruth Overhiser, a descendant of the founder of the family business, George Overhiser. In his carriage-making and cabinet-making shop, located at 37 Union Street, Overhiser built caskets to order. Years ago, funerals were conducted at home; only in more recent times have they been held in funeral parlors. This photograph dates from about 1890.

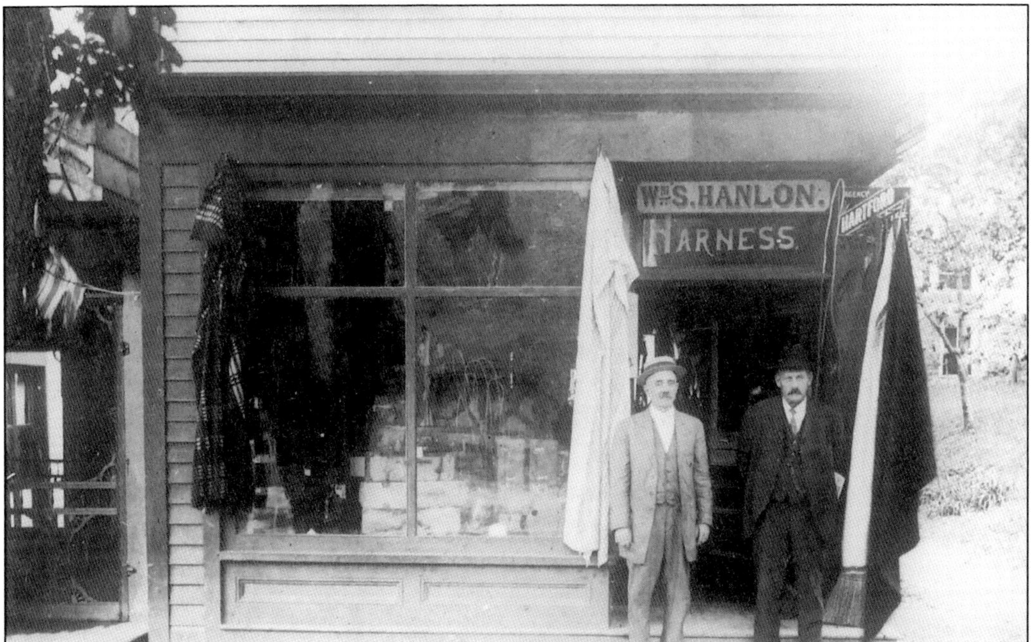

The Hanlon Harness Shop was located in the building occupied today by the Village Sampler. The harness shop was founded by William Hardenburgh and, in 1878, was taken over by William S. Hanlon. Originally Charles Borland's law office, the building dates from the early 1800s.

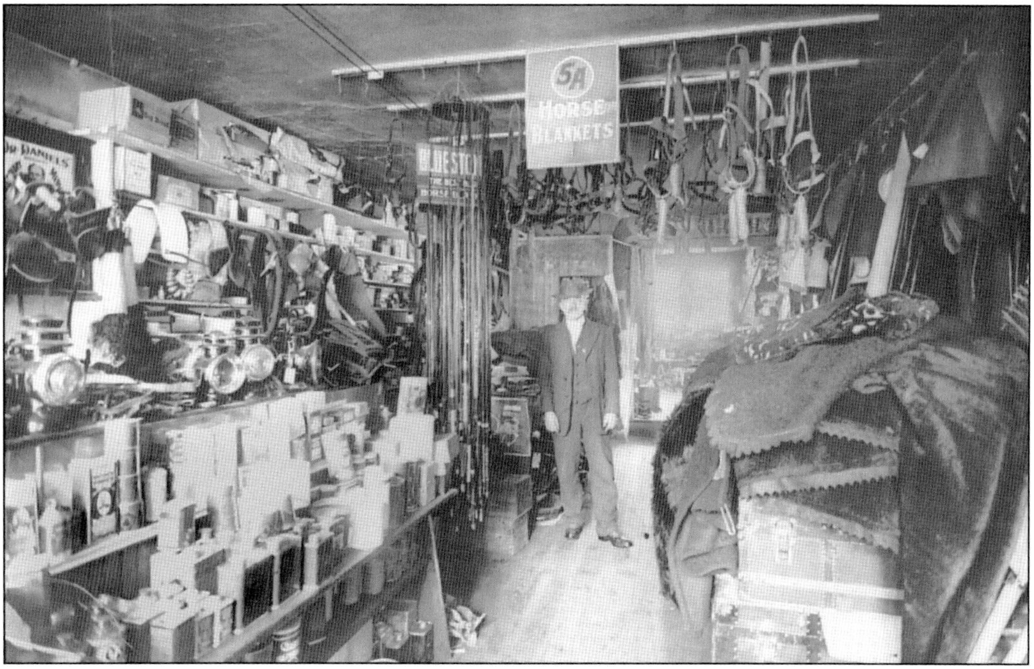

This interior photograph of the Hanlon Harness Shop dates from about 1910. To this day, many village residents remember the smell of freshly tanned leather that dominated the store. Sold here were harnesses, leashes, horse whips, and various leather goods. Today, the smell of leather has been replaced with that of homemade chocolate.

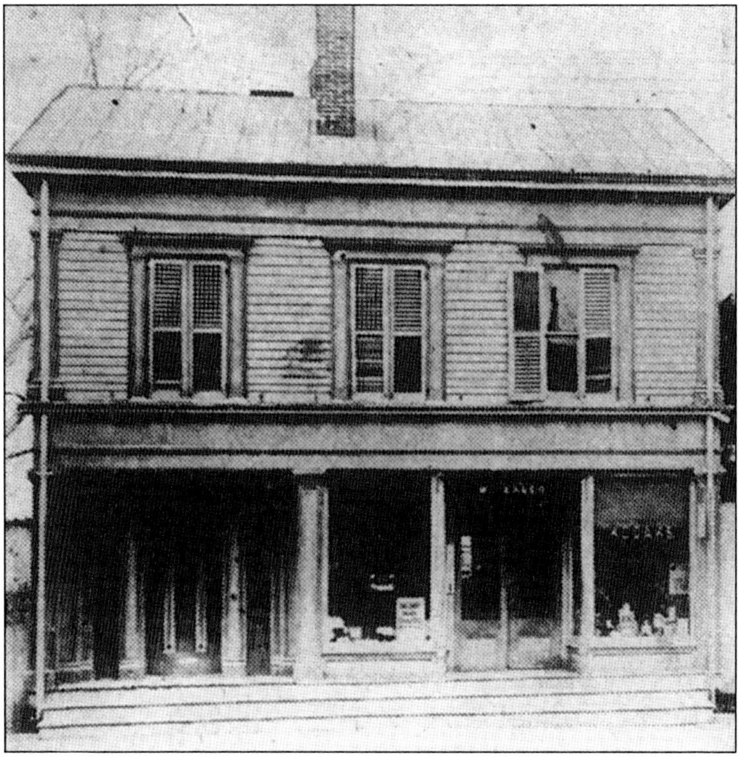

When Eager's Pharmacy closed in 1945, it was said to be the second-oldest drugstore under continuous operation by one family in New York State. Established in 1816 by Dr. George Eager, the building on Clinton Street was built about 1840. Today, the Greek Revival-era doorway on the left remains, the storefront is enclosed, and the building serves as a private residence.

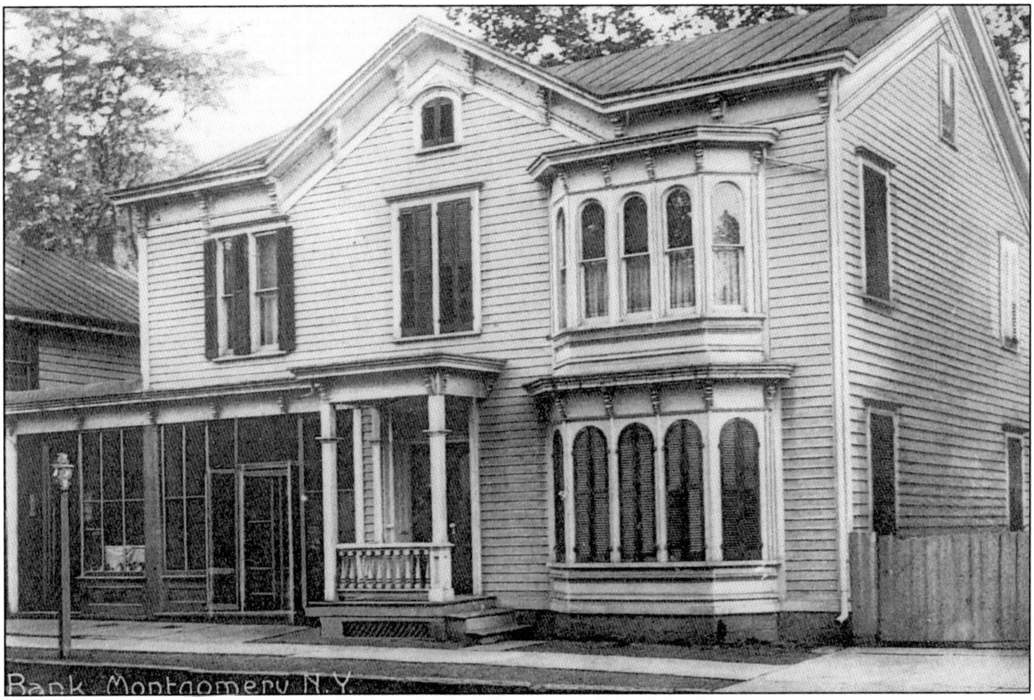

Shortly after the turn of the century, a bank was located in this Victorian-era edifice on Clinton Street. Next door was the former Eager Pharmacy. In the 1890s, Puff's Barber Shop was located here. Today the commercial portion of the building serves as a pizzeria.

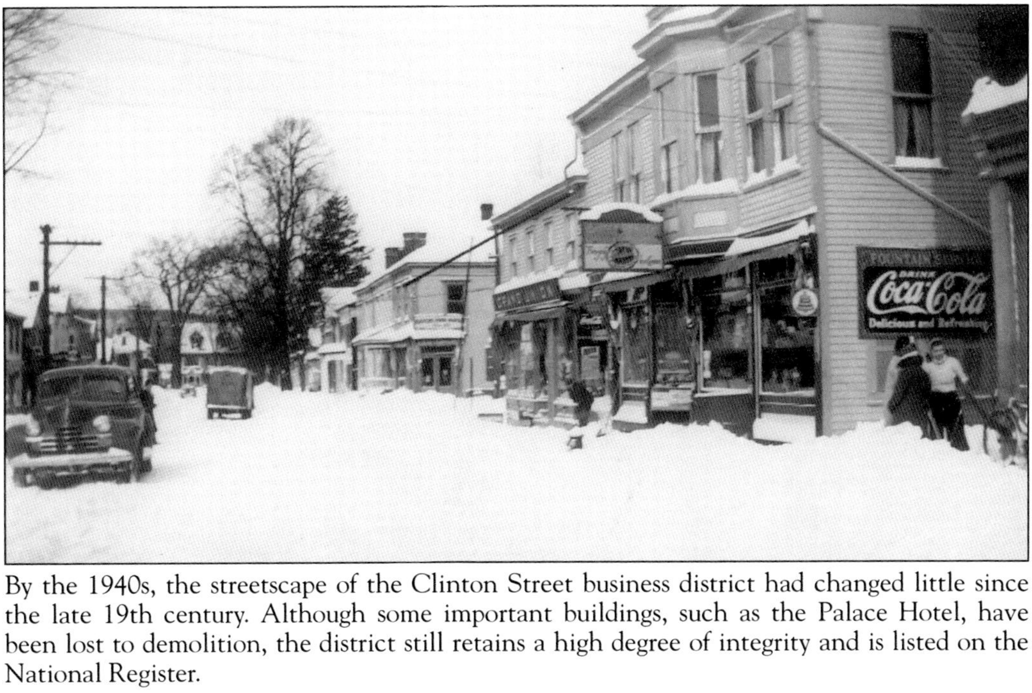

By the 1940s, the streetscape of the Clinton Street business district had changed little since the late 19th century. Although some important buildings, such as the Palace Hotel, have been lost to demolition, the district still retains a high degree of integrity and is listed on the National Register.

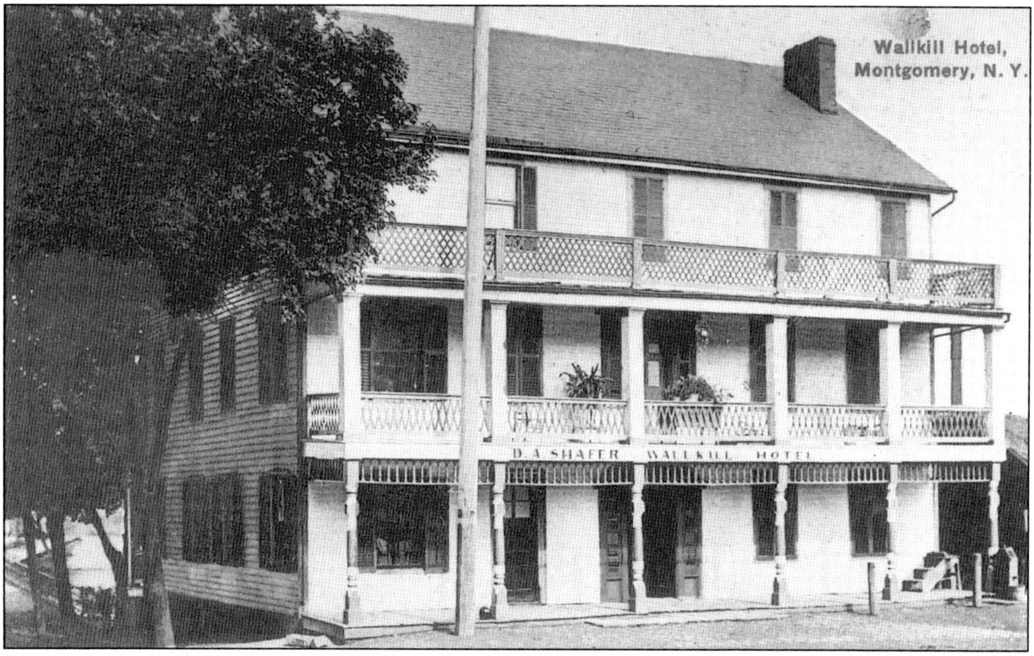

Through much of the 19th century, the village had four hotels to comfort the weary traveler. The Wallkill Hotel was located on the corner of Ward and Bridge Streets. Originally the site of the Widow Smith's Tavern, the Wallkill Hotel was built in the 1820s in the Federal style. It contained a fanlight transom over the first-floor front doorway and a carved sunburst over the second-floor doorway. After fire damaged the attic floor in 1903, an additional story was added.

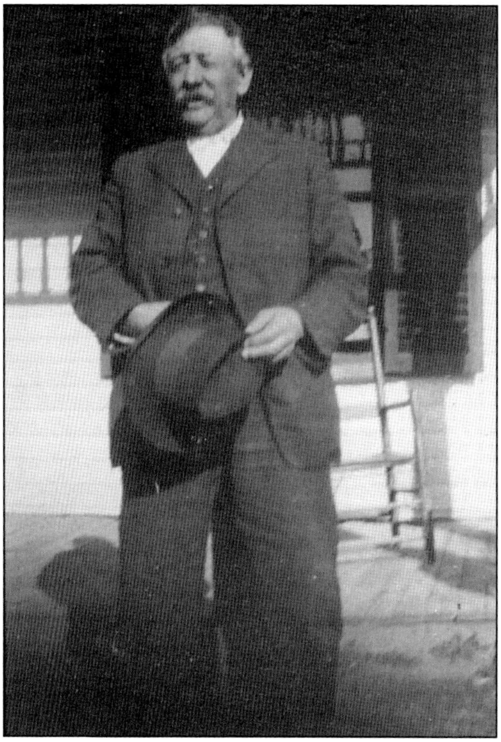

Daniel Alanson Shafer purchased the Wallkill Hotel from D.F. Bull in 1868. In 1880, it became the property of Shafer's son and namesake, pictured here. The hotel was noted for its clambakes held in the rear yard on the bank of the Wallkill River. It was also known for the livestock auctions that were held behind the barn. The hotel remained in Shafer's ownership until 1917 and was demolished in 1956. A parking lot now occupies the site.

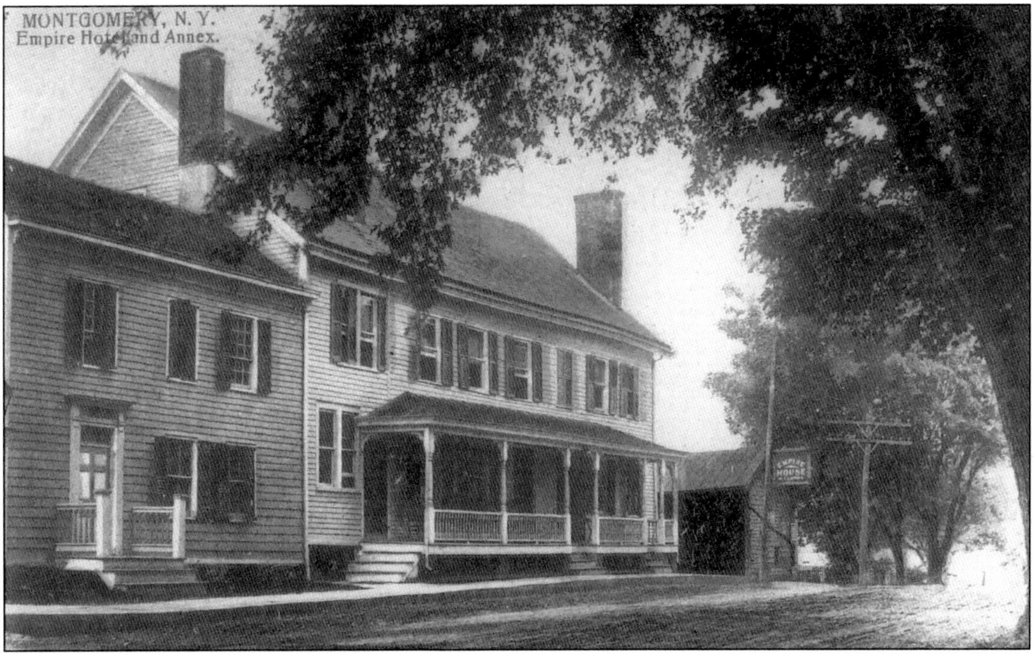

The old Empire House, located on Ward Street just east of Union Street, is currently C.B. Driscoll's restaurant. Dating from the 1820s, the Empire House was operated by the Lodge family for many years. Note the smaller wing attached to the east gable of the building. The wing was removed some years ago. Like D.A. Shafer II, William T. Lodge ran a distillery in addition to his establishment. Lodge's distillery was located in nearby Burnside. Shafer's was located near Franklin Square.

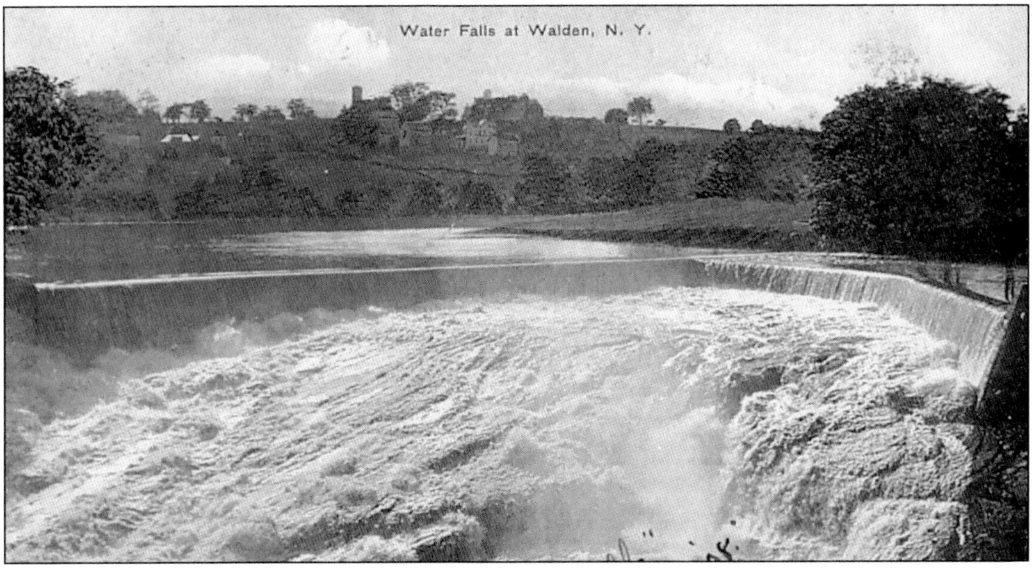

Jacob Treadwell Walden, a shipping merchant from New York City, recognized the potential of the high falls of the Wallkill River. He and other investors bought land on both sides, formed several companies to take advantage of the waterpower, and encouraged businesses to relocate to the area. The 1831 development map made by the investors named the community the "Village of Walden." This view of the falls dates from around 1900.

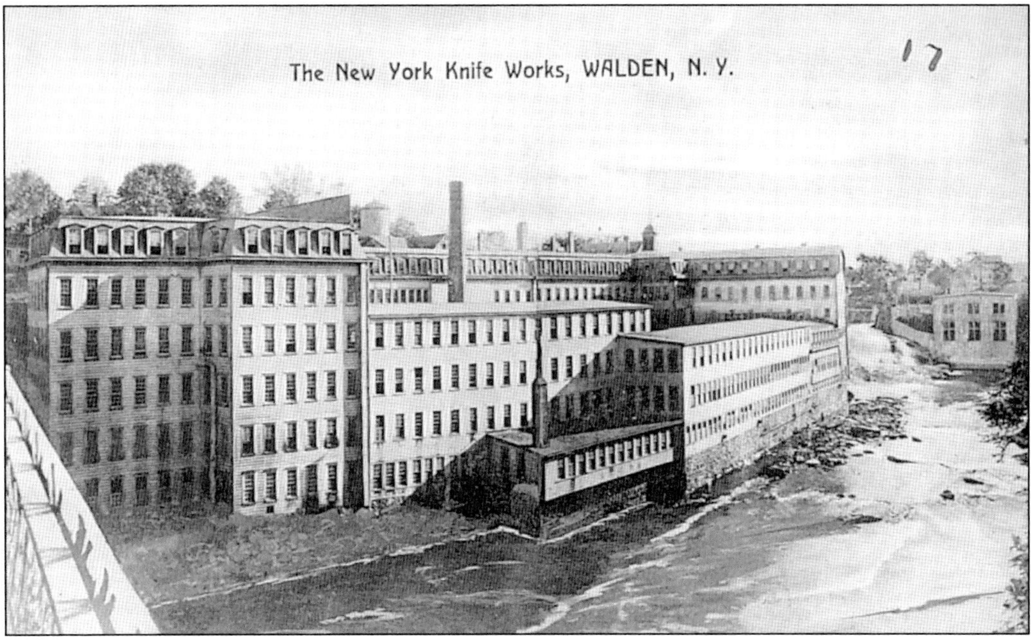

By 1900, the buildings of the New York Knife Company had extended far along the Wallkill River, from below the falls to the bridge on the east bank. Organized in 1852, the company moved to the village in 1856. By 1881, it was one of the largest cutlery producers in the U.S. Business declined and operations ceased in the 1930s. In the 1940s, the buildings were demolished. Today, the ruins of the extensive foundation remain at the site.

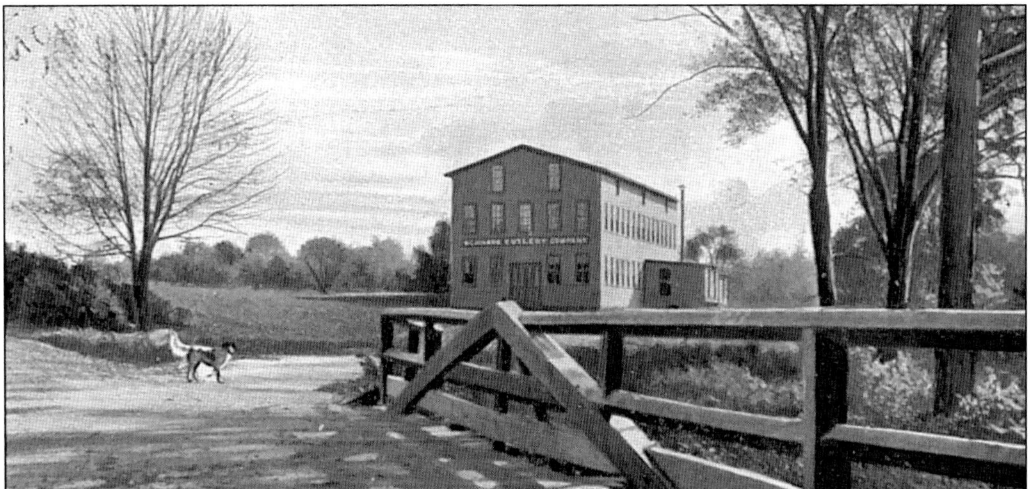

Cutlery manufacturing was big business in Walden. During its peak years, the village was referred to as the Sheffield of America. The Schrade Cutlery Company began in Walden in 1904. The Schrade building, located on Route 52, was destroyed by fire in the 1960s. The dog shown in this 1906 postcard belonged to the night watchman. A bell, located in the gable peak, was rung for the workers. Schrade closed the Walden facility in 1958, consolidating it with the Ellenville operation.

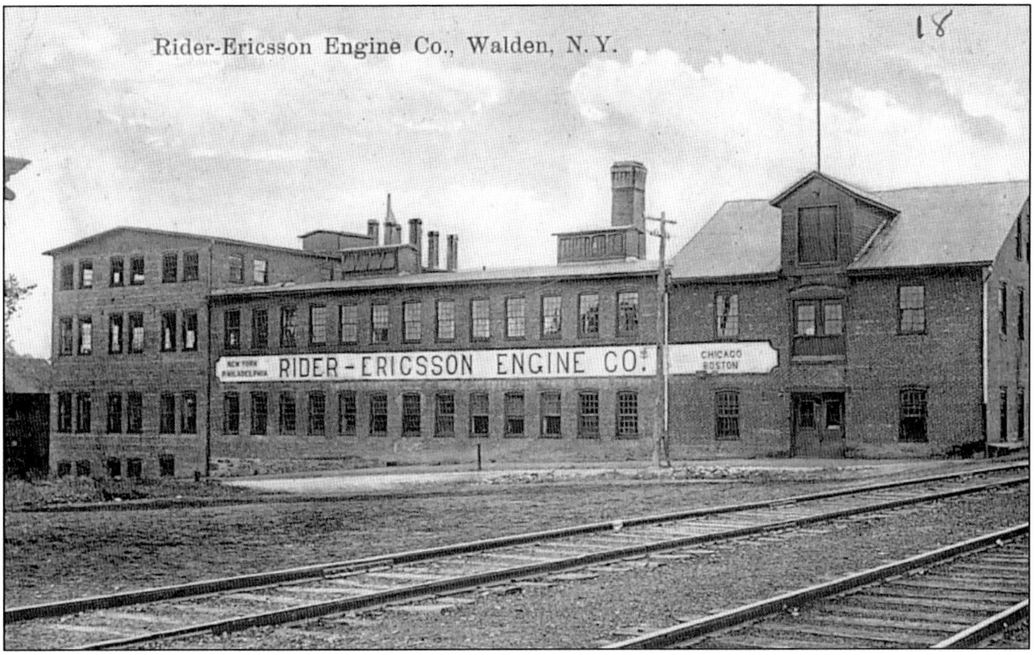

Dating from the 1870s, the Rider-Ericsson Company (originally Rider, Wooster & Co.) was located in the village of Walden in a large brick building on Grant Street, now occupied by Packaged Lighting. The company originally manufactured steam and hot air pumping engines. In 1908, it employed 125 men. Rider-Ericsson was succeeded by Spence Engineering, a manufacturer of steam regulation valves now located on Coldenham Road.

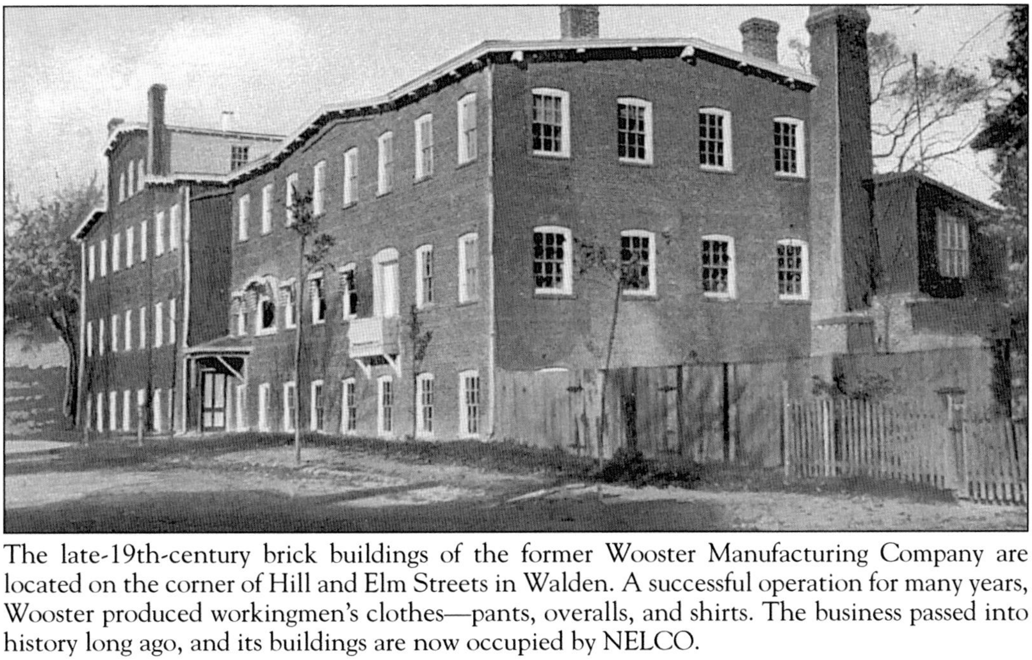

The late-19th-century brick buildings of the former Wooster Manufacturing Company are located on the corner of Hill and Elm Streets in Walden. A successful operation for many years, Wooster produced workingmen's clothes—pants, overalls, and shirts. The business passed into history long ago, and its buildings are now occupied by NELCO.

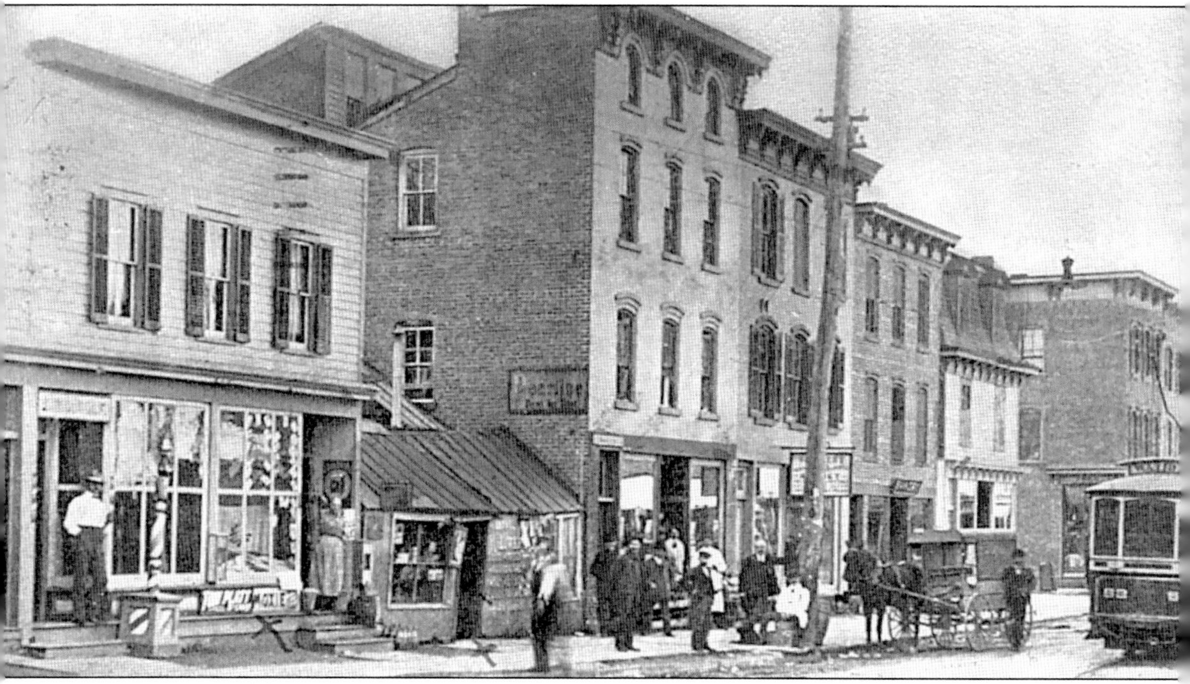

By 1900, Walden was the busiest of the town of Montgomery's three villages. This view shows the south side of Main Street, as seen from a point near the McKinley Memorial. Note the Walden-Newburgh trolley. On the far left, Ed Dewolfe stands at the entrance to his barber shop. Next door is Mrs.Coddington in the doorway of her candy shop. The low, dilapidated building is a cobbler's shop. On the right is a building that housed the Scribner Grocery Store. The Fowler & Decker Hardware building is next door. On the corner is the Caleb Birch Shoe Store. On the opposite corner of Orchard Street is the H.E. Williams Hardware Store.

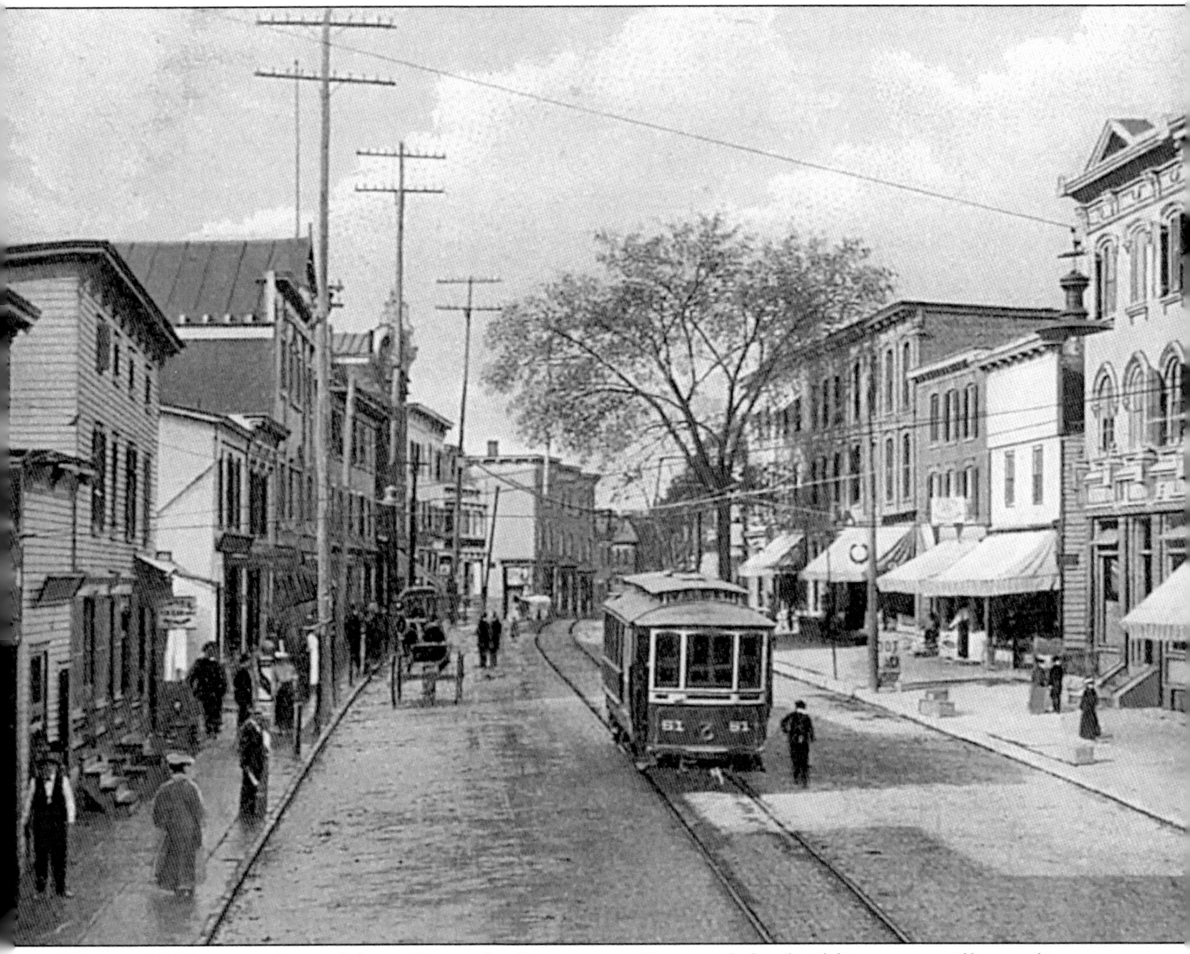

This *c.* 1908 view shows Main Street looking west. Some of the buildings are still standing. The one at the far right housed Carl Lustig's dry goods business. The one next door housed the National Bank of Walden. Diagonally across the street was the Didsbury Theater, which dated from 1903 and was demolished in 1974. People went there to see plays, minstrel shows, and silent movies (later, talkies). Singer Enrico Caruso was featured there once, as was John Philip Sousa's band.

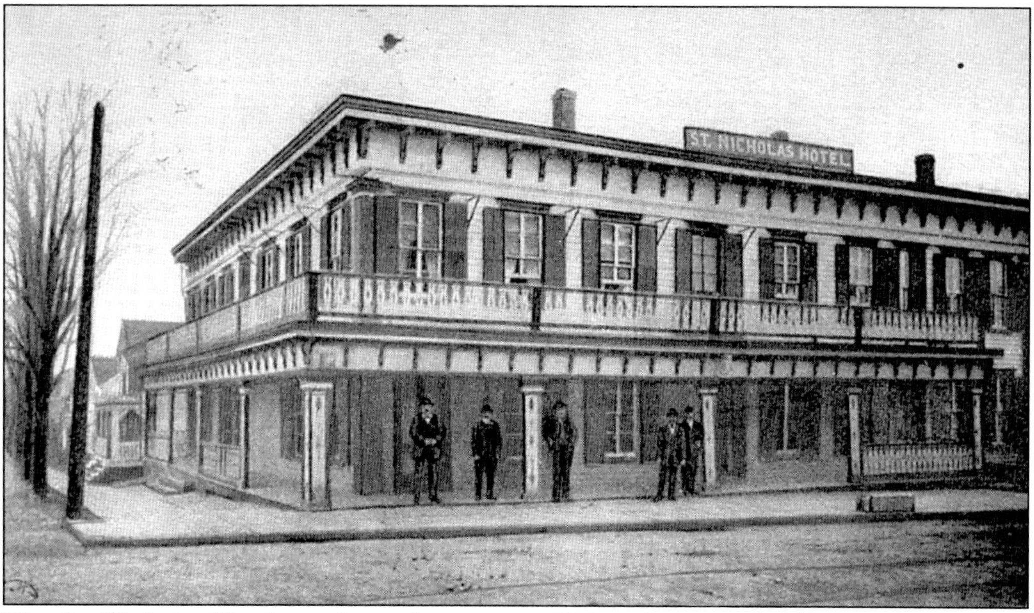

The St. Nicholas Hotel stood on the corner of Main Street and Ulster Avenue, where Walden Federal now stands. Probably built during the Greek Revival period, the hotel was updated during the mid-Victorian era in the Italianate style. Note the carriage stepping-stone alongside the roadway. In the 1930s, this old hotel gave way to Johnston's Service Station and Burton's Diner.

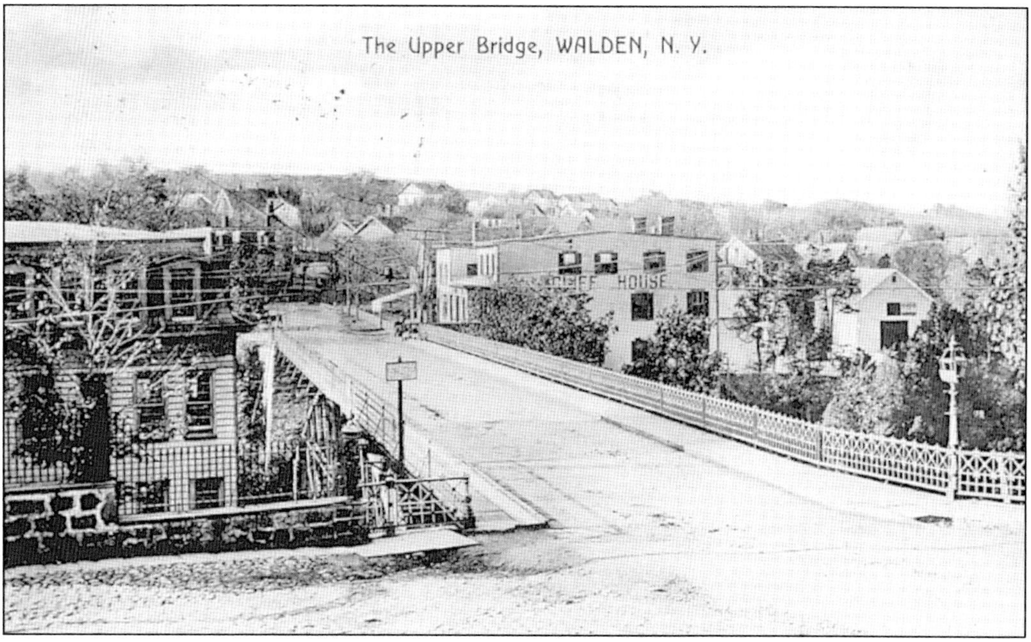

This 1900s view shows the upper bridge over the Wallkill River. Like the bridge in Montgomery, this iron span was manufactured by the Berlin Iron Bridge Company. Note the old lamp. The Cliff House, visible on the opposite side of the bridge, was a boardinghouse that has been converted into apartments. A portion of the New York Knife Co. appears to the left of the bridge. In the 1930s, this bridge was replaced with the current one.

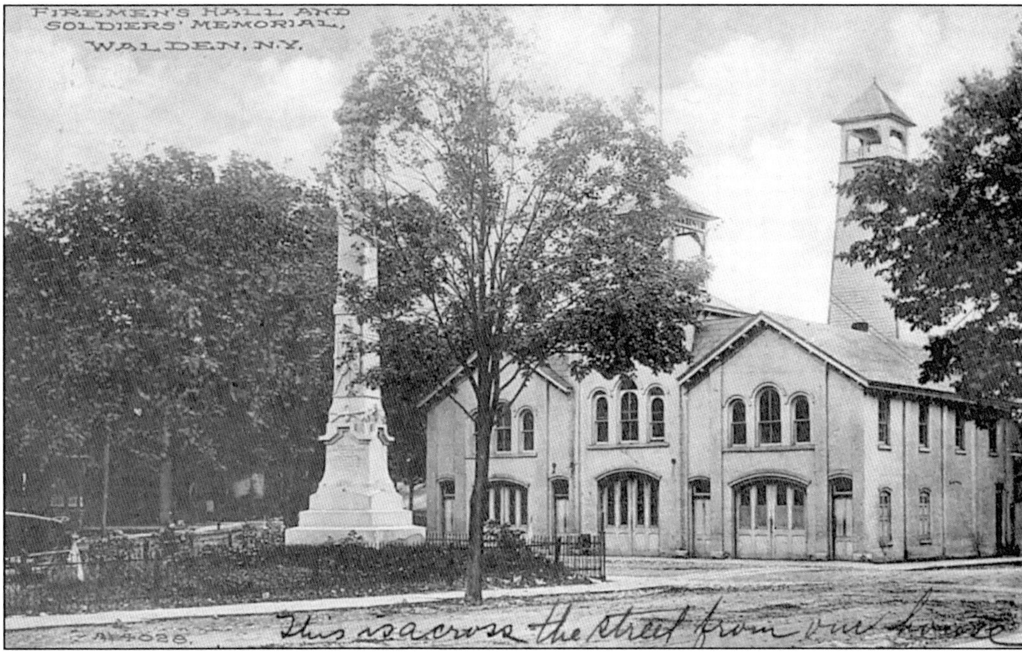

The old Victorian-era firehouse, pictured above, was replaced by the Walden Municipal Building, seen below. Note the tower behind the old building. It was used as a lookout, as well as a place to dry the hoses. Col. Thomas W. Bradley, Walden's most influential businessman, made a substantial contribution toward the construction of the new building, with certain stipulations as to the naming of the library (Josephine-Louise, after his wife and daughter) and the assembly room. Built in 1915, the building contains not only the library, but also municipal offices and the firehouse. It is also the cultural center of the village. The large monument in front was erected in 1890 in honor of Montgomery's Civil War veterans.

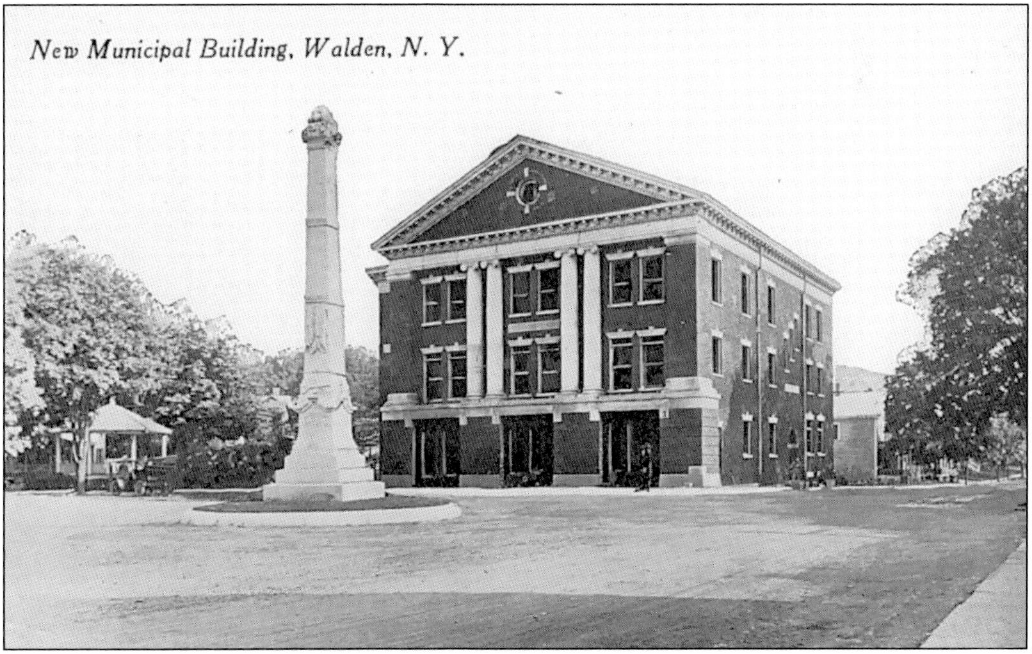

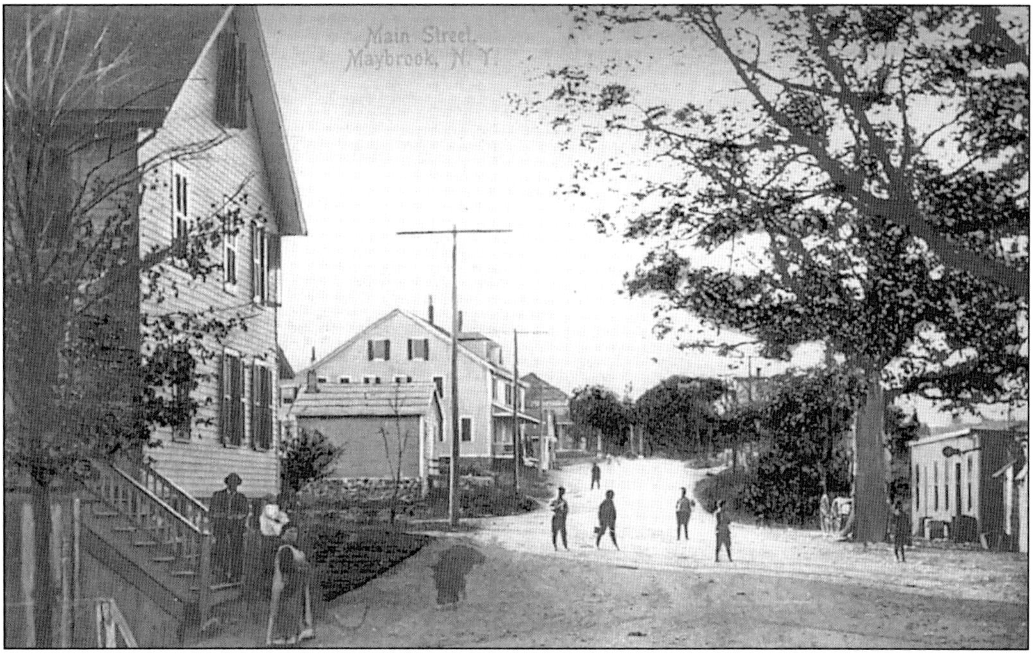

Maybrook as a village traces its roots to the late 1880s, when work on a rail line commenced from Campbell Hall to the bridge over the Hudson River at Poughkeepsie. This new line enabled goods to be transported from the western markets to New England and overseas. Initially called Orange Junction, it was renamed Maybrook Junction. These postcards, *c.* 1900, show the same area of Main Street—one from the bottom of the hill and the other from the top.

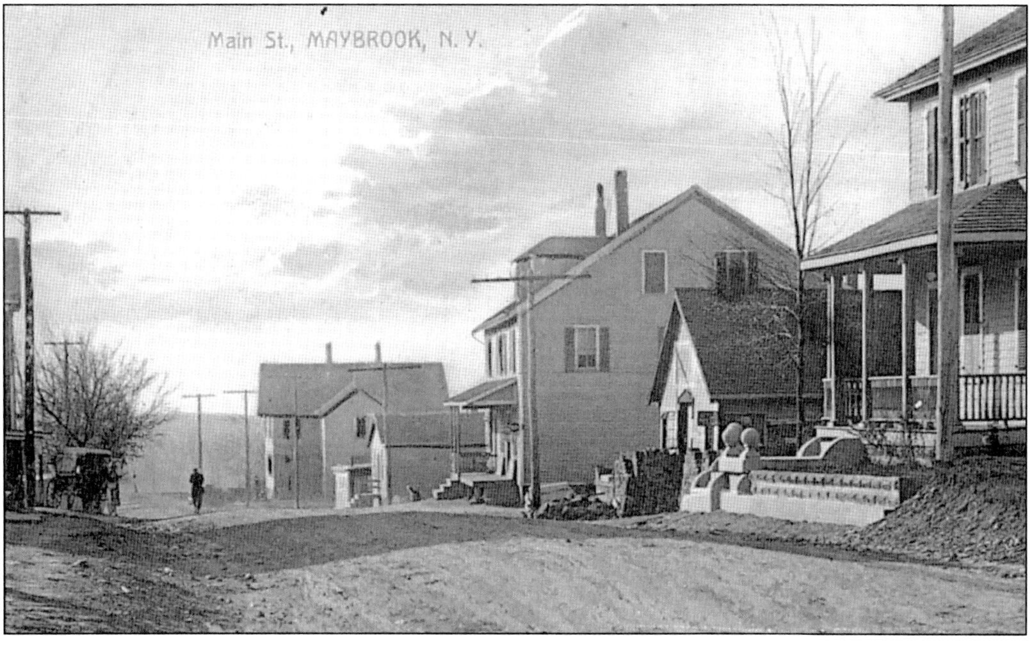

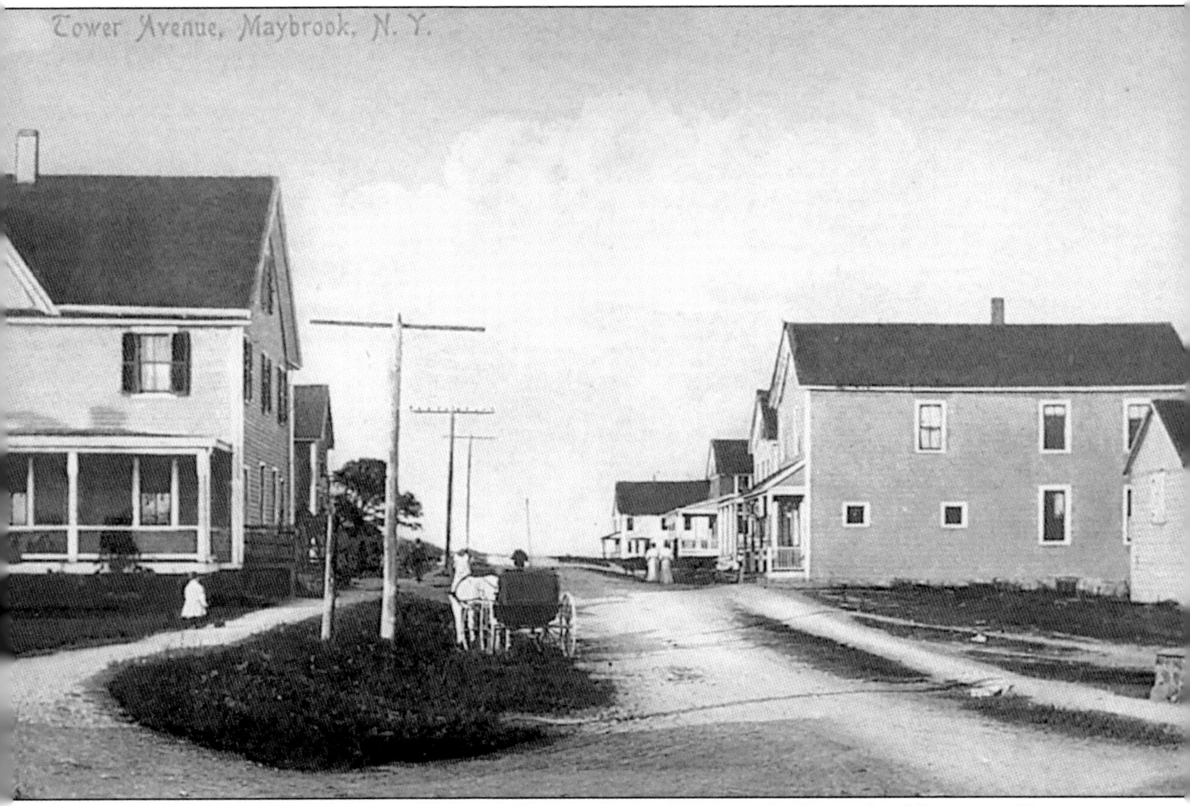

Taken from the corner of Main Street, this *c.* 1910 photograph shows buildings on Tower Avenue, many of which are still standing. The large house at the left once housed Sweeney's Hotel and Bar. By 1900, Maybrook had a large number of rooming houses. Among them were the Yellow Dog, the Red Onion, the Green Turtle, the Blue Goose, and Ma Hawks's House of Blazes.

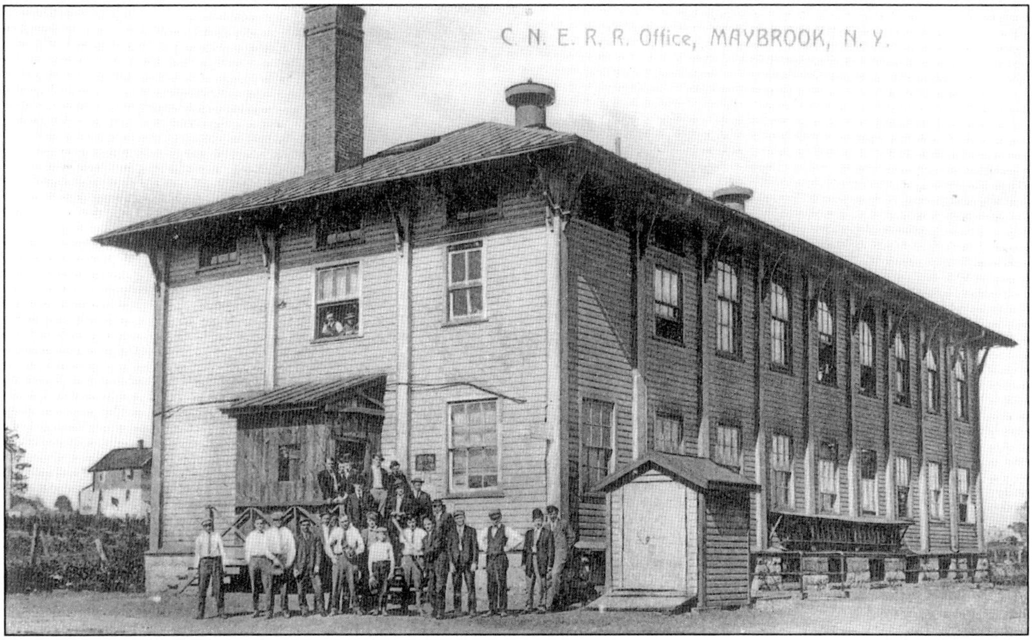

The Central New England Railroad built its office at the end of Main Street, where the lumberyard is today. The office served the administrative purposes for the operation of the Maybrook terminal. By 1900, the terminal consisted of three tracks for receiving trains of the western lines and three for the Central New England trains to be delivered to the western lines.

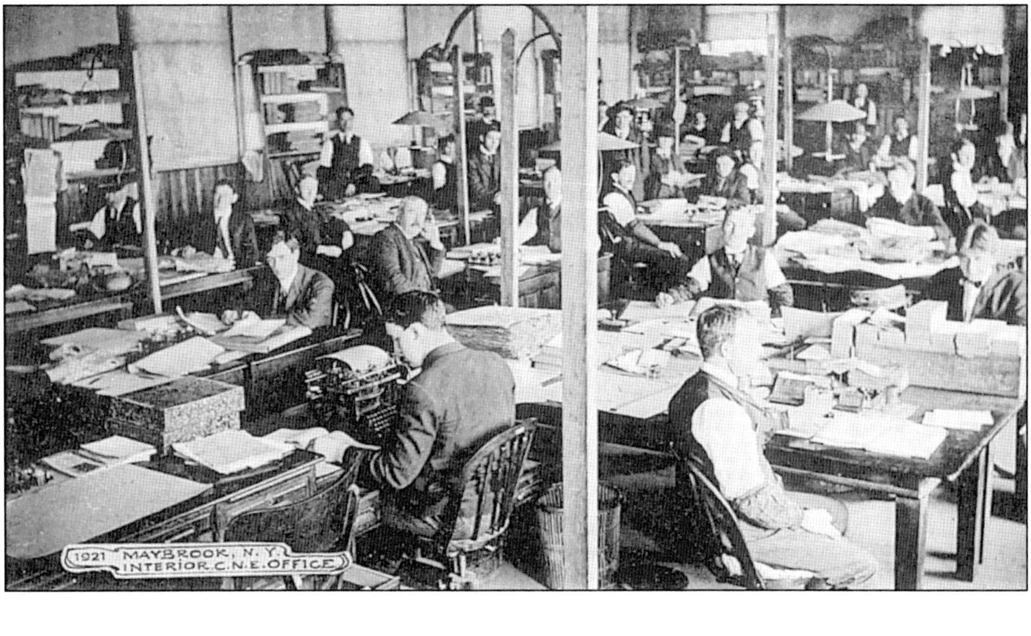

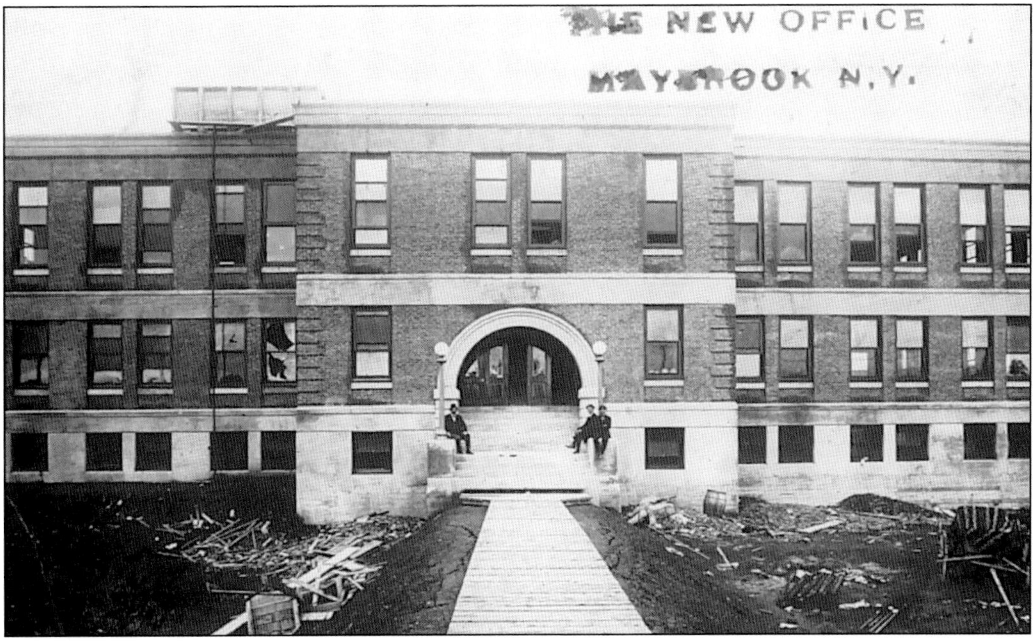

In 1906, the New York, New Haven and Hartford Railroad acquired a half interest in the Central New England Railroad at Maybrook. Soon afterward, the railroad initiated plans to construct a switching terminal, which later became one of the largest east of the Mississippi. New buildings were constructed, including those to house repair shops and car building shops. This photograph, c. 1912, shows the new general office building. Abandoned long ago, the office still stands to the east of Yellow Freight's yard.

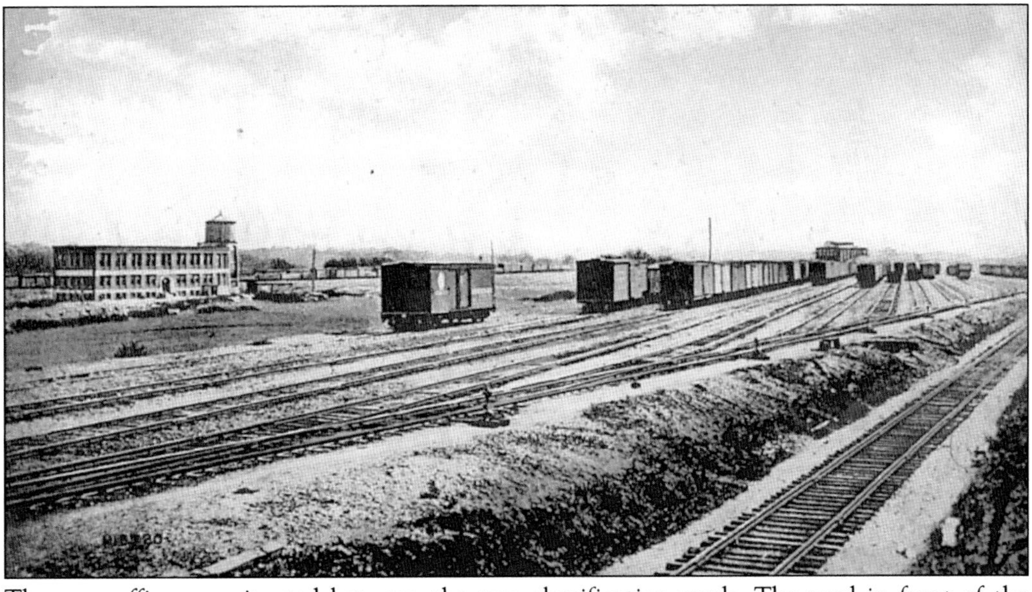

The new office was situated between the two classification yards. The yard in front of the office served as the westbound yard (much of this area is now occupied by Yellow Freight). Behind the office was the eastbound yard. The foreground of this 1918 view shows the main, an unobstructed track that allowed passenger trains through the terminal. In its peak years during World War II, the terminal employed 1,500 people and had a weekly payroll of $150,000.

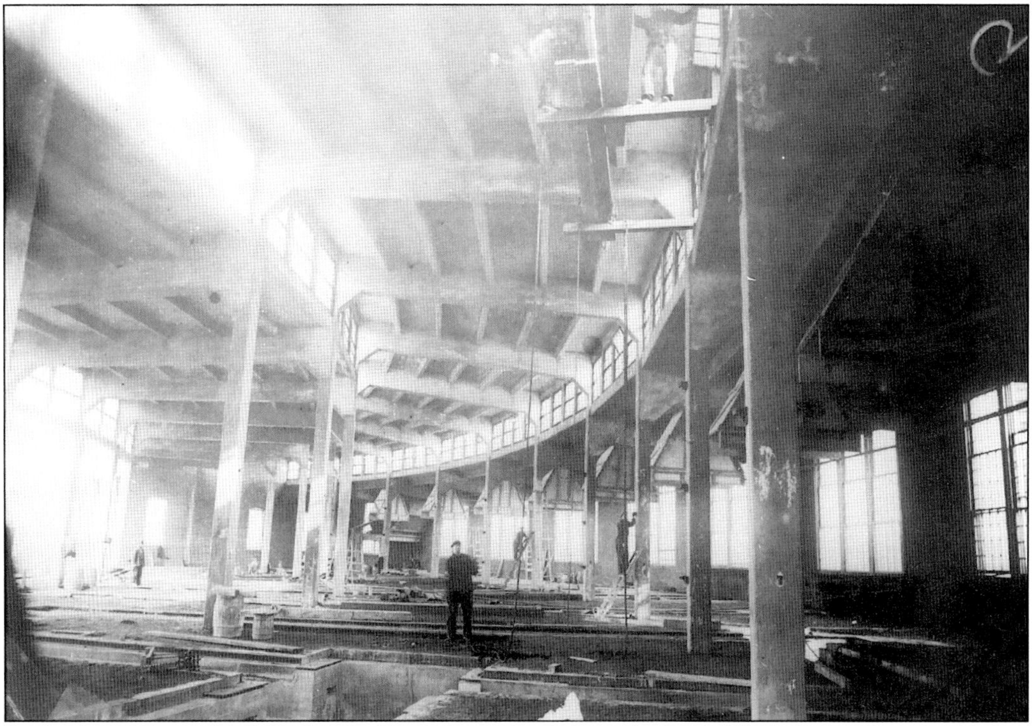

The roundhouse served as a repair shop for the engines. The exterior view dates from the 1940s, and the interior view dates from 1912, when the building was under construction. A portion of the roundhouse was removed in the early 1960s, when cars were rerouted, causing the Maybrook facility to undergo a reduction in service. In 1974, after the bridge fire in Poughkeepsie, all activity at the Maybrook facility ceased. Yellow Freight removed the last portion of the roundhouse in recent years.

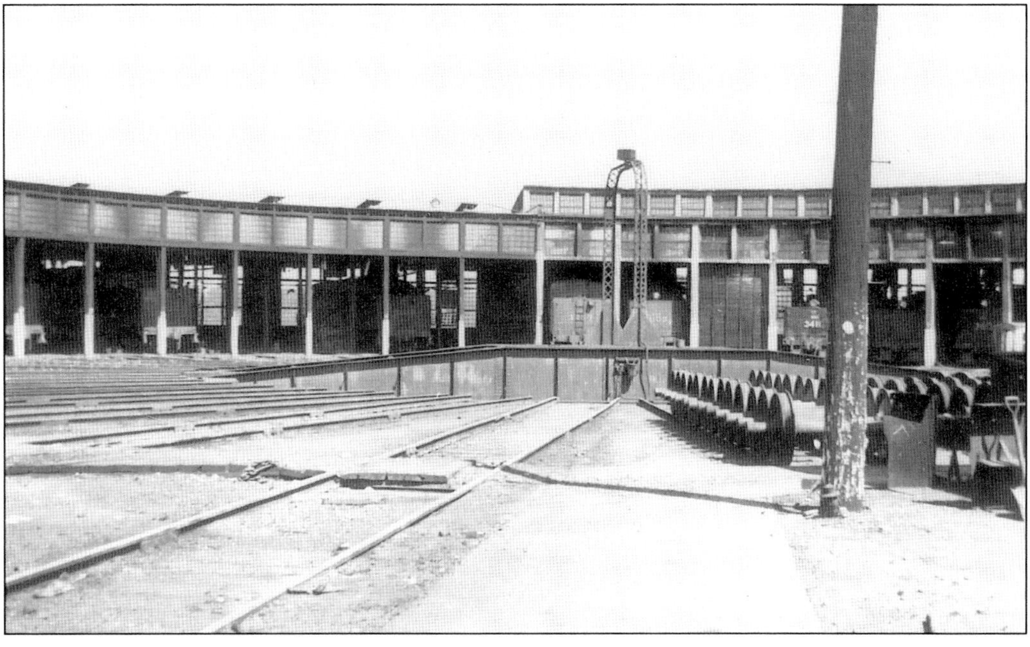

Five

Recreation

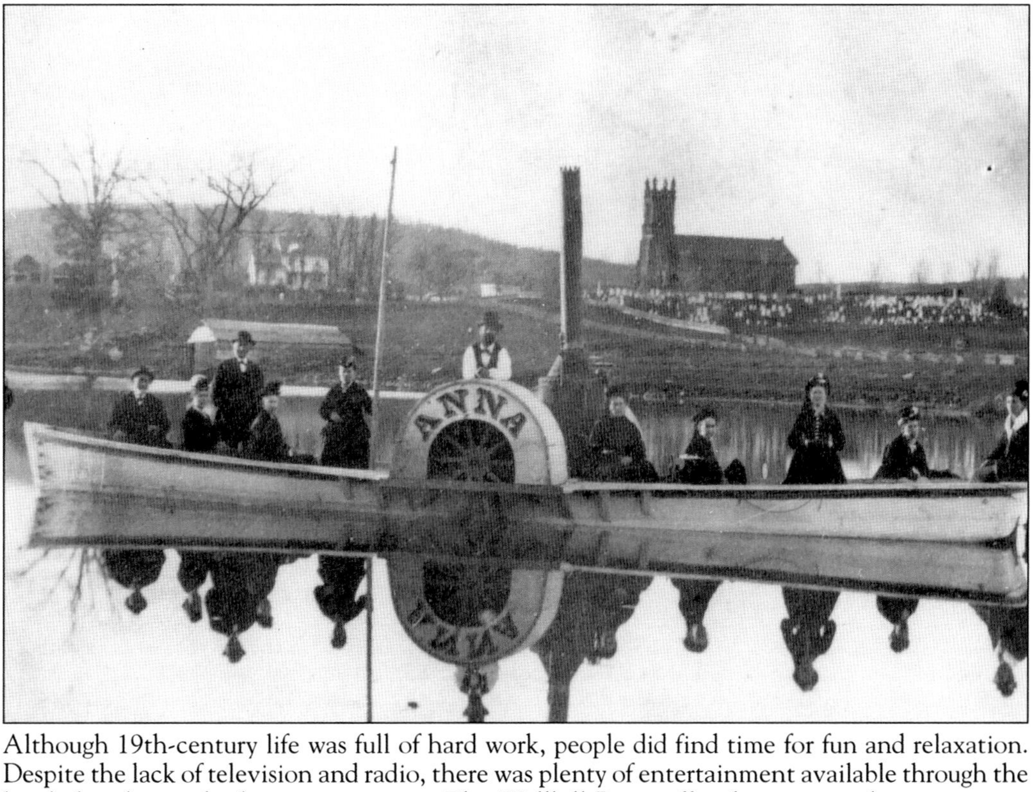

Although 19th-century life was full of hard work, people did find time for fun and relaxation. Despite the lack of television and radio, there was plenty of entertainment available through the local churches and other organizations. The Wallkill River offered recreational opportunities to both young and old. All along the river were favorite swimming holes and fishing spots. This photograph, c. 1870, shows the small steamboat *Anna* on the river above Ward's Bridge. Note the Brick Church in the distance, with its original spire configuration.

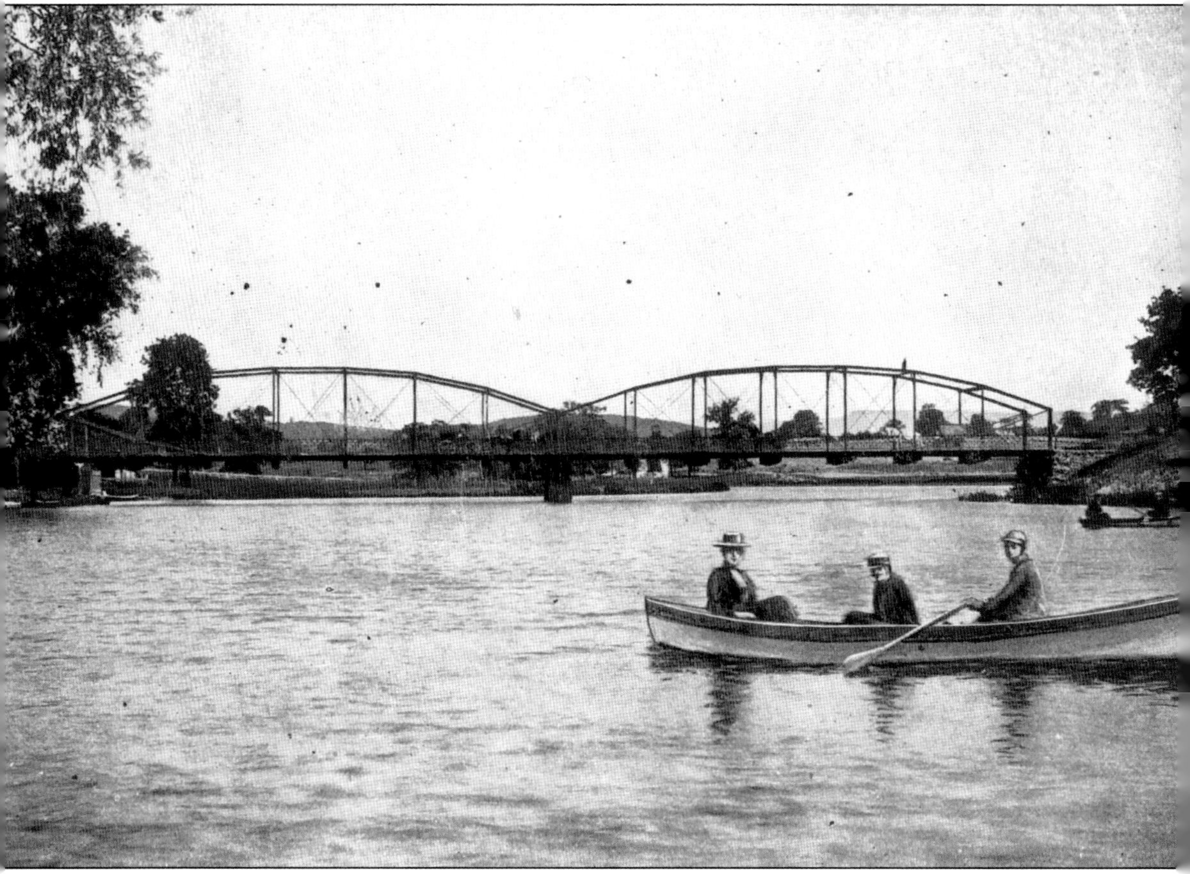

A leisurely sojourn in a rowboat above Stratton's Dam was a favorite pastime of years ago. Boaters shown here were probably patrons of D.A. Shafer's Wallkill Hotel. The hotel made boats available to hotel guests and friends. The hotel also had a dancing pavilion, which was an exciting place to be in the summer months of the 1890s. The Berlin Iron Bridge in the background was built in 1887 to replace an earlier span.

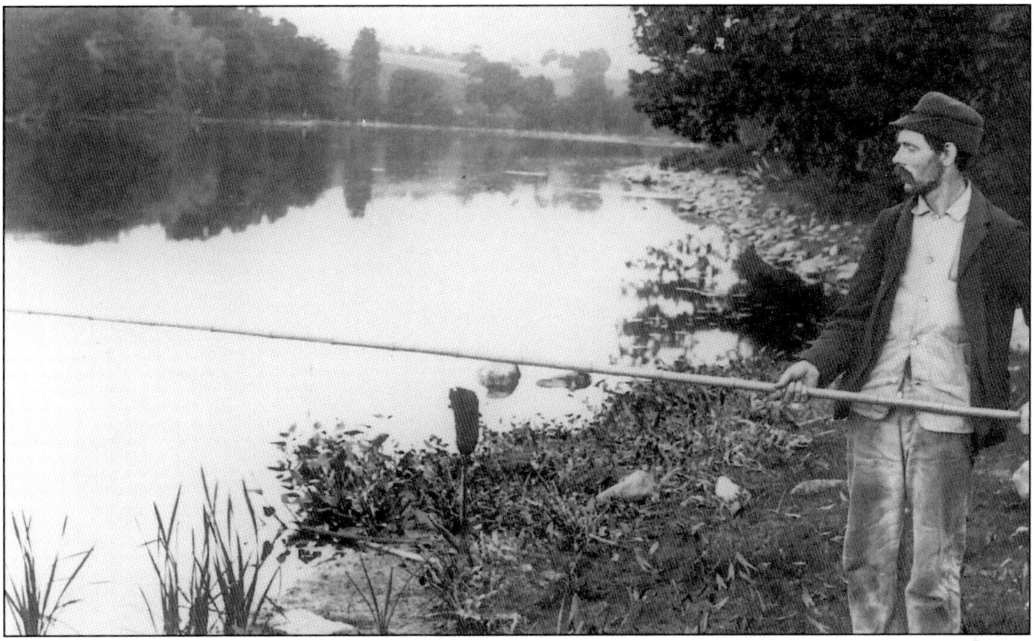

On the south shore of the Wallkill River, above Crabtree's Dam, was a favorite fishing and swimming area. Note the crude fishing rod in the above photograph. In this earlier era, most fishing rods were nothing more than poles with strings attached. The lower photo shows bathers using the river—a reminder that, at one time, the water was clean enough for swimming and other recreation. Today, as the area continues to develop, the water quality of the river will decline.

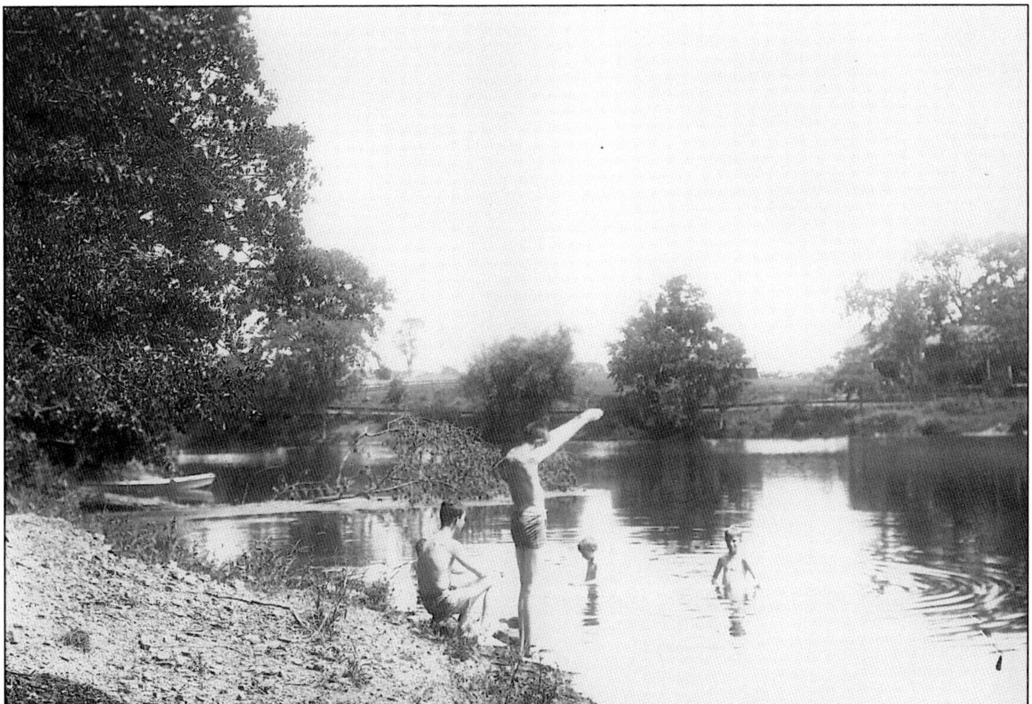

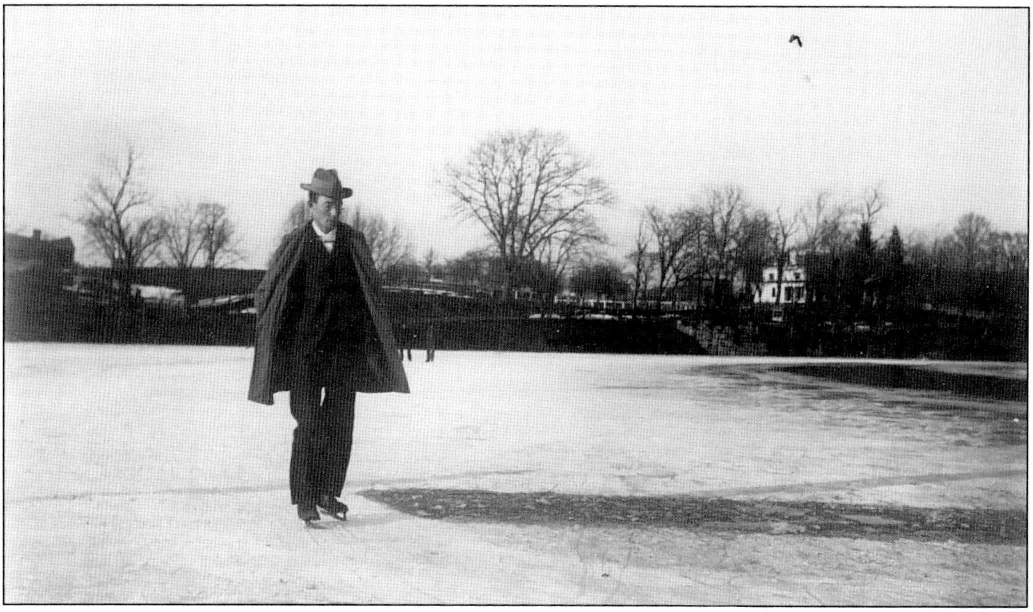

During the winter months, the frozen millponds of the Wallkill provided a source of entertainment. Skating was a great social event, often enjoyed on pleasant Sunday afternoons. This photograph, *c.* 1898, shows John Crabtree. It was taken from above the Crabtree Mill, in the village of Montgomery. John's daughter, Lemma Crabtree, recalled that, in her youth, it was her Uncle Charlie's job to make sure the ice was thick enough for skating.

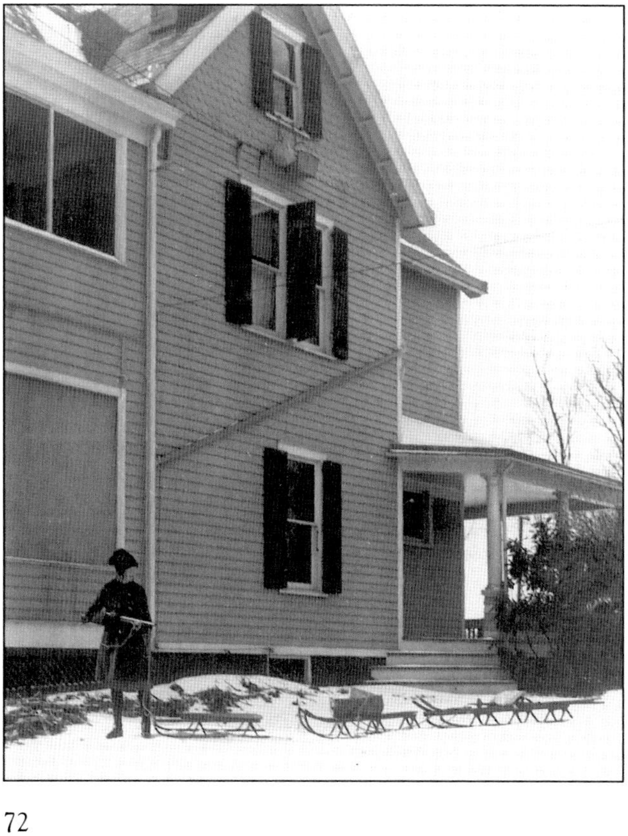

As in our time, children of years ago enjoyed sledding down steep hills. This photograph of Lemma Crabtree was taken on the side of the John Crabtree residence on Factory Street about 1924. The Crabtree children made good use of the hill behind their grandfather's house, which sloped down into the meadows. Note the baskets hanging from the north attic window; pork was stored in them during the winter months.

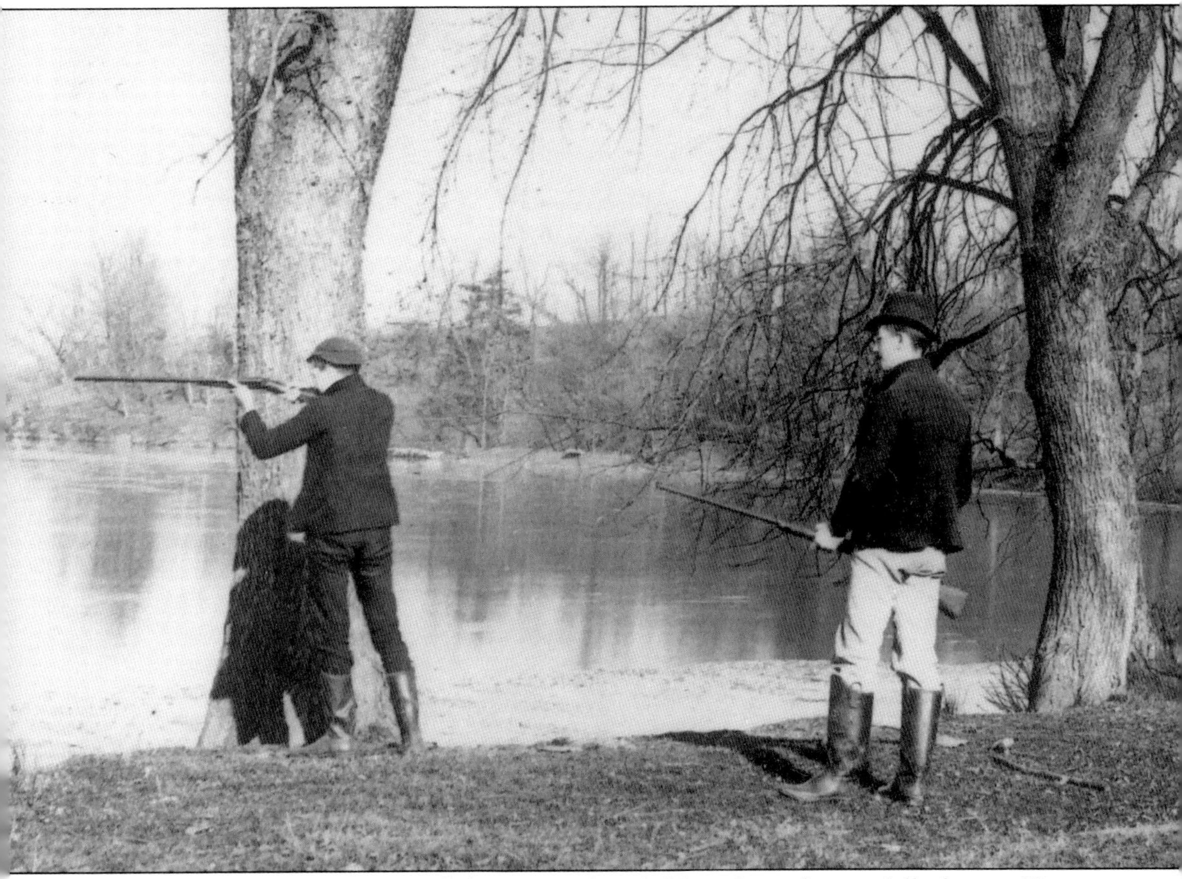

Hunting was a favorite pastime, and the surrounding fields and woods were full of game. Here, the Crabtree brothers, Charles and Harry, hunt along the Wallkill River. A story handed down in the Shafer family tells of the time when Jim Gill stopped at the Wallkill Hotel and told his friend Dan about the fox he was in pursuit of in the Comfort Hills. The gentlemen then parted company. A short time later, Dan decided to try his luck as well. While en route to the hills, Dan spotted a fox crossing the road, successfully bagged it, and went back to the hotel with his prize. Later, when Jim returned empty-handed, Dan revealed his good fortune.

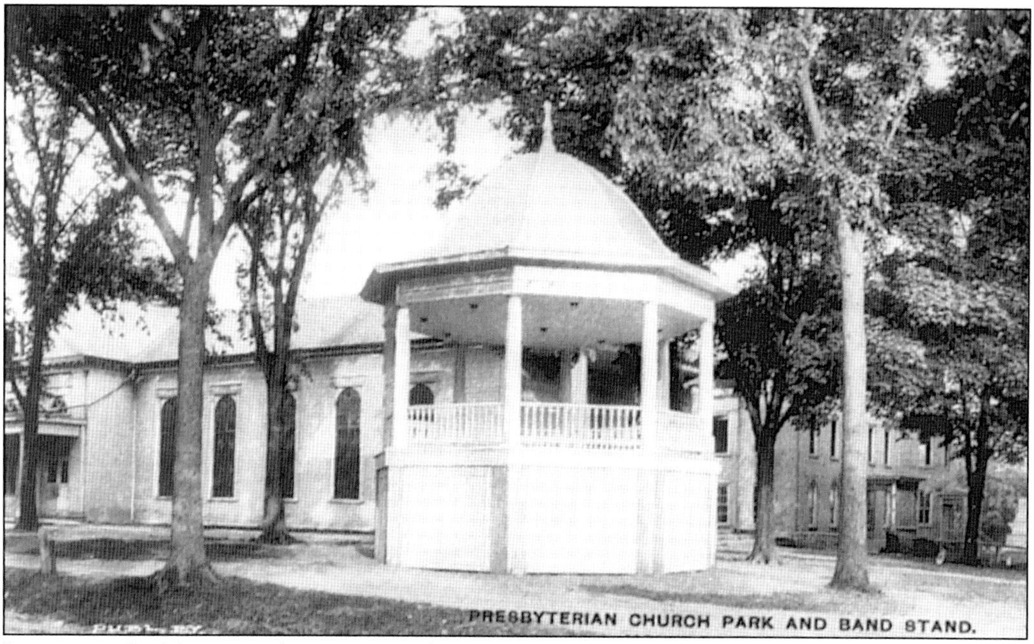

It was wonderful to spend a summer afternoon or evening listening to the local band in the village center. The bandstand pictured above in this postcard, c. 1913, stood adjacent to the Presbyterian church in the village of Montgomery. Long since vanished, the bandstand was built in the early 1900s as a replacement for an older stand. At that time, there were several small bands in the town of Montgomery.

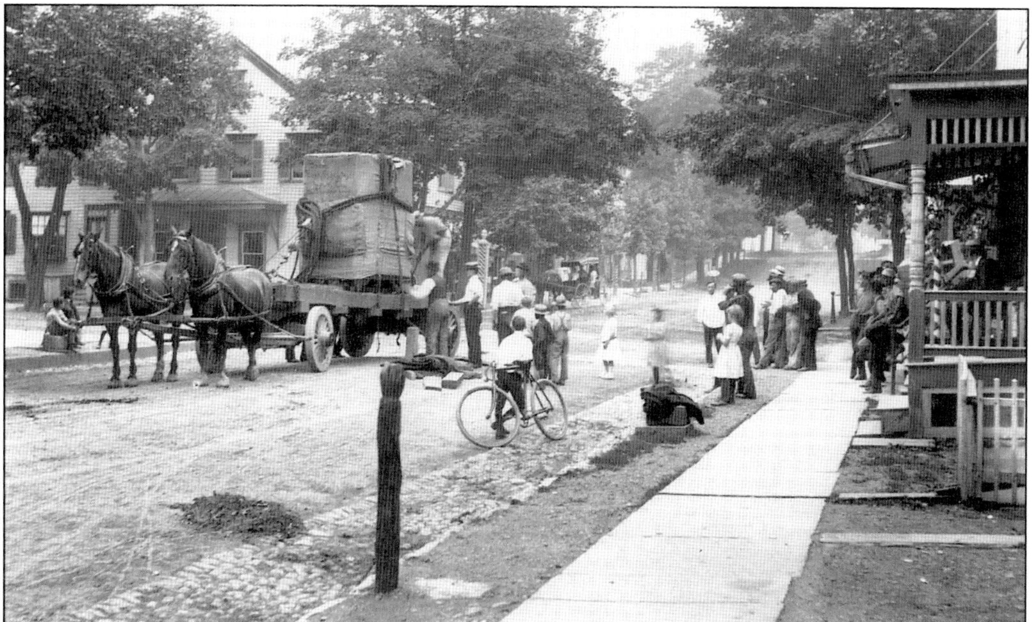

Local out-of-the-ordinary events provided excitement for people of all ages. This postcard, c. 1905, shows the bank safe being moved to its new location on Clinton Street, where the village pizzeria is located today. Some of the anxious spectators appear to be wondering how something so large and heavy can be moved by hand.

Six

The Crabtree Photographic Legacy

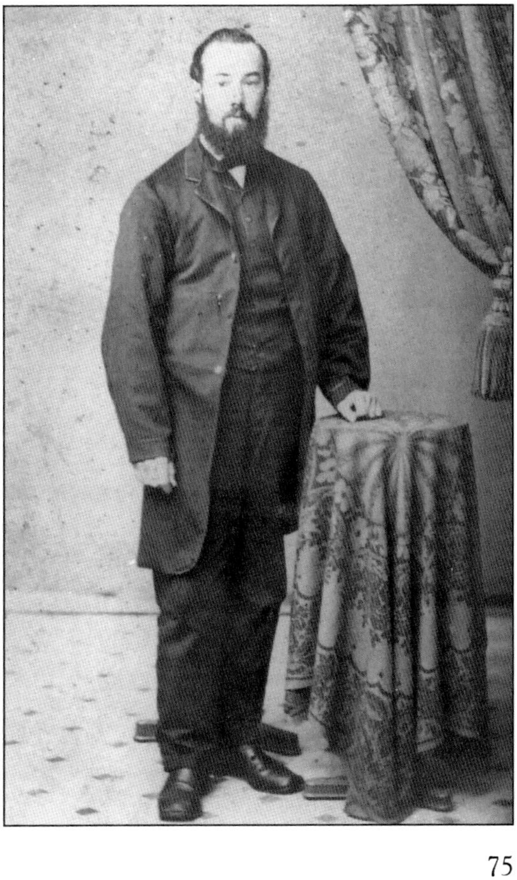

William Crabtree emigrated from Yorkshire, England, to the U.S. in June 1864 in search of a life of prosperity. He returned to England three years later to marry Harriet Patchett, and the two moved to William's home in Philadelphia, where they began their family. They were eventually joined by Harriet's brother Arthur, who, no doubt, was enticed to America by Will's favorable reports. In 1880, the brothers-in-law formed a partnership, determined to acquire a textile mill of their own. They heard of the availability of Edmund Ackroyd's mill in Montgomery, and after inspecting it, they decided to purchase it. The business proved to be profitable for many years, and the Crabtree and Patchett families were included among the upper class of the town. William was a hard-working businessman who always found time to spend with his family and develop his hobbies. He was an admirer of the splendors of nature, and by 1890 he had developed an interest in photography. He was a common sight in the 1890s, traveling through the area with his bulky photographic equipment.

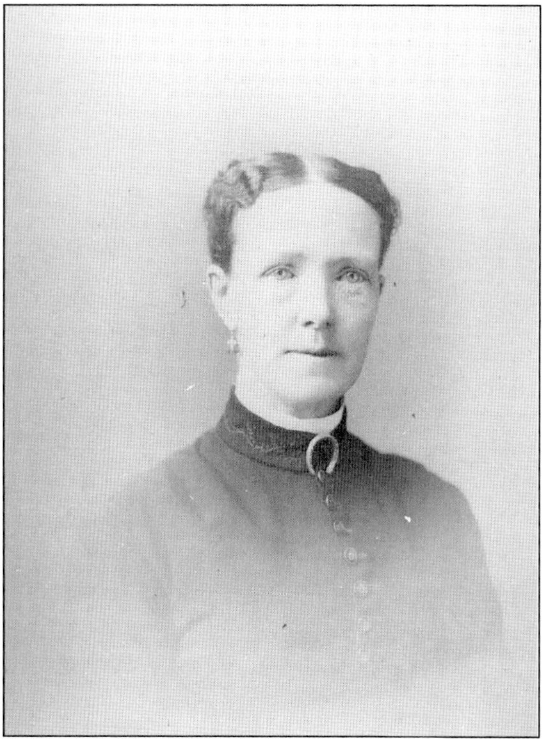

Harriet, also a native of Yorkshire, was probably Will's childhood sweetheart. While living in Philadelphia, the Crabtrees had four sons: Harry, Edmund, John, and William. In the *c.* 1880 photograph below are, from left to right, Harry, John, and Edmund. After moving to Montgomery, Harriet and Will had a fifth son, Charles. All five sons eventually became involved in the family worsted mill on Factory Street in Montgomery.

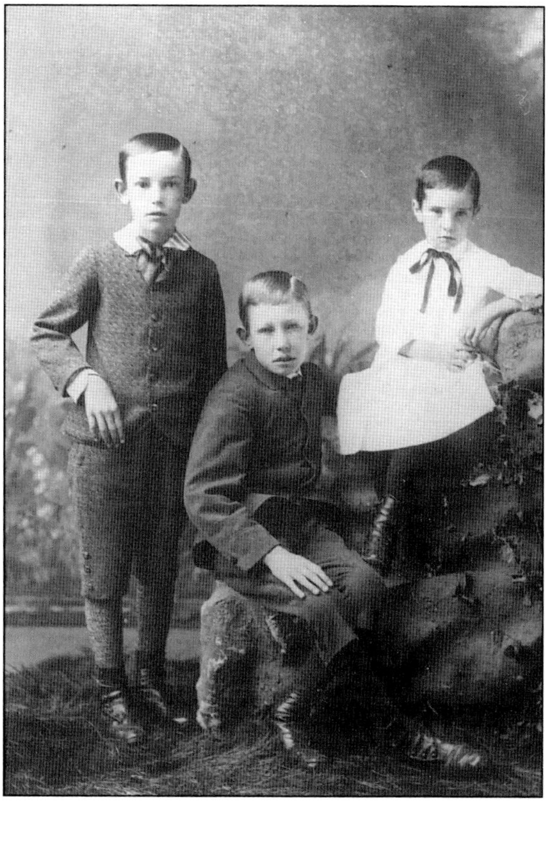

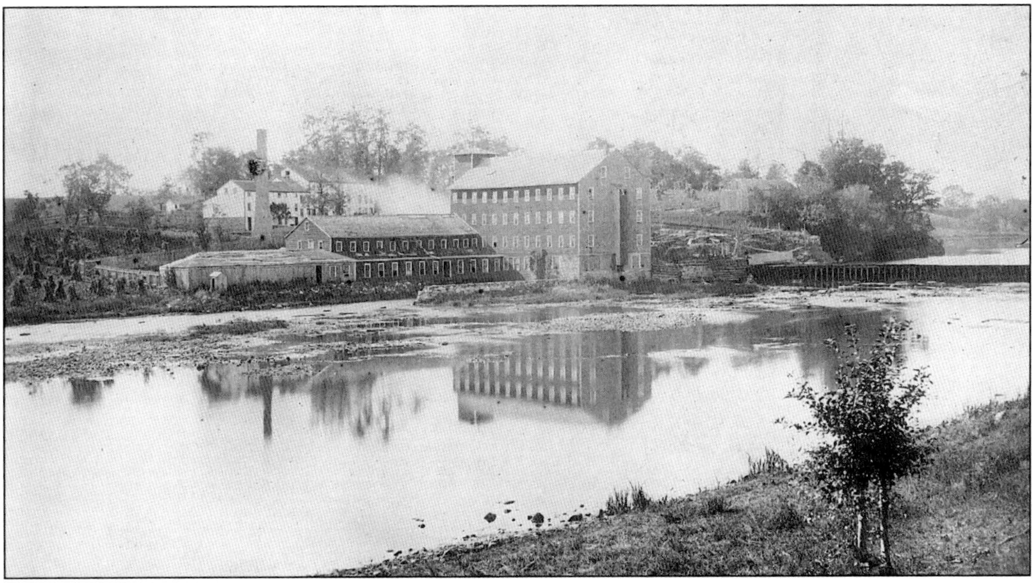

The mill on the Wallkill River was quite different in 1880, when William Crabtree and his partner came to Montgomery. The large frame block was built in the early 1800s by a group of local entrepreneurs. The frame wing was probably the first addition to the original mill. In the 1870s, a brick section was added by Edmund Ackroyd. Dating from the 1880s, this is the earliest known photograph of the mill.

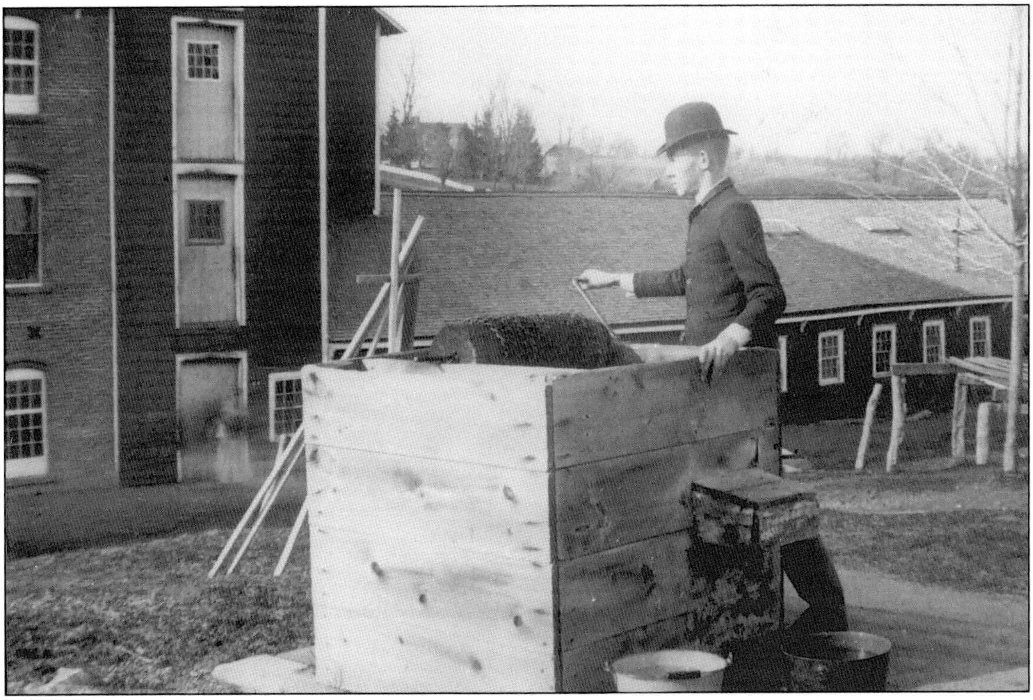

Will wanted to catch his subjects doing everyday activities but would usually have family members pose for him. Here, John Crabtree is at the well in front of the old mill in the early 1890s. Note the full pails of water beside the well. Also, note the blur in front of the mill's lower-floor doorway—a woman walking out of the mill.

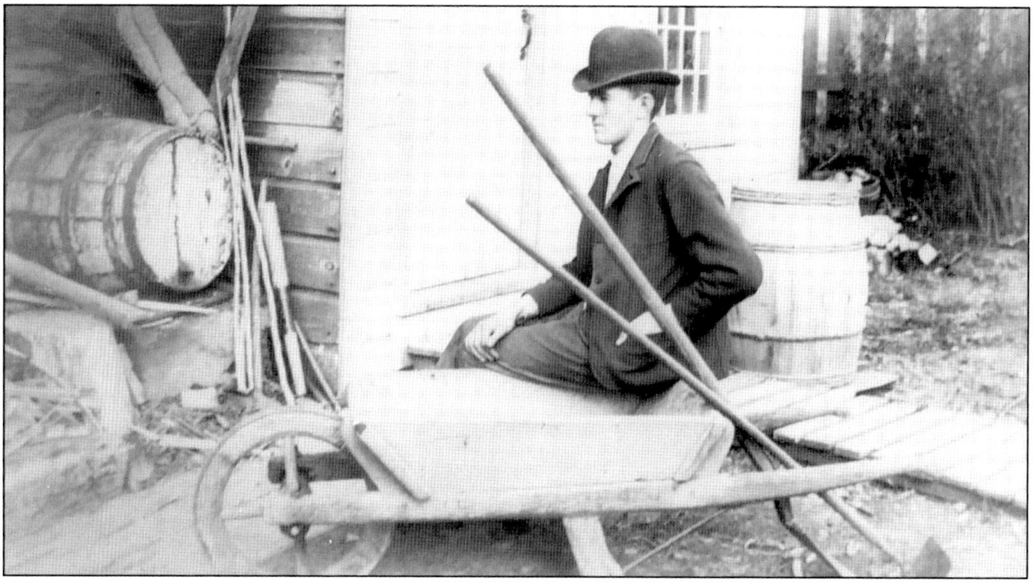

Ed Crabtree posed for this artistic view in front of the woodshed, located behind the row house. Note the early wheelbarrow and the wooden boardwalk. After William Crabtree Jr. built his house on Factory Street in 1903, he moved the woodshed to his backyard, where it still stands today.

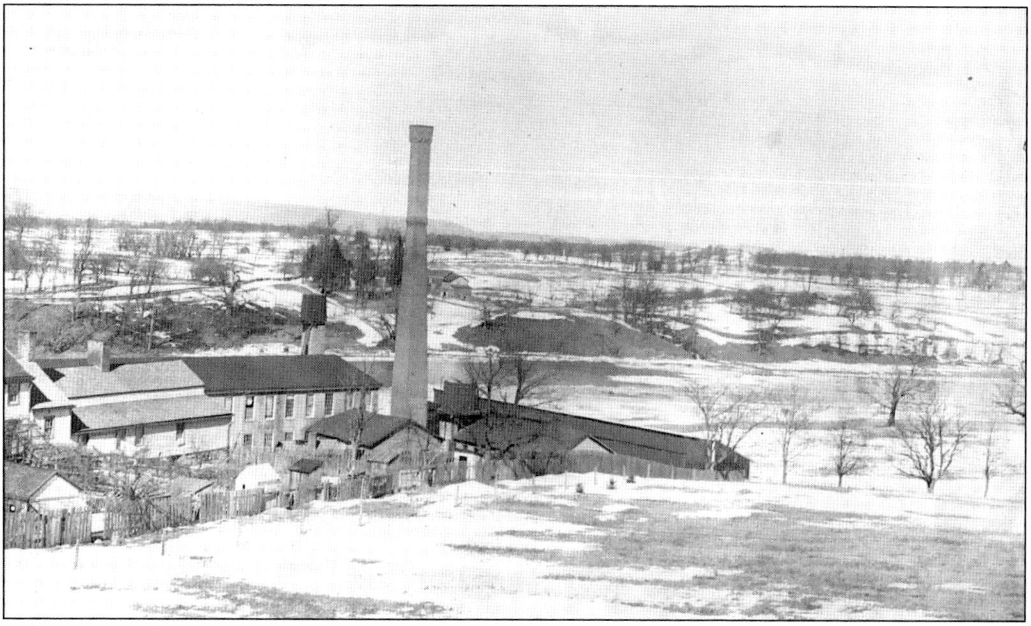

Adjacent to the mill was a building referred to as the row house, built to house mill workers. The row house included six units, the oldest dating from 1826. This photograph, *c.* 1898, shows a portion of the row house at the left. In 1880, the row house became the home of William Crabtree and Arthur Patchett and their families. To the right of the smokestack are the barns of the Sears farmstead on River Road. The barns are now gone, but the farmhouse still stands.

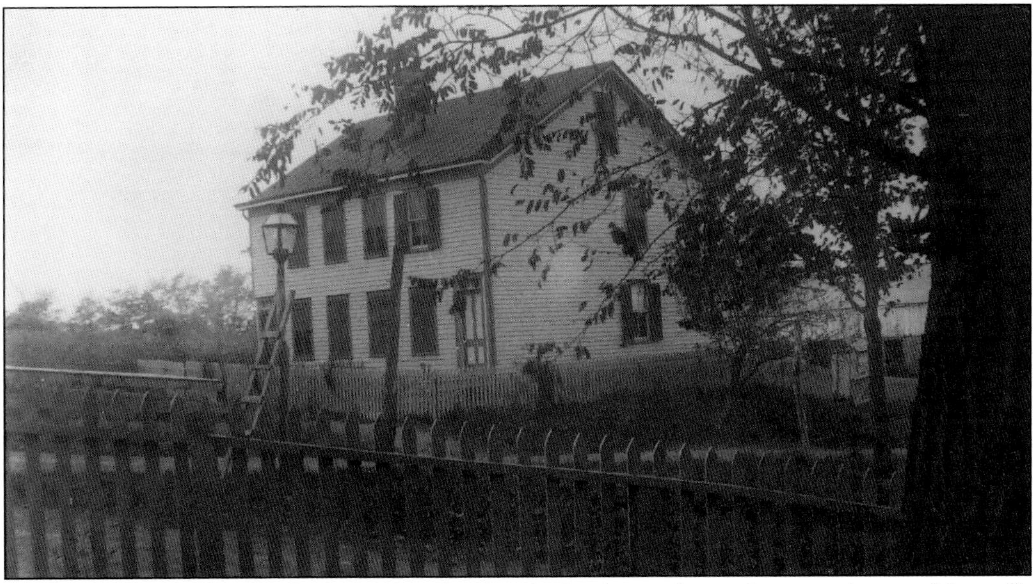

Built by local contractor Chauncey Brooks, this duplex house for workers stood west of the mill. Like the row house, it no longer stands. Notice the old lamp post. The rungs on the post allowed the lamplighter to lean a ladder against it to light the wick of the kerosene lamp. William took this photograph in the 1890s.

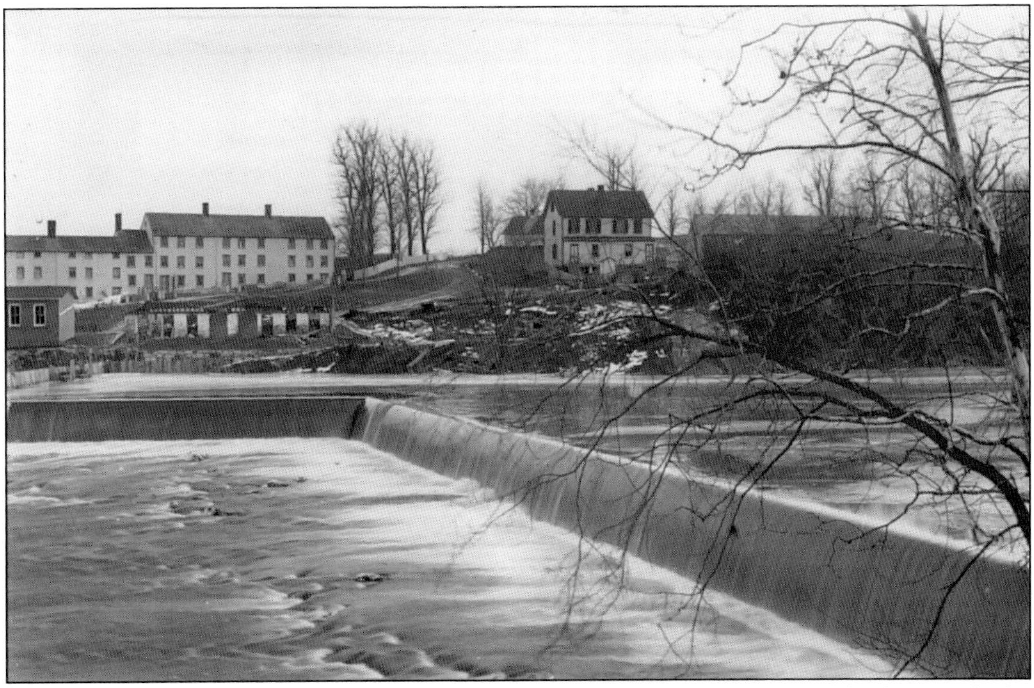

On Election Day of 1891, Crabtree and Patchett's operation was destroyed by fire. With the insurance money they received and the dream still burning in their hearts to run their own operation, they picked up the pieces and started anew. The brick mill was built in 1892, adjacent to a portion of the remains of the old plant (the office of the new mill appears at the far left). The business was back in operation in the summer of 1892.

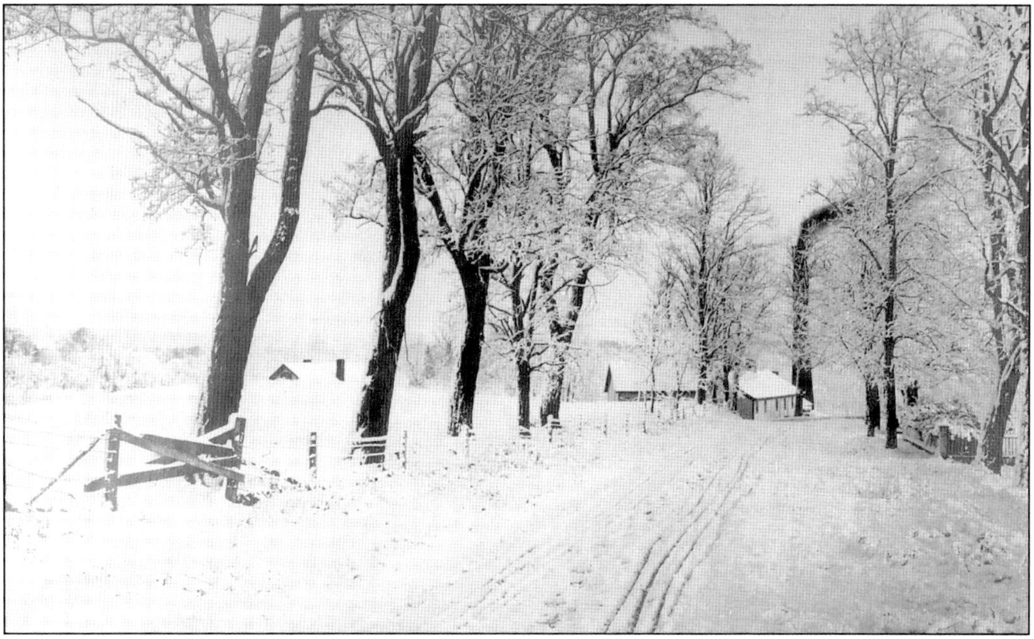

William was always looking for a good photo opportunity, such as this winter view of the mill from Factory Street. Notice the black smoke billowing from the smokestack. The old stack still exists but is deteriorating. This photograph, *c.* 1899, was taken shortly after William's large home had been constructed on Factory Street.

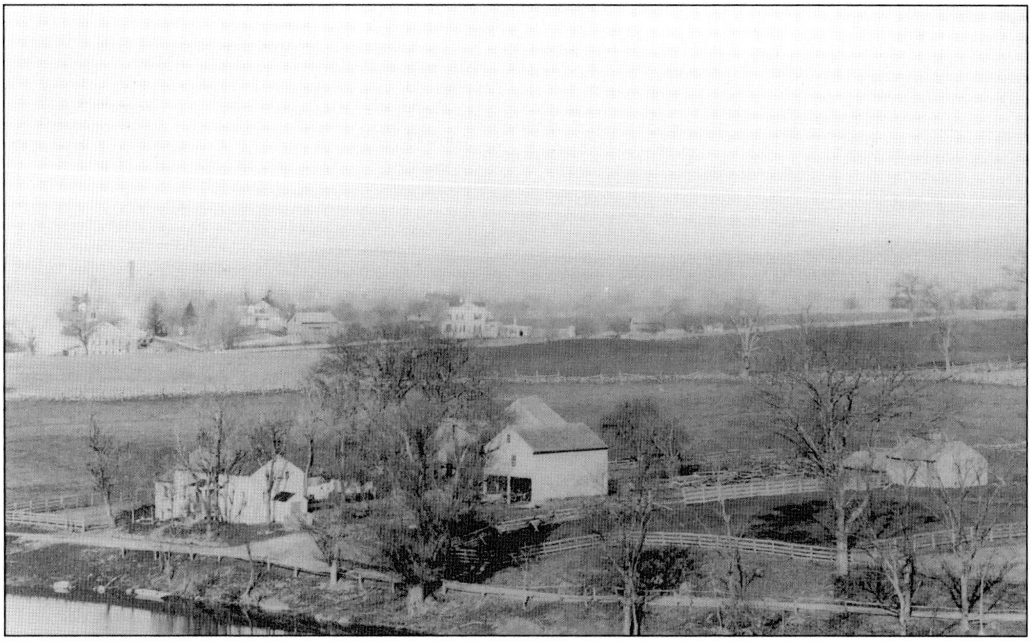

A great deal of effort was required to take this 1892 photograph. Bulky photographic equipment had to be carried up on the scaffolding surrounding the chimney stack, which was under construction. The photograph shows River Road along the Wallkill River and points north. The farmstead in the foreground has been replaced with a modern dwelling. The house in the center is the Devine home (see p. 108). To the far left is the paper mill.

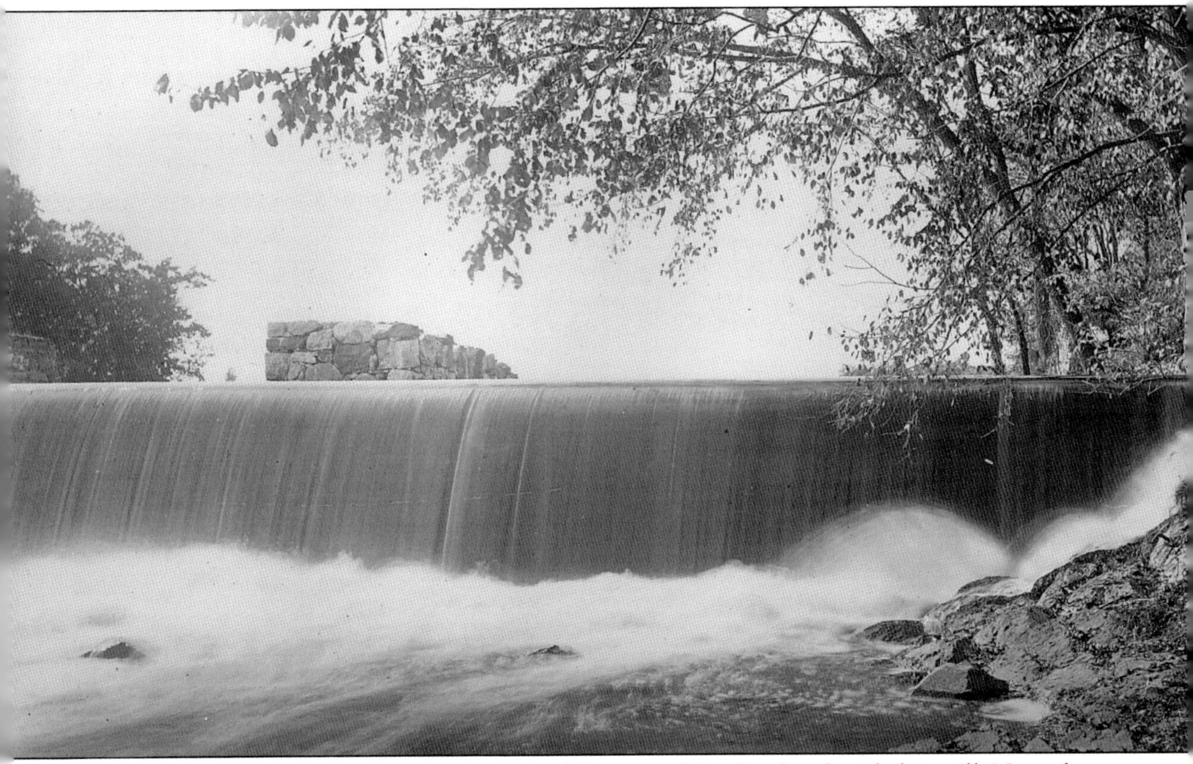

About 1892, William took this picture of the falls created by the dam beside his mill. Note the stonework above. The abutment and stone pier are the remains of an early bridge that dated to about 1818. The bridge was built as a cooperative undertaking by farmers who used a gristmill located on the north shore. During the morning of March 18, 1862, a portion of the bridge was destroyed, and it was never rebuilt. Some of the stonework survives even today, including a small portion of the center pier, which is usually covered by water.

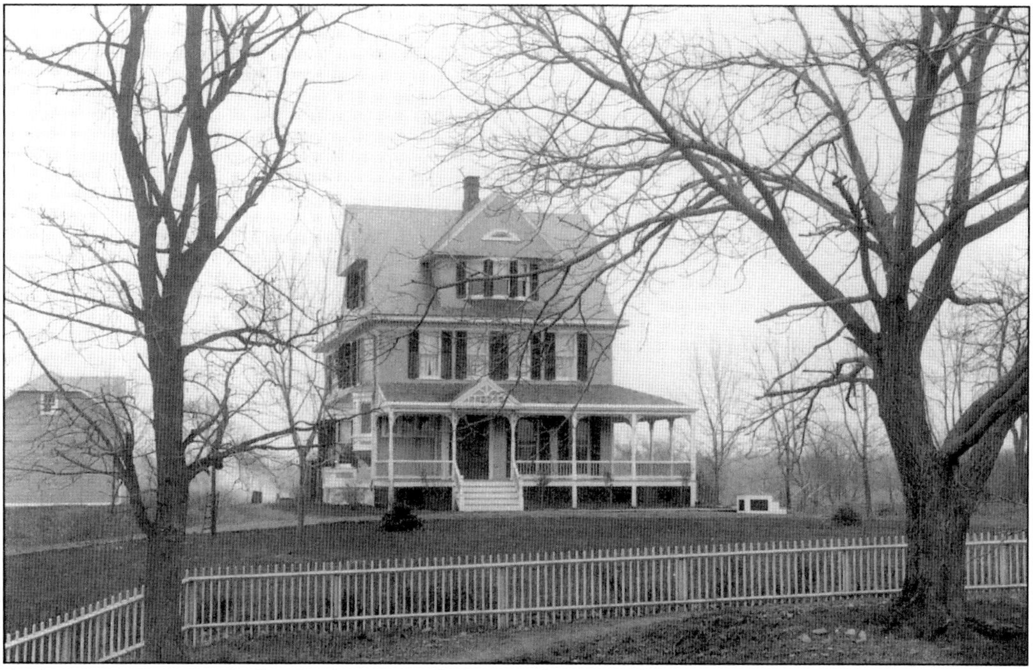

As business prospered, the Crabtrees and the Patchetts exchanged their cramped conditions in the row house for more substantial accommodations. Arthur Patchett purchased the large brick house on the corner of Factory and Ward Streets that still bears his name. Will contracted with Chauncey Brooks in 1896 to build this large Queen Anne Victorian-style house, which still stands on Factory Street, above the mill. This photograph was taken about 1897.

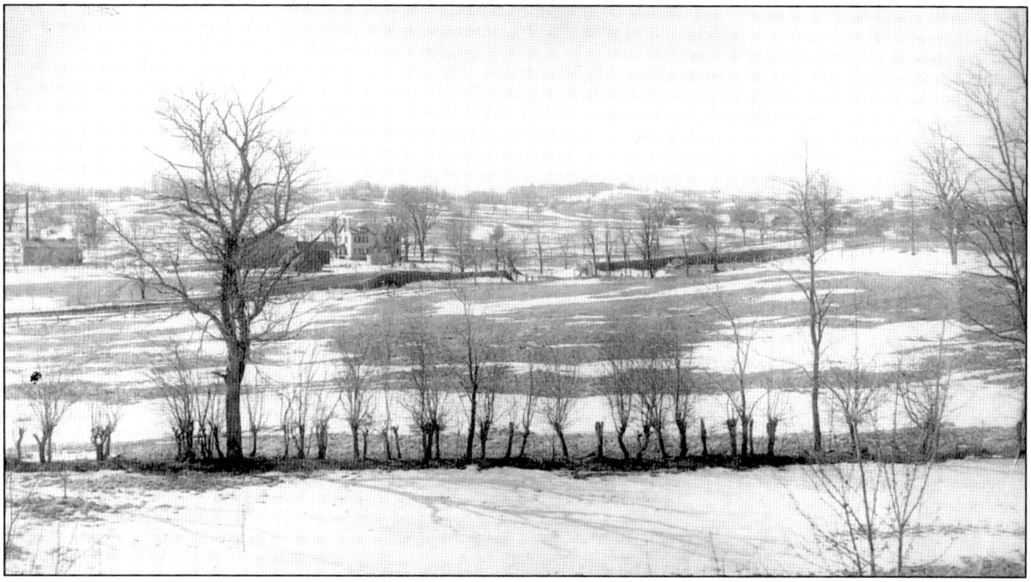

Dating from the late 1890s, this view from the attic of William Crabtree's new house shows points west. The house in the center left of the photograph is the Patchett homestead, on the corner of Ward and Factory Streets. The old brick waterworks building, built in 1895, is to the left of the Patchett homestead. A view of this area today would show vast changes, as apartments, condominiums, and commercial buildings occupy much of the open space.

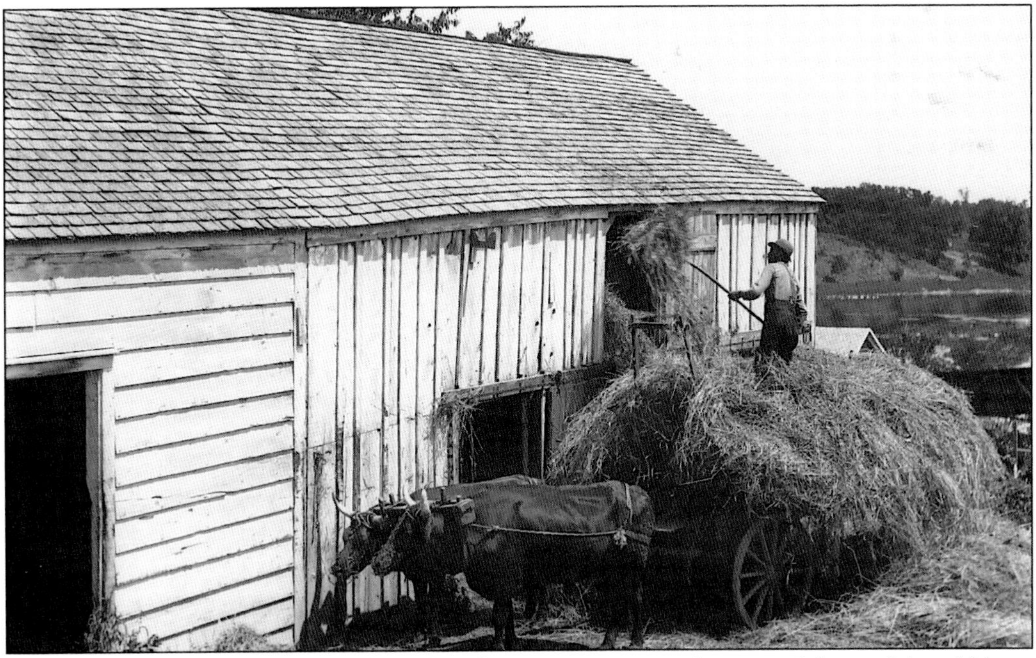

This photograph of a worker pitching hay from a wagon into the second floor of the old barn was one of Will's more noted views. It became a popular postcard view at the turn of the 20th century. The barn stood a short distance west of the mill. Torn down after 1900, it was replaced with a new gambrel-roofed barn.

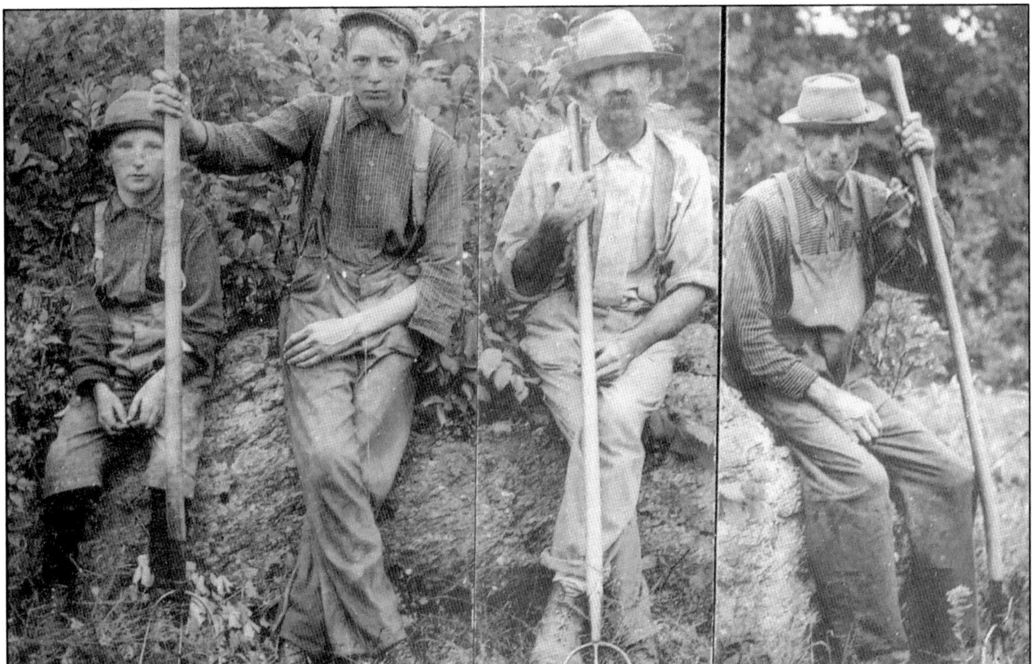

William used his photography to capture the everyday life of his time. This rare view shows two farm workers with their young helpers, taking a break. Dating to about 1900, this may have been taken on Crabtree's farmland.

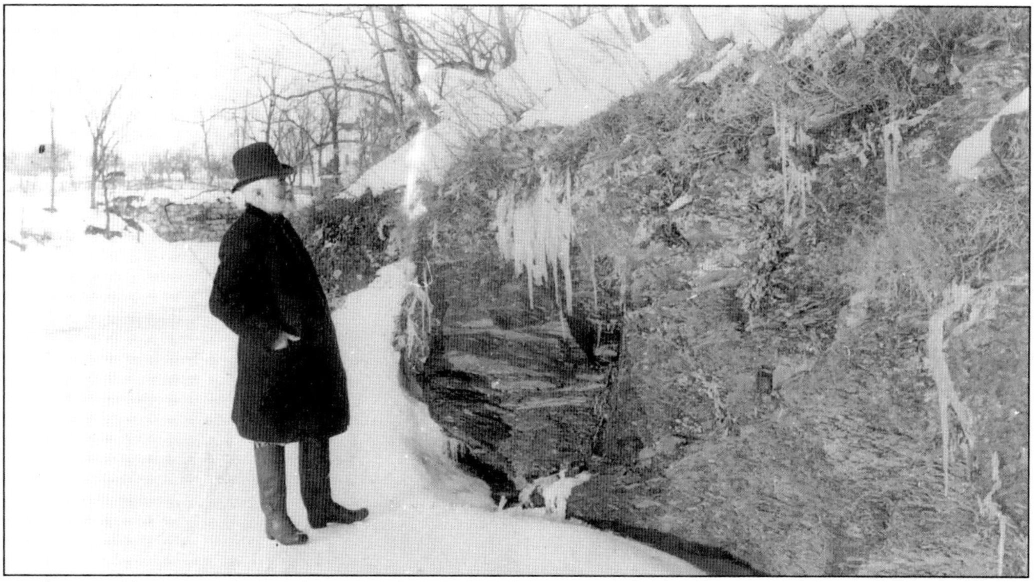

Will passed his interest in photography along to his son John, who took this photograph about 1896. It shows William exploring one of his favorite botanizing ledges, a short distance above the Crabtree Dam. William also shared his great interest in botany with John. Behind William is the stonework of the bridge abutment on River Road.

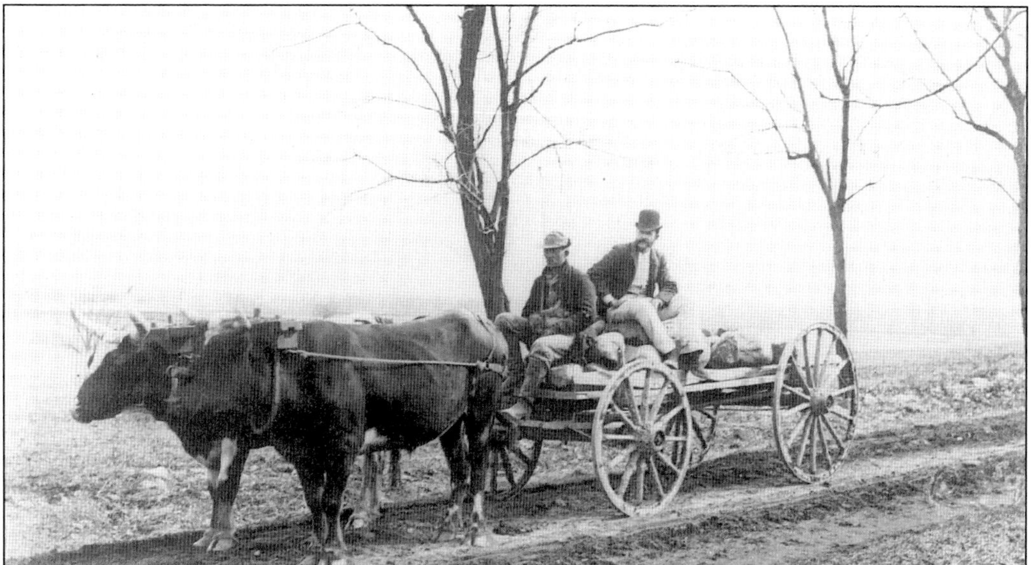

This photograph, taken by John in late 1899, was labeled "The Field Where Our Home Now Stands." It shows the stone boat delivering stones for the foundation of his new home, which was completed in the spring of 1900. This venerable building remains in the Crabtree family and has recently been placed on the National Register of Historic Places.

John's house was built by Chauncey Brooks at a cost of $1,925. The house was designed by W.J. Keith of Minneapolis in the Queen Anne Victorian style. The front attic room was used as John's personal photography studio. For more than 80 years, scores of his and his father's glass-plate negatives were stored there on shelves.

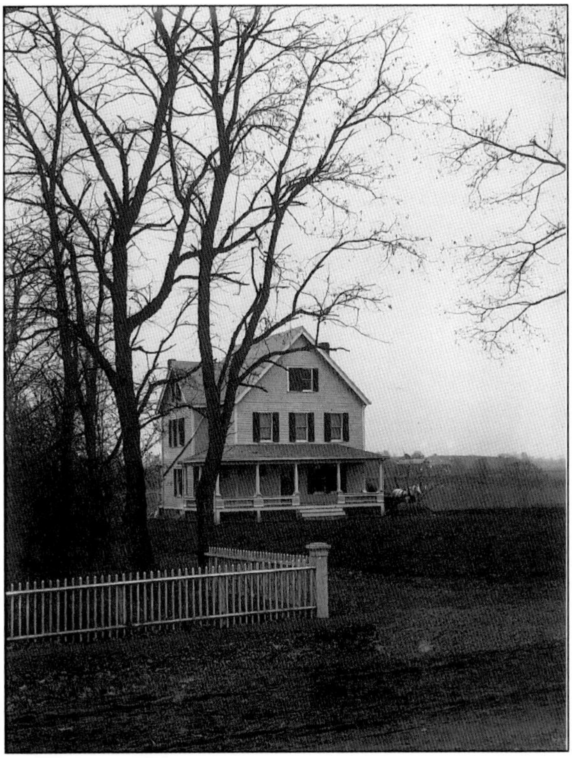

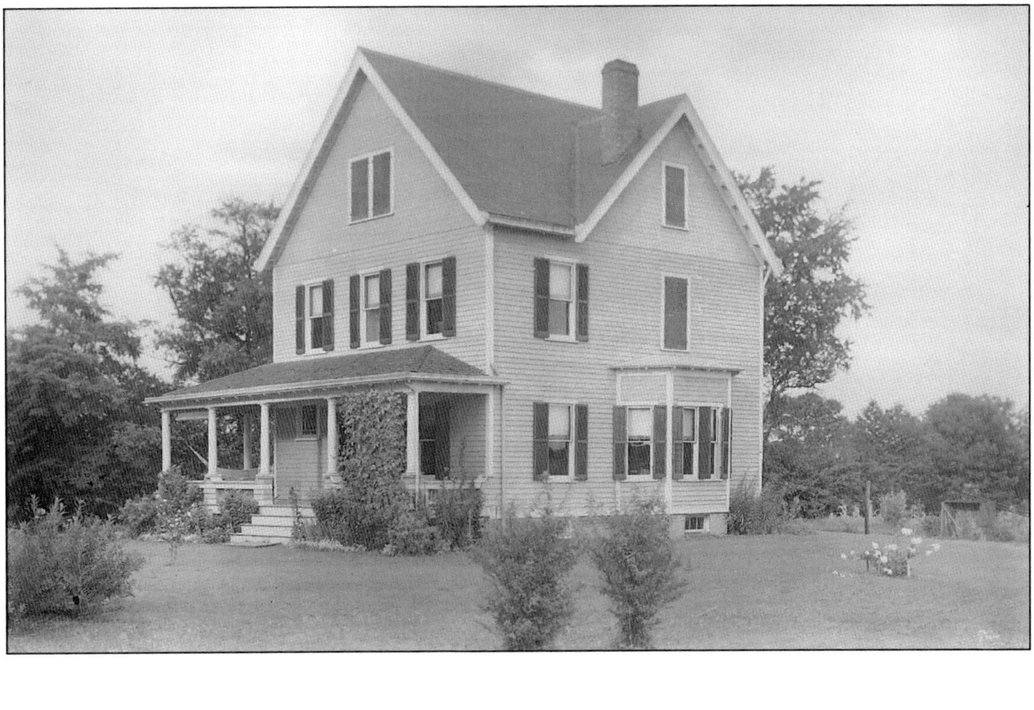

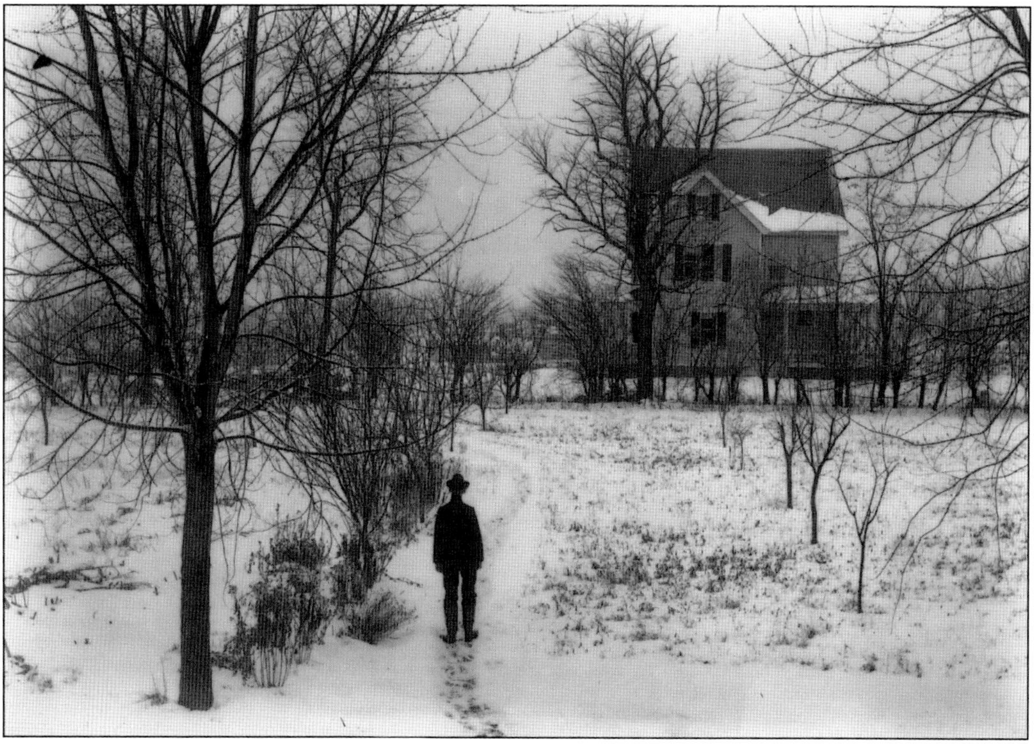

William Crabtree took this photograph from his home about 1902. It shows John returning home next door. One year later, William Jr., John's brother, constructed his home on this parcel.

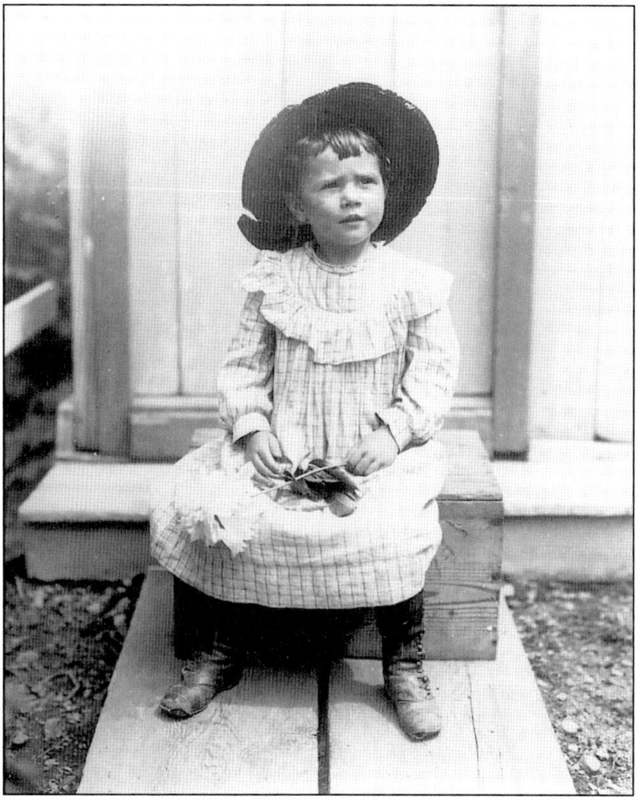

May Crabtree, Will's granddaughter, sits on a soapbox in front of the family outhouse. Note that she is holding a flower. Also note the wooden sidewalk, not uncommon in the late 1800s and early 1900s.

Will and his family were members of the Brick Church, and naturally, this site proved to be one of his favored photograph subjects. Both views date from the 1890s. The photograph at right was taken from the east bank of the Wallkill River, near Riverside Cemetery in the village. The photograph below was taken at the rear of the church and shows a portion of the old cemetery.

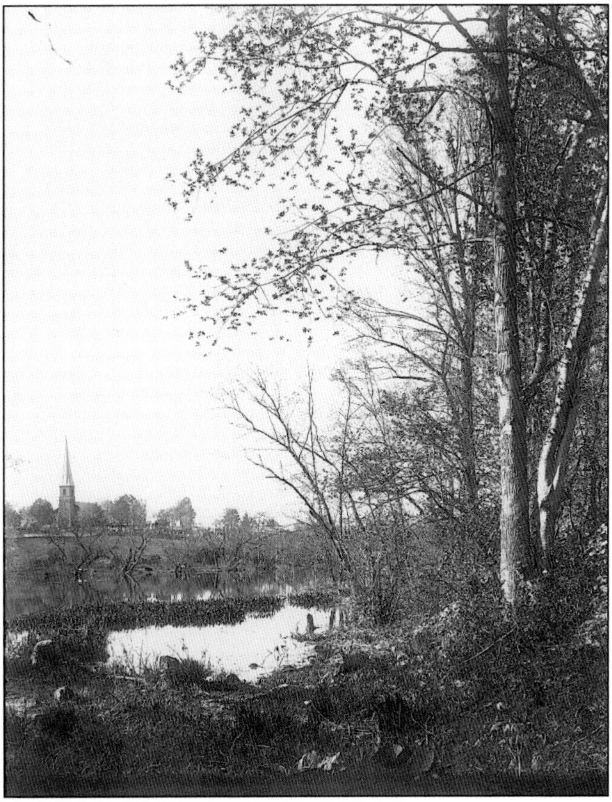

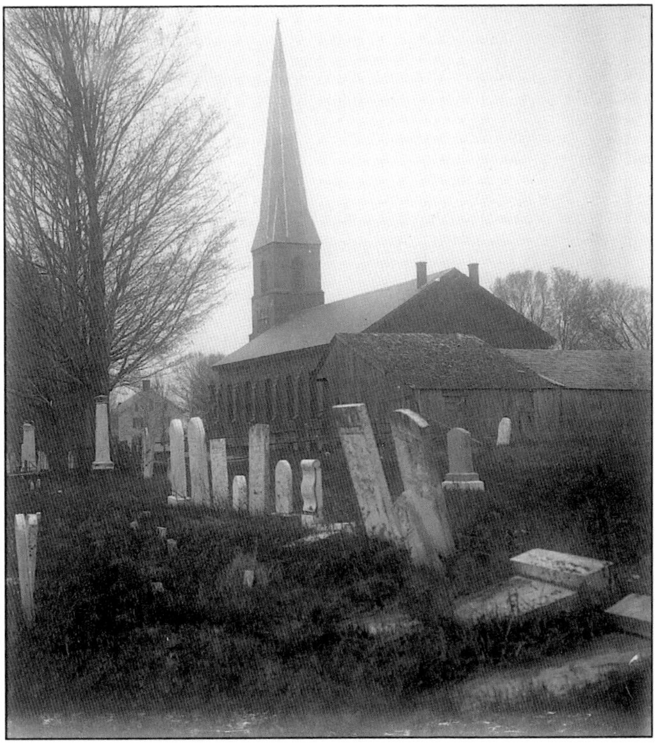

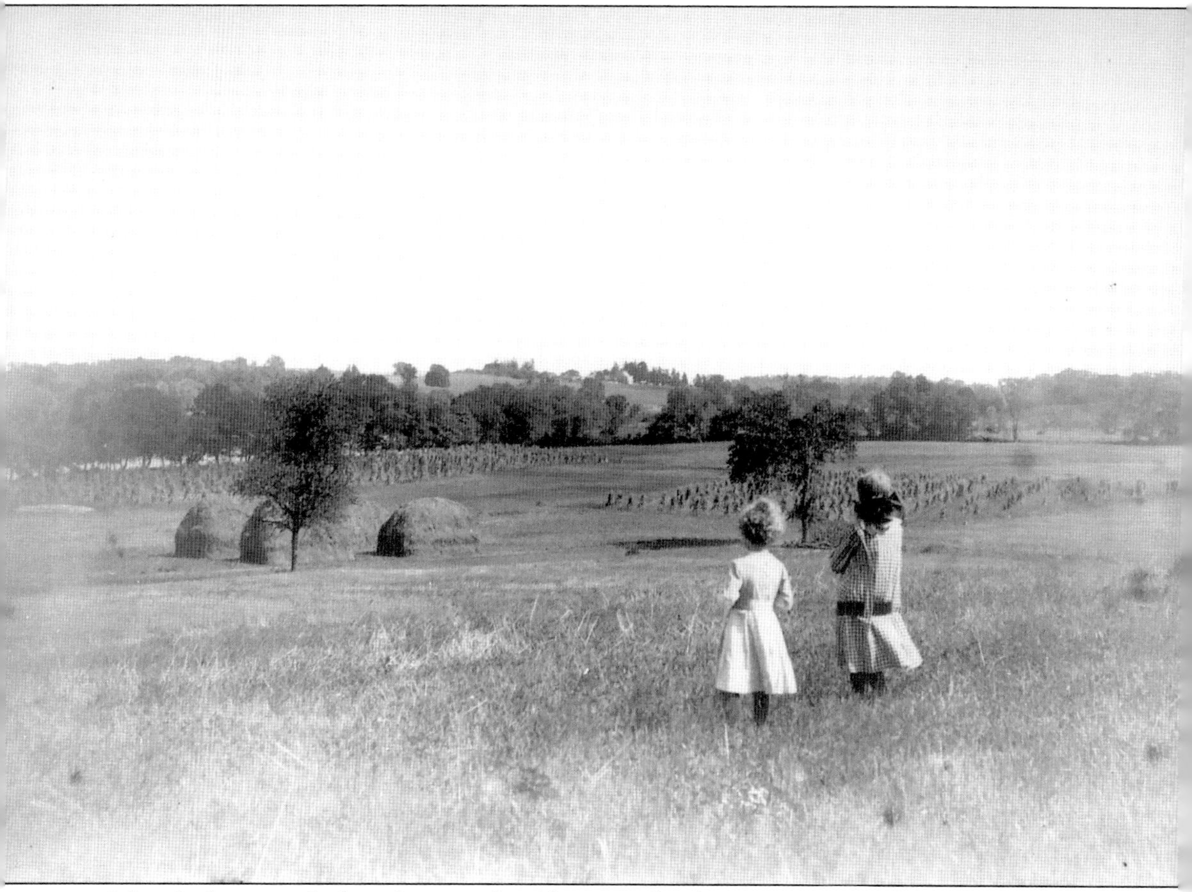

John Crabtree took this photograph of his two daughters, Lemma and Eleanor, c. 1914. It shows the field behind William and Harriet Crabtree's home that now holds a large apartment complex. The farm in the distance is the Bergen-Suydam Farm, located on Bailey Road.

William Crabtree died in 1903, and John carried on with photography until his interests waned. Through their collective hard work, they captured, in picture-perfect images, a cross-section of an era for posterity.

Seven

HISTORIC SITES

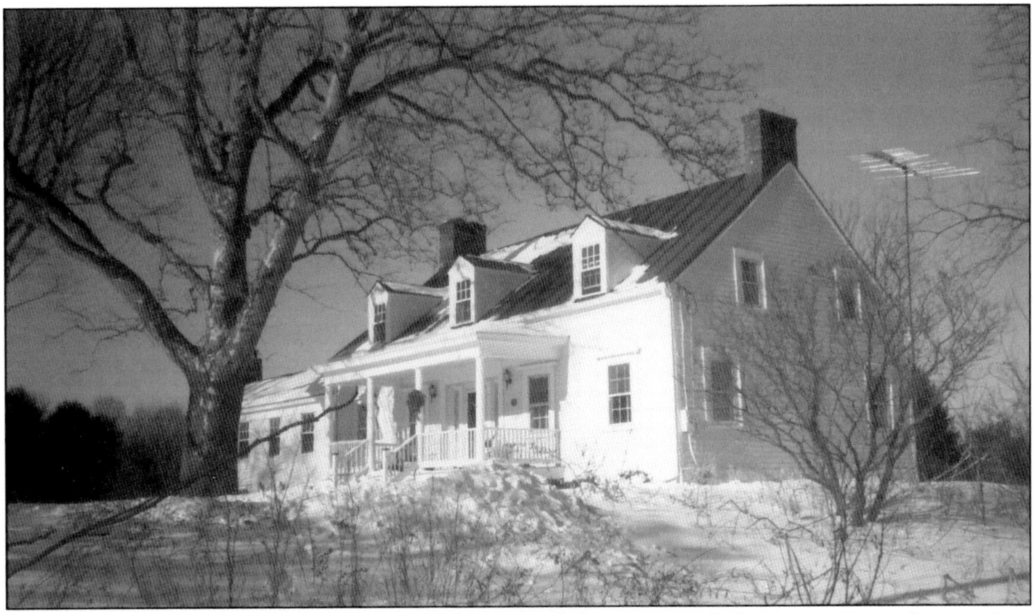

The town of Montgomery is recognized for its rich heritage and the tangible evidence of its past, ranging from homesteads to public buildings and burying grounds to archaeological sites. In recent years, two cemeteries and nine homesteads have been added to the town's already impressive list of National Register sites. Jacob Bookstaver was one of the earliest pioneers of the town of Montgomery, having first settled in the vicinity of the Brick Church in the early 18th century. He soon relocated to what is now known as the Schmitt Farm, which is tucked away at the end of a long dirt lane, off Albany Post Road. His original house may have been a log structure. The oldest portion of the homestead shown above is believed to have been built by him, and on a collar beam in what was once an attic room in the gable end of the large block is carved the date 1779. A couple of the doors in the house retain their Germanic-style strap hinges, which may have been forged by Wilhelm Smidt, a blacksmith who resided in a stone house on Albany Post Road, adjacent to the beginning of the lane.

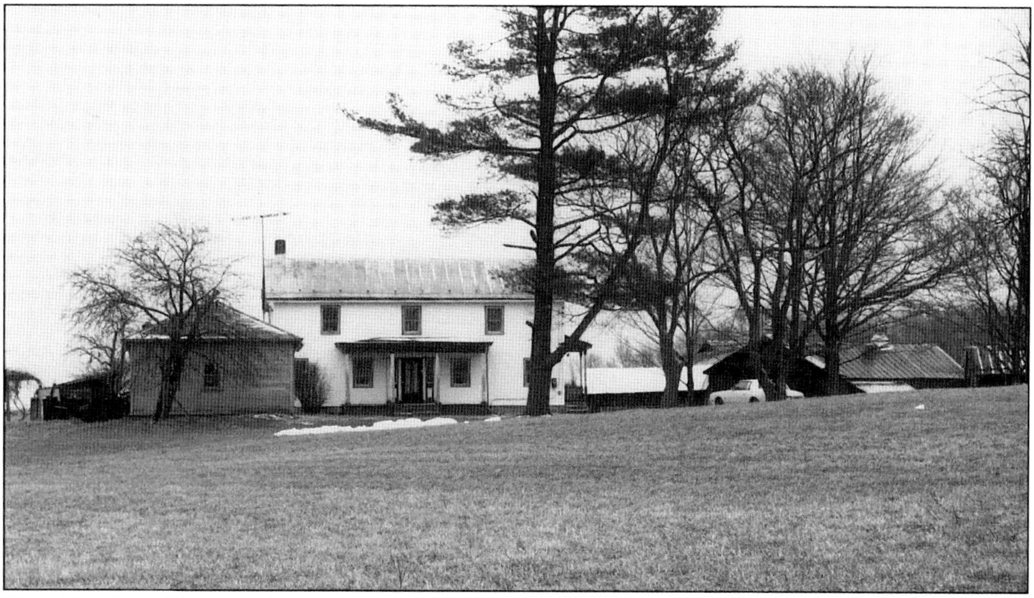

The Comfort Farm is located on Searsville Road, opposite Rowe Lane. Documentation reveals that Lawrentz Crist settled on this site in 1730. Like many early farms, this one was updated with new buildings during its long and useful existence. About 1850, the pioneer structure was replaced by the present house. The Dutch door from the original dwelling was reused on the cellar entry, and one of the old barns, which has a beam inscribed with the date 1775, was retained.

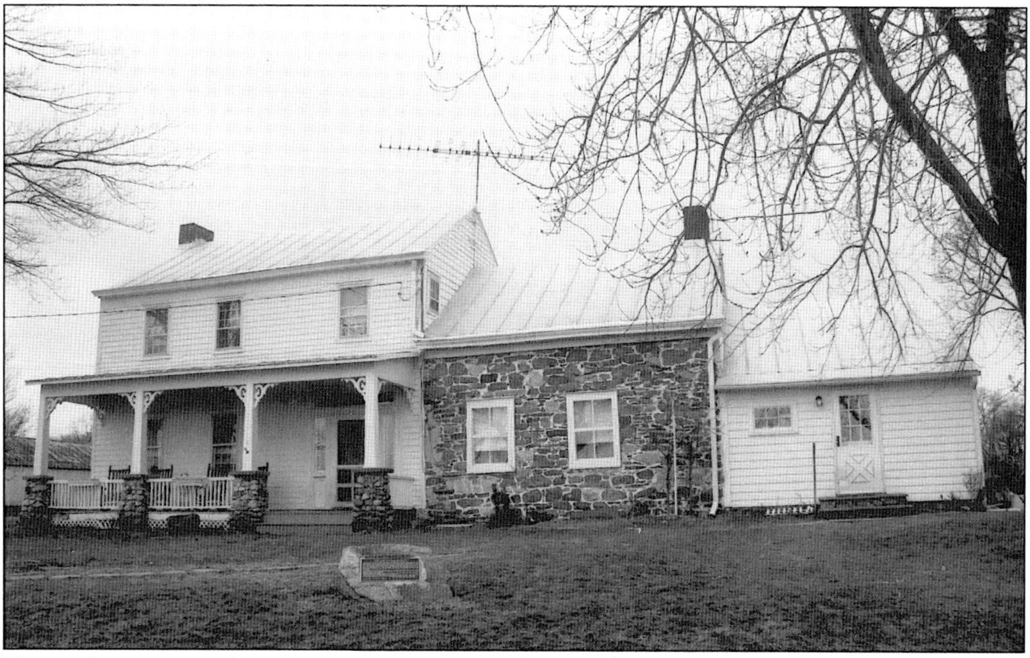

The Gideon Pelton farmstead stands at the end of Rockefellow Lane, off Beaver Dam Road. Gideon Pelton, an ex-Revolutionary War soldier, purchased the farm in the third quarter of the 18th century. His son Gideon added the Greek Revival section to the stone portion about 1830. This venerable farmstead was listed on the National Register in 1995.

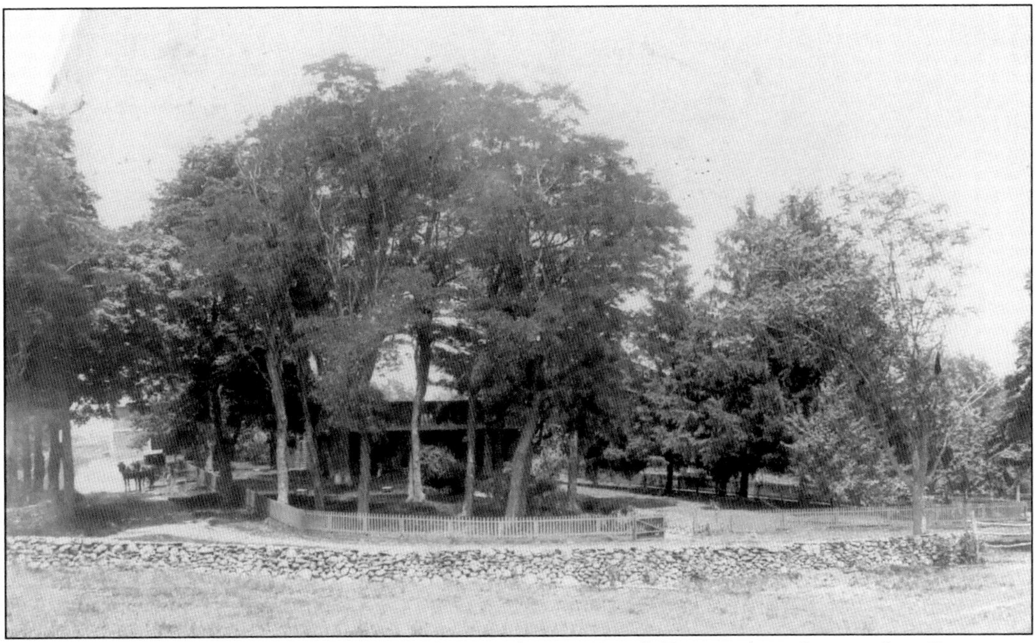

The Haddon-Scott farmstead is located on Coleman Road. Research indicates that Benjamin Haines built the original house as early as the mid-18th century. The house was updated in the Federal, Greek Revival, and Victorian eras, and as a result, it contains a wide array of architectural detailing. The photograph above dates from the 1890s, and the one below was taken in 1995, before renovations.

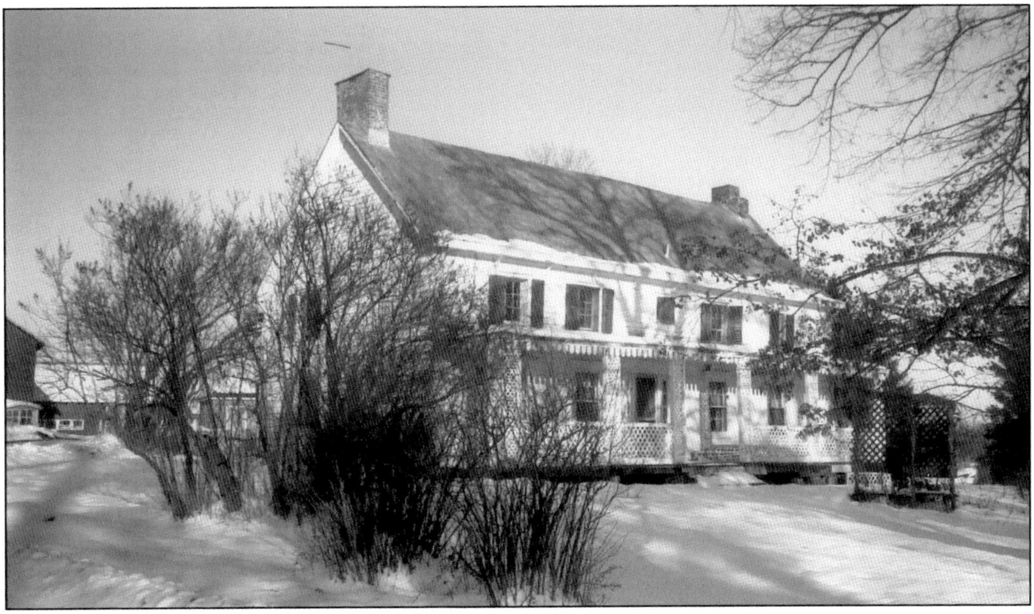

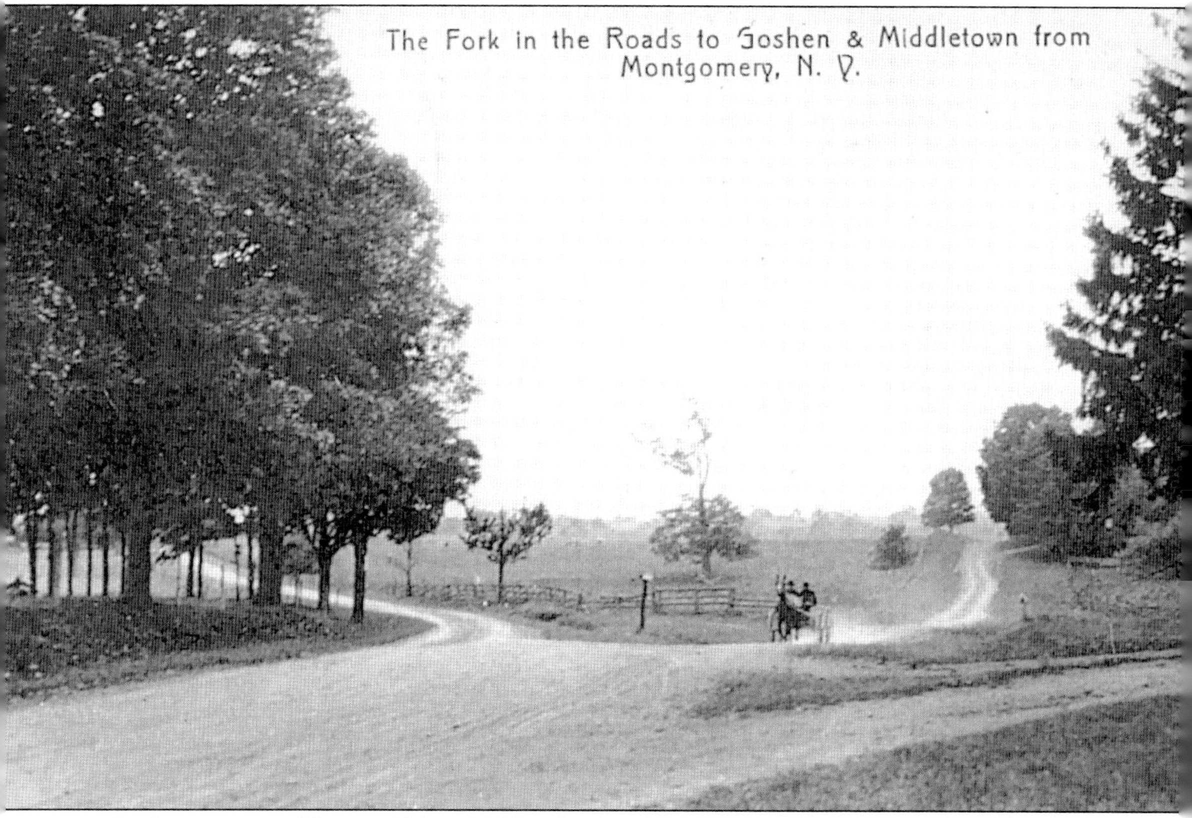

At the junction of Routes 211 and 416 is the Germantown Cemetery, one of the oldest burying grounds within the town. The location is also the site of the log Hebron Lutheran Church, established early in the 18th century but discontinued prior to the American Revolution. Samuel Eager, in his Orange County history, records that one marker was inscribed with "Born in 1686, died in 1759, A.M.M." No one knows whom this marker memorialized. There is known to have been another stone in the cemetery with the inscribed date of 1764. Unfortunately, both of these markers have vanished over the years. During restoration, these stones were replaced, and one was added for Dederick Shafer, who is known to have been interred here. In 1997, the site was listed on the National Register of Historic Places. This view, taken in the early 1900s, shows the cemetery to the left of the road, beneath the stand of trees.

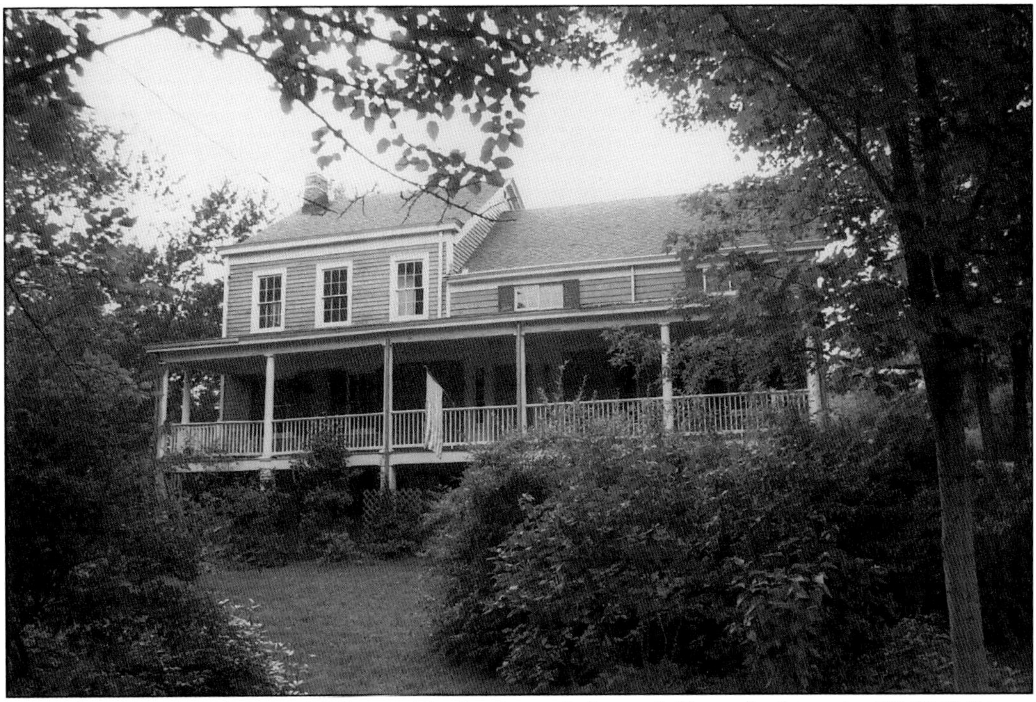

In the late 1720s, Johannes Miller and his bride settled on a hill overlooking the Wallkill River, on what is today Canning Road. Their permanent residence was a stone dwelling that stood on top of the hill. About 1840, the house was replaced by one of their descendants, Elmer Miller. In this photograph, the original portion of that dwelling is shown on the right side.

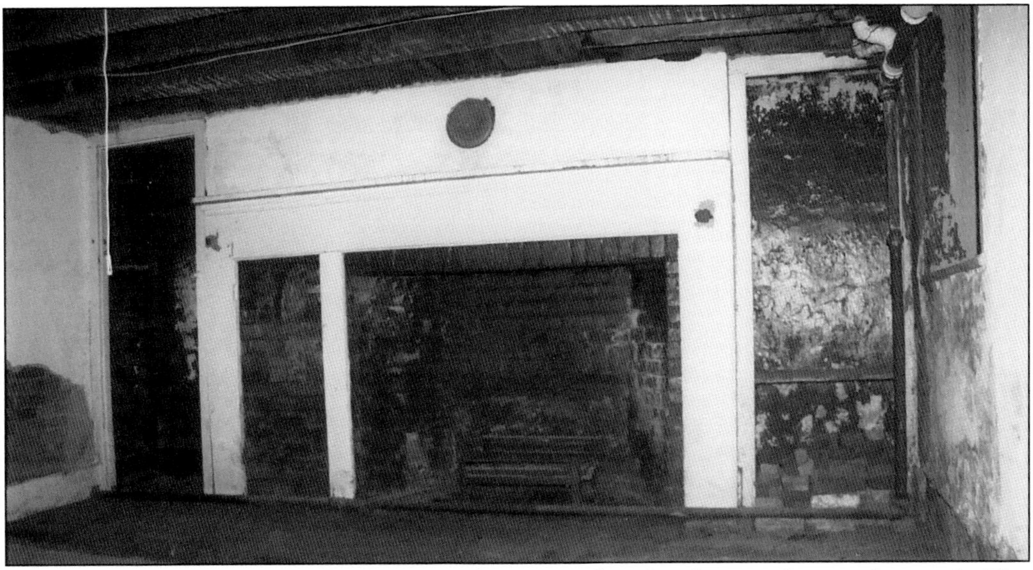

The *c.* 1840 block of the Miller homestead contains four fireplaces with period mantels. The basement contains a spacious keeping room with a large hearth and the remains of a beehive oven. The oven was used for baking breads and cakes. It required a great deal of effort and know-how to heat to the correct temperature.

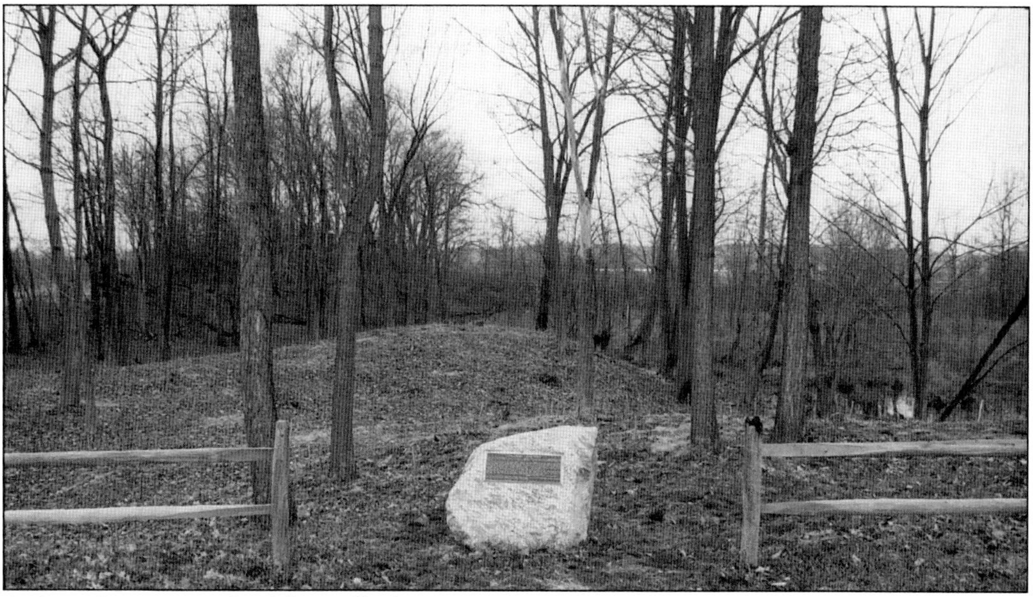

A short distance north of the Miller homestead, on an abandoned stretch of old Route 416, lies one of Montgomery's most significant historical sites: the "Colored Cemetery." The cemetery was established on the Miller property in the 18th century for enslaved African-Americans. Research indicates that it was used as recently as 1900. The earliest section of the cemetery sits on a small knoll. There, one of the stones bears the lightly inscribed date of 1756. The inscribed stone pictured below is also located on the knoll. The base of a marble slab lies closer to the road bed. The Miller family cemetery, located across the road on a high knoll, was obliterated in recent years.

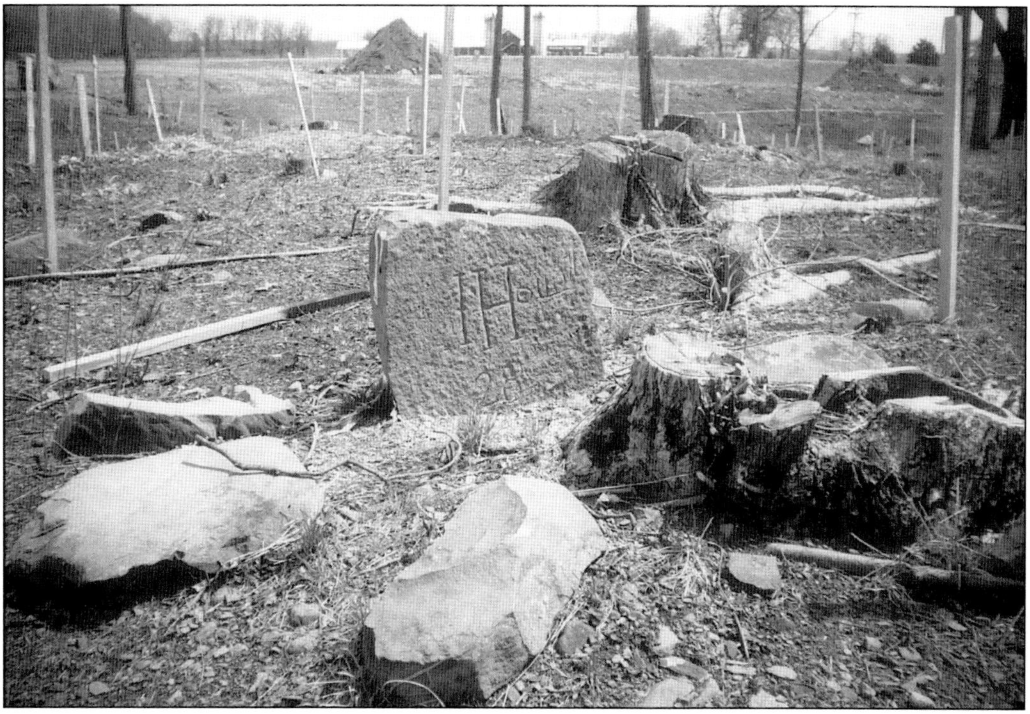

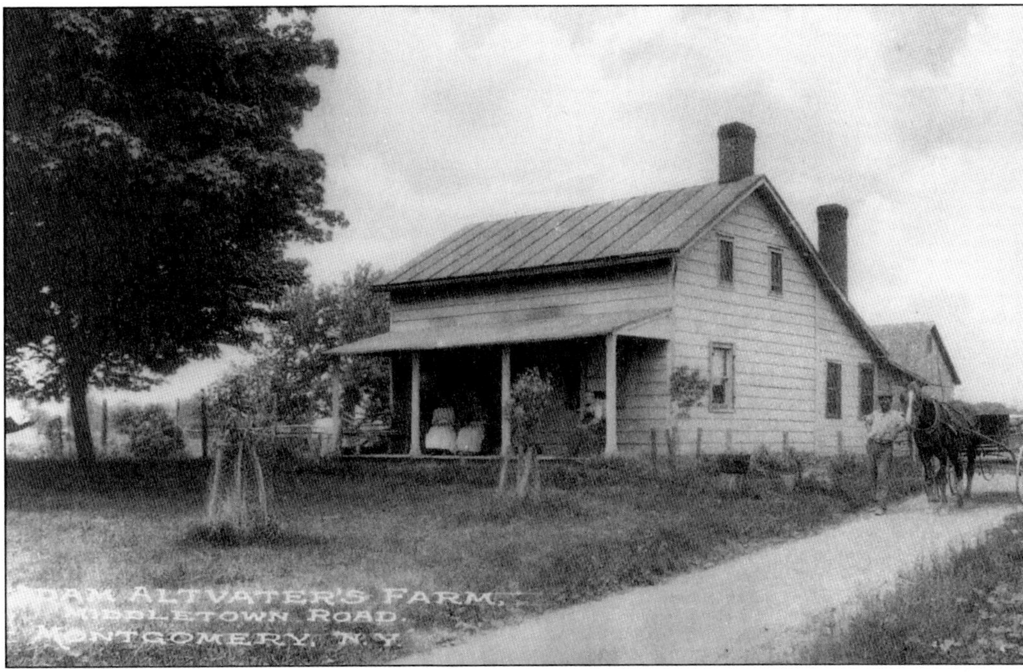

The small Rockafellow house serves as a reminder that not all of Montgomery's older homes stand on their original site. This house, probably dating from the mid-19th century, was once on property off Route 211 that is now part of Orange County Airport. The house was moved to its present site on the east side of Route 211 in the 1940s, when the airport was built.

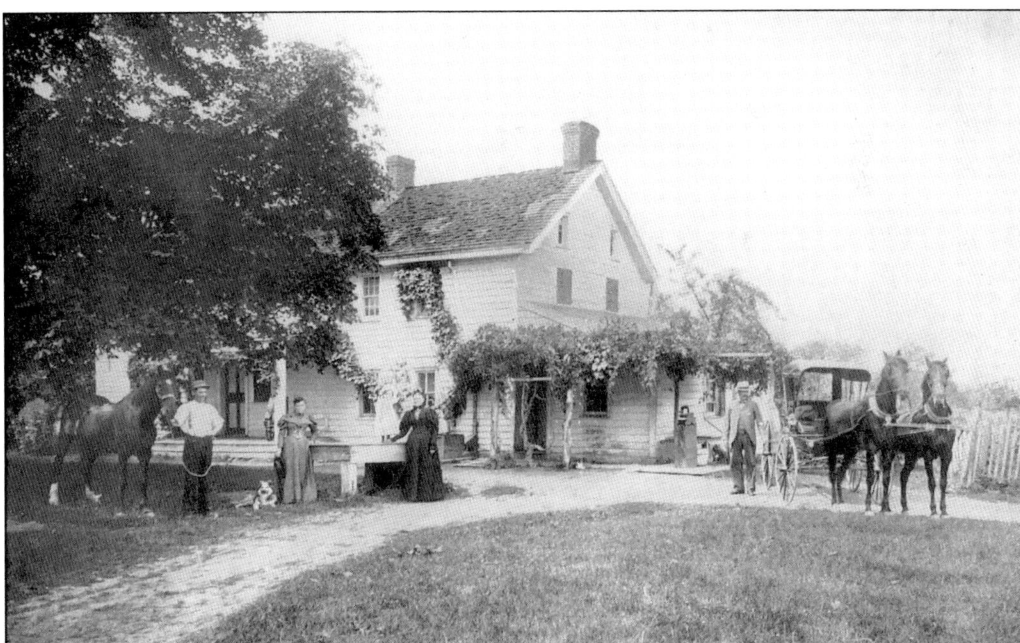

The Galatian homestead on Wallkill Road, north of the village of Walden, dates from the 18th century. It once contained a beautiful Dutch door, shown in this photograph, *c.* 1890, as well as other period details. Many of these venerable features were lost during a recent remodeling.

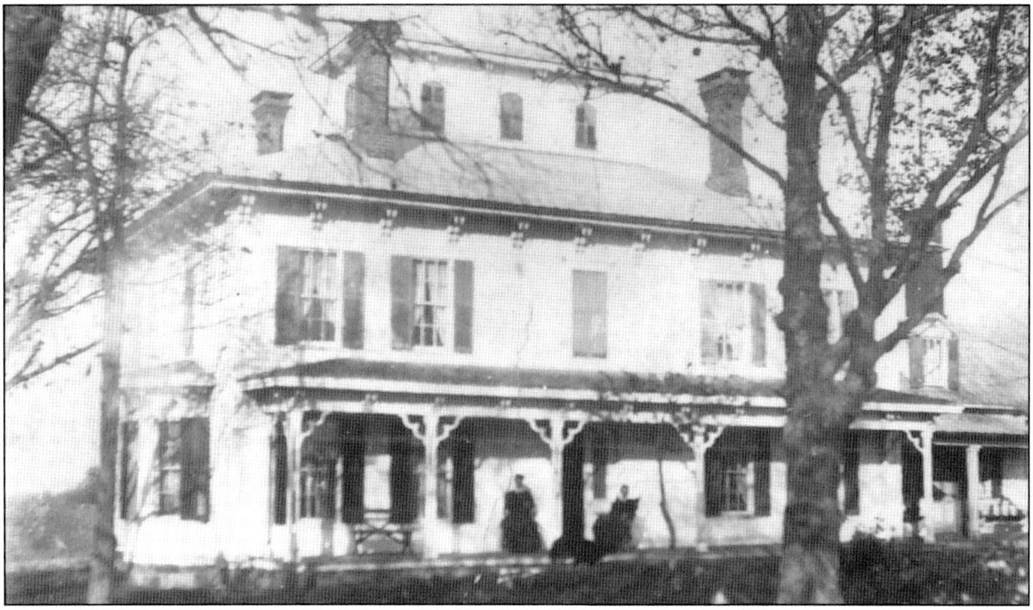

The Bodine homestead is located on the east side of Wallkill Road, a short distance north of Route 52. Although heavily Victorian in appearance, a portion of the house appears to date from the 18th century, and an old map shows that Peter Bodine settled in the vicinity as early as 1750. One of Bodine's descendants updated the house about 1870, and today it is undergoing restoration. This photo was taken at the turn of the 20th century.

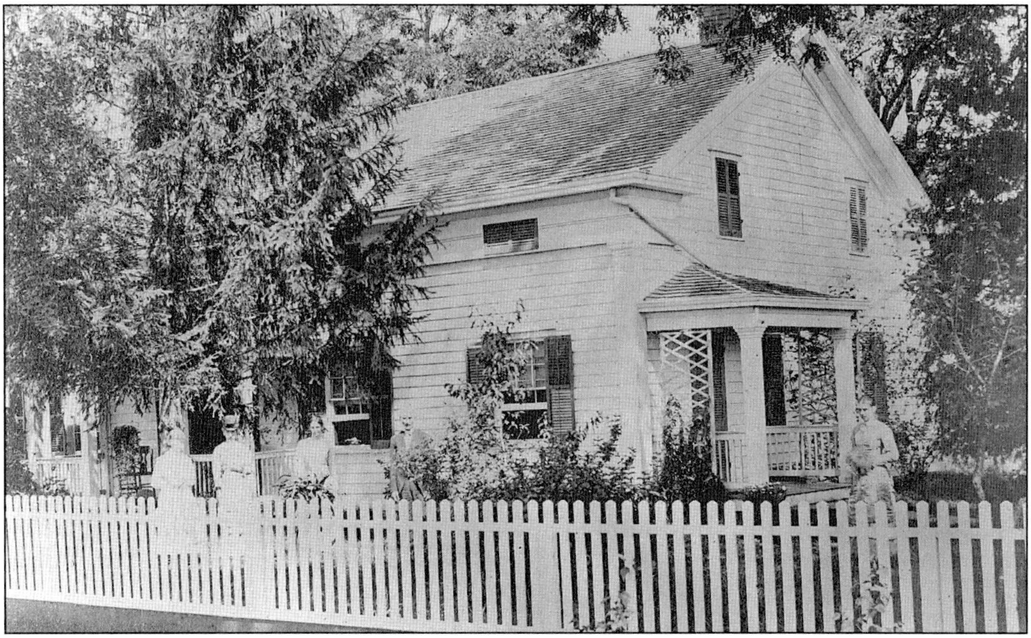

Research indicates that Riverside Farm, located on Wallkill Road north of the Bodine homestead, was built in the 18th century as a tenant house on the Bodine Farm. In 1851, L. Nathaniel Dubois purchased the property and remodeled and enlarged the house. The property changed hands several times before it was purchased by the Phelps family in 1922. This photograph dates from the 1890s.

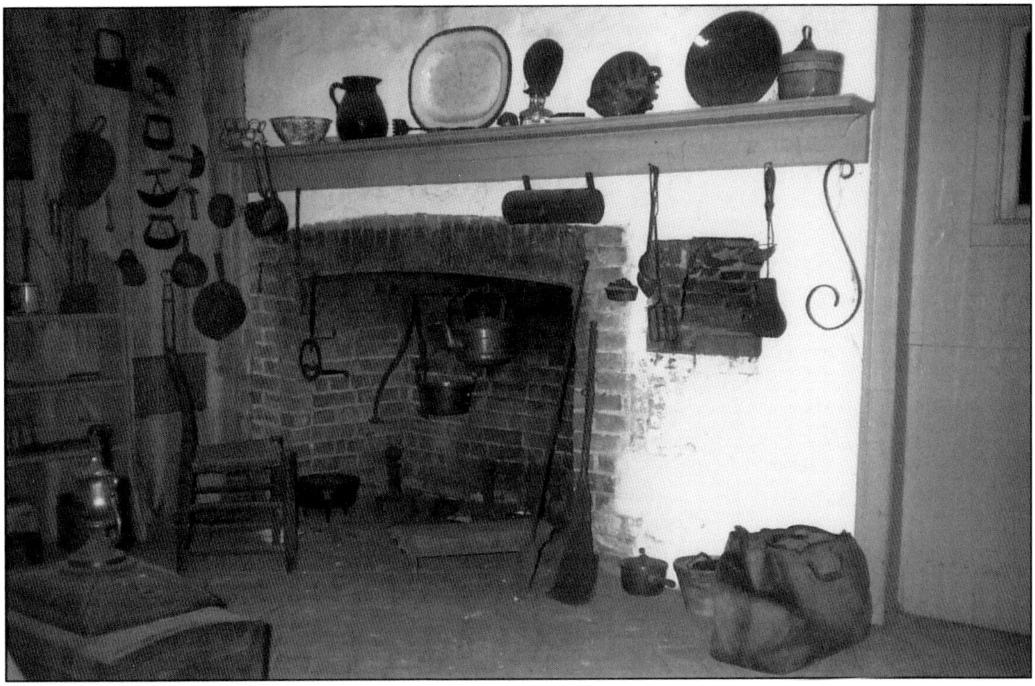

The original keeping room in the Dubois-Phelps homestead is located in the basement of the original block. It has been beautifully and sensitively restored by current owner Sam Phelps, a master mason. In 1997, Riverside Farm was recognized for its historic significance and listed on the National Register of Historic Places.

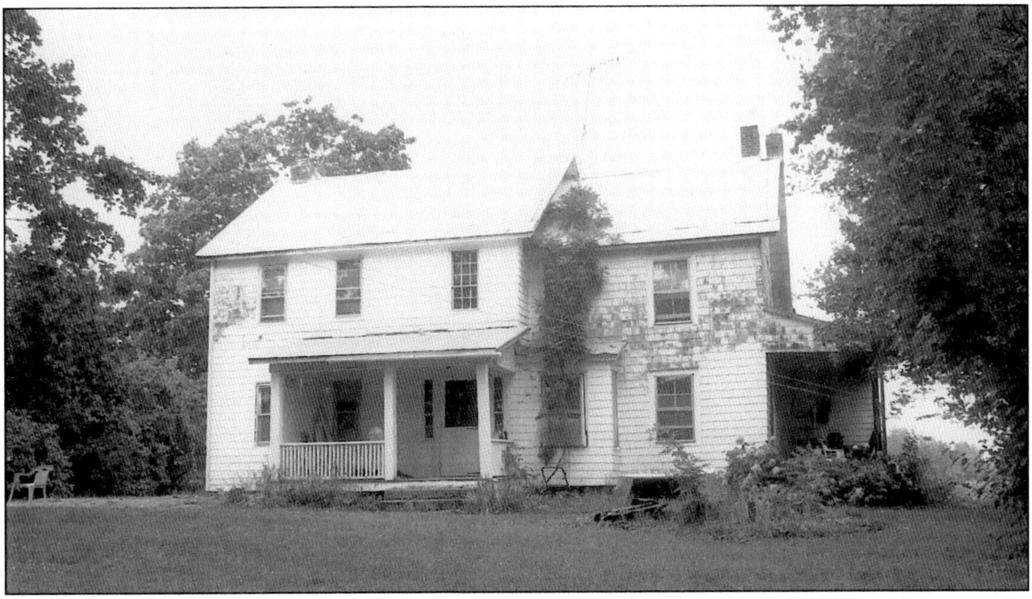

The Constable farmstead is located a short distance north of Riverside Farm, at the end of a dirt lane. An early map reveals that Benjamin Constable settled this site in 1739. The original portion of the house is on the first floor of the right block. The large left wing was added c. 1810. A second floor and attic were added to the pioneer block during the Victorian era. This venerable farmstead is now the home of John Roebuck.

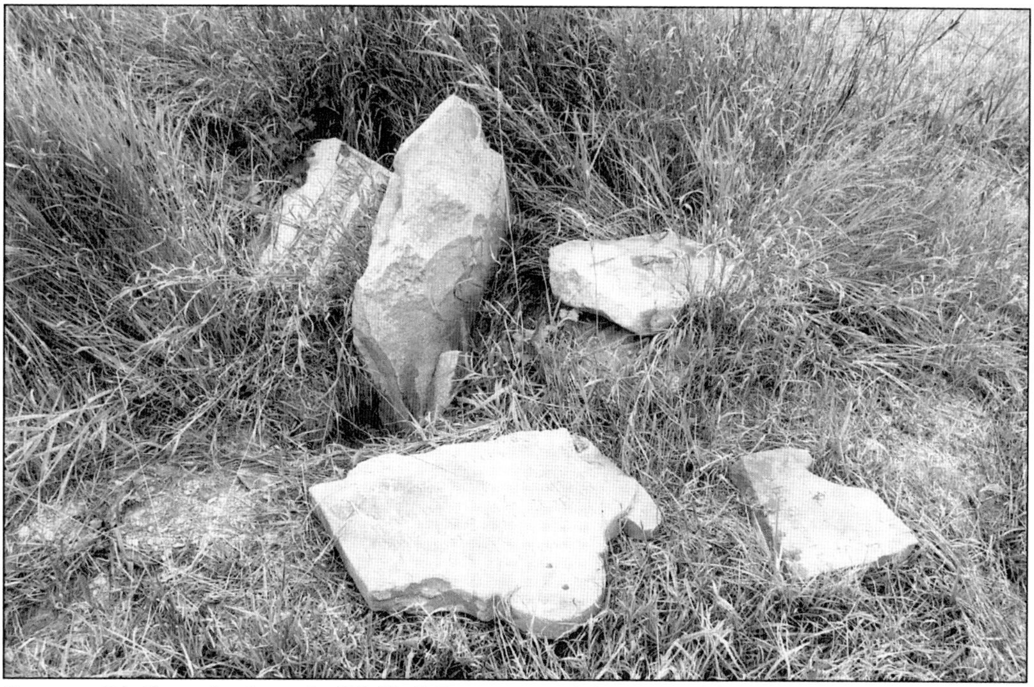

On a small hill overlooking the Wallkill River, east of the Constable farmhouse, lie the remains of an early family cemetery. Most of the stones have been broken, and none are in their original spot. The cemetery contains the remains of two Revolutionary War soldiers: Matthew Warner and James Galatian. A number of similar small cemeteries survive in Montgomery, some of which have long been forgotten.

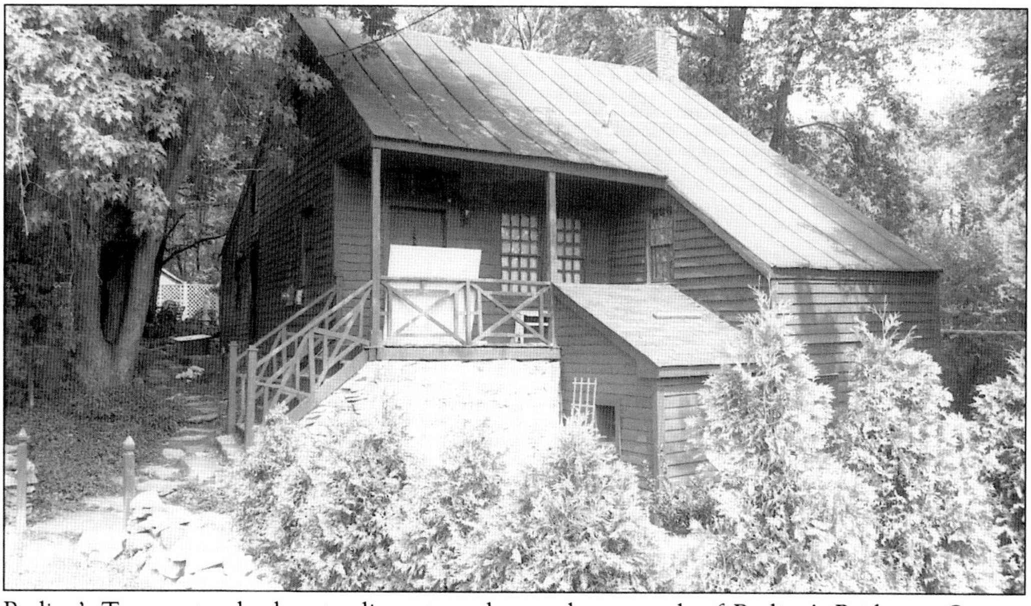

Bodine's Tavern stands almost adjacent to the south approach of Bodine's Bridge at Orange County Airport. Dating from the early 1800s, the building contains much of its architectural integrity. One of the highlights is an old taproom with corner fireplace and built-in warming cupboards above the mantel shelf. This fine, old landmark recently underwent restoration.

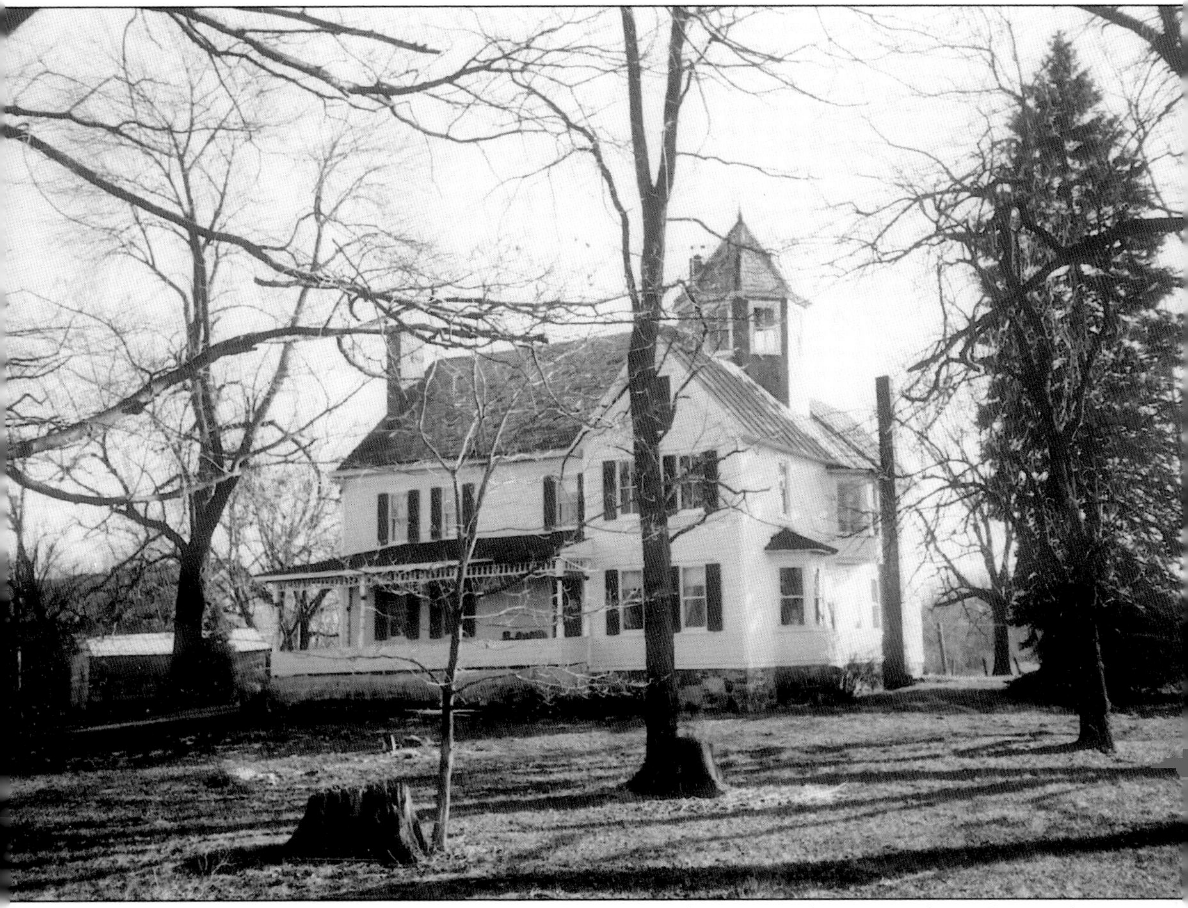

Peachcroft, located on River Road, is listed on the National Register of Historic Places. Research indicated that the property was first settled by Philip Millspaugh in the first half of the 18th century. A Millspaugh descendant replaced the original house with the left block of the present house, shown here in the early 1800s. In 1891, J.W. Brown gave the house and farm to his daughter and son-in-law as a wedding present. Daughter Anna and her husband, J.M. Hawkins, contracted with Chauncey Brooks to have the house remodeled and expanded. The gambrel roof on the left block was modified with the present roof. Much of the Victorian-era detailing, including some period wallpaper, survives.

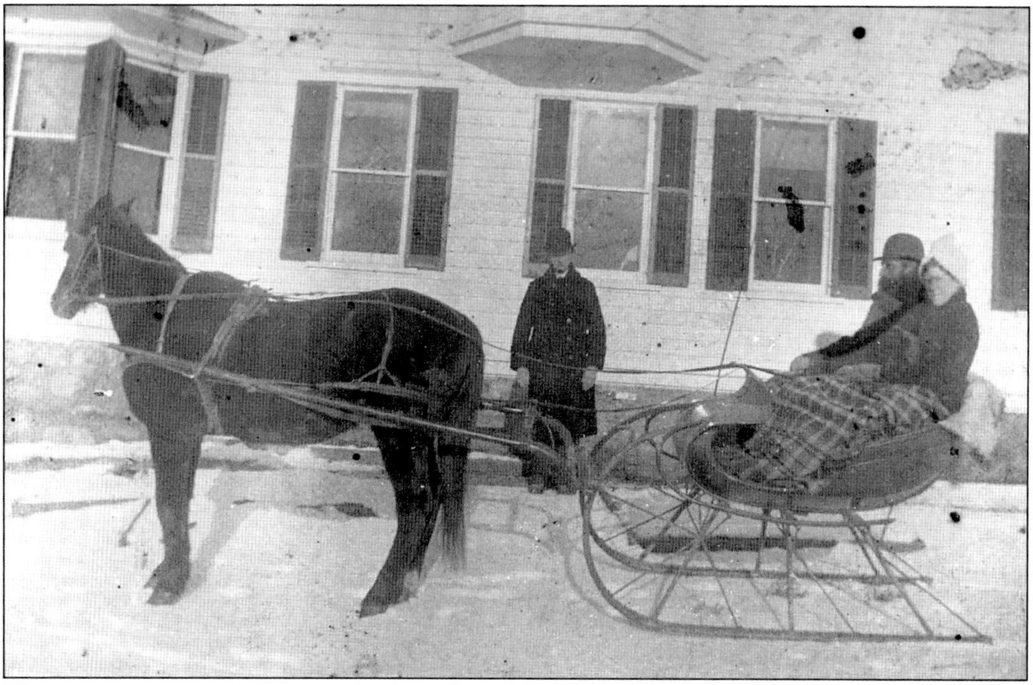

This winter scene was photographed on the side of Peachcroft *c.* 1900. It serves as a reminder that winter travel was far different years ago from what it is today. In the sleigh are J.M. Hawkins and his wife. Peachcroft, which has remained in the Hawkins family, recently underwent an exterior restoration.

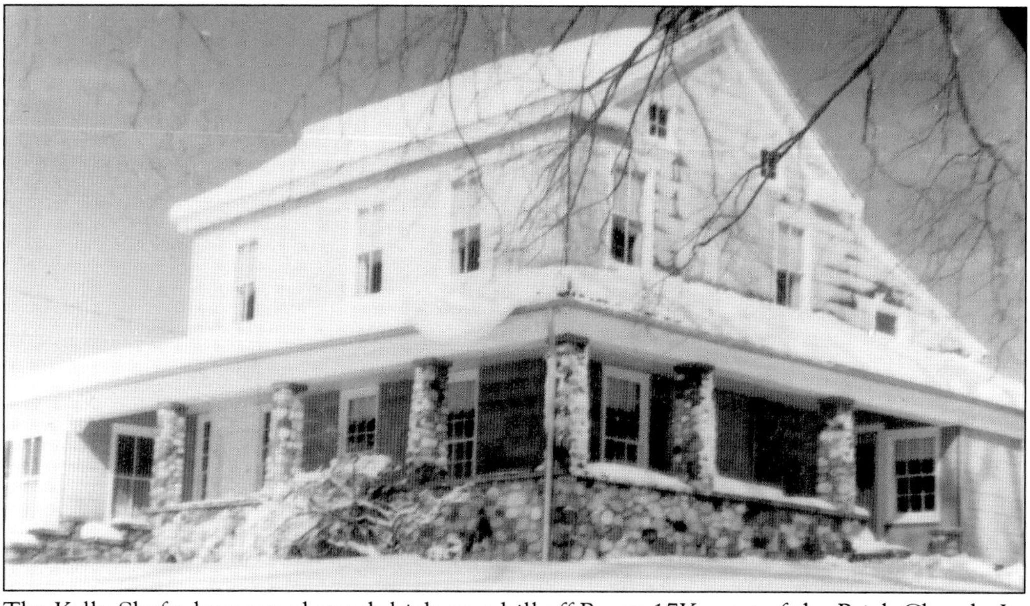

The Kelly-Shafer homestead stands high on a hill off Route 17K, west of the Brick Church. Its original builder and exact date of construction remain a mystery, but based on the homestead's architectural details, it is thought to date from about 1810. It contains a beautiful carved fan and two quarter fans over the front doorway and two nicely carved interior mantels. A recent remodeling project removed much of the homestead's original woodwork and windows.

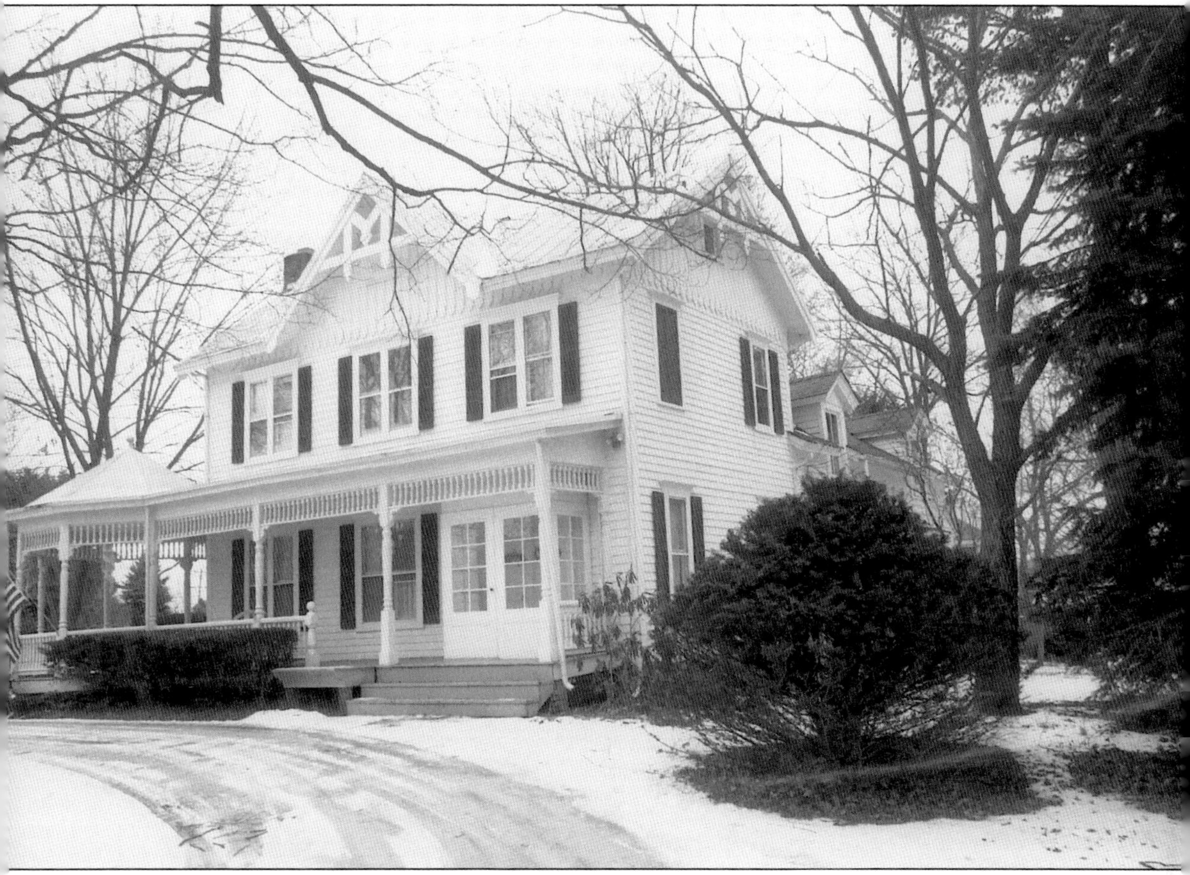

On the east side of Bailey Road stands the Milliken homestead. Research indicates that the rear wing of the house was built by Capt. James Milliken in 1770. Milliken and his bride moved into the new home, but with the seeds of war being sewn, tragedy was about to strike. In 1777, James and his two brothers were killed defending the patriot cause at the Battle of Fort Montgomery. The house remained in the family for several generations. The large front block was probably built about 1890 for Harvey Smith, who lived there at the time.

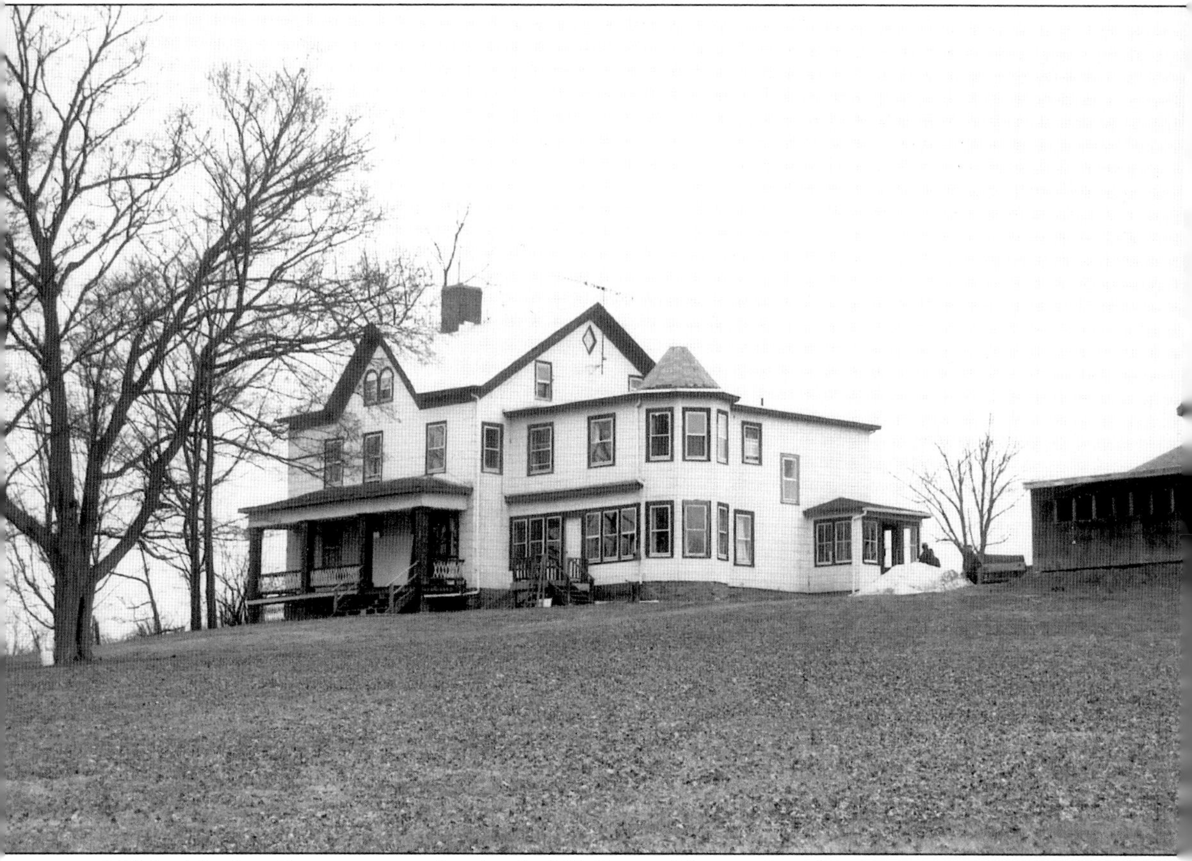

Mildred Parker Seese states in her book *Old Orange Houses* that the property on the corner of Coleman Road and Route 208 was initially the pioneer farmstead of Alexander Milliken (the father of Capt. James Milliken). Alexander, who died in 1780, may have been responsible for the construction of the original kitchen wing of the present house. In the early 1800s, the large main block of the dwelling was built in the Federal style. The 1862 Town of Montgomery Farm Map records this as the farm of Peter Eager. In 1890, it passed to the Coleman family, who replaced the original kitchen wing with the present Victorian-era wing. The Colemans no longer own the house, but the surrounding fields continue to be farmed.

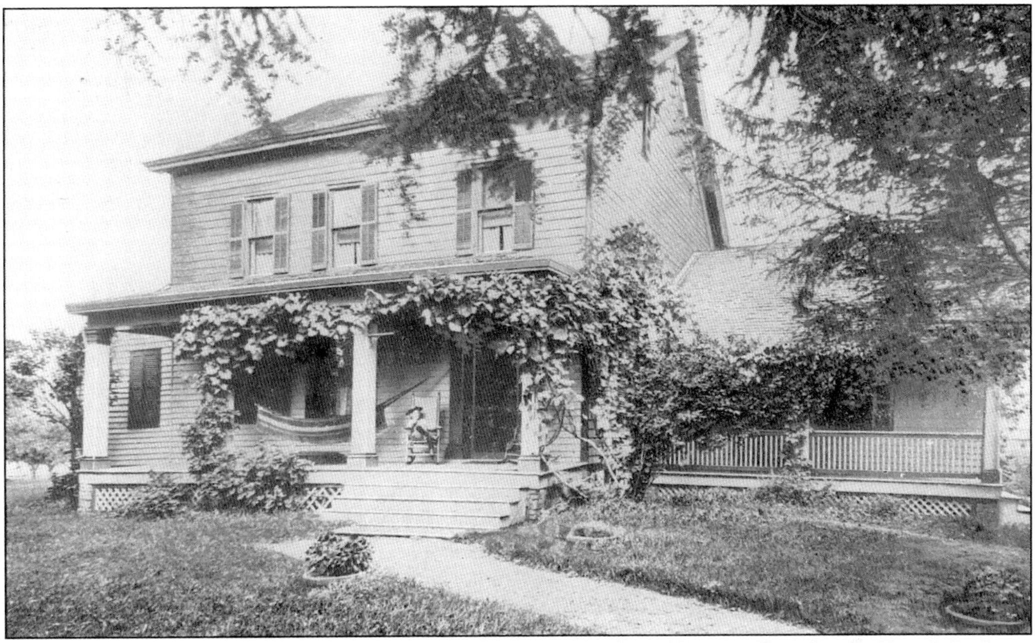

The Bowne homestead stands at the end of a long, tree-lined lane, off Coleman Road. It dates from the first half of the 19th century and was probably built for Cyrus Bowne. Cyrus's son Samuel achieved worldwide renown in the early 1900s as the proprietor of the elixir Scott's Emulsion. Samuel had the mansion on the hill to the north constructed for his younger brother, Cyrus, who had been residing in the family homestead.

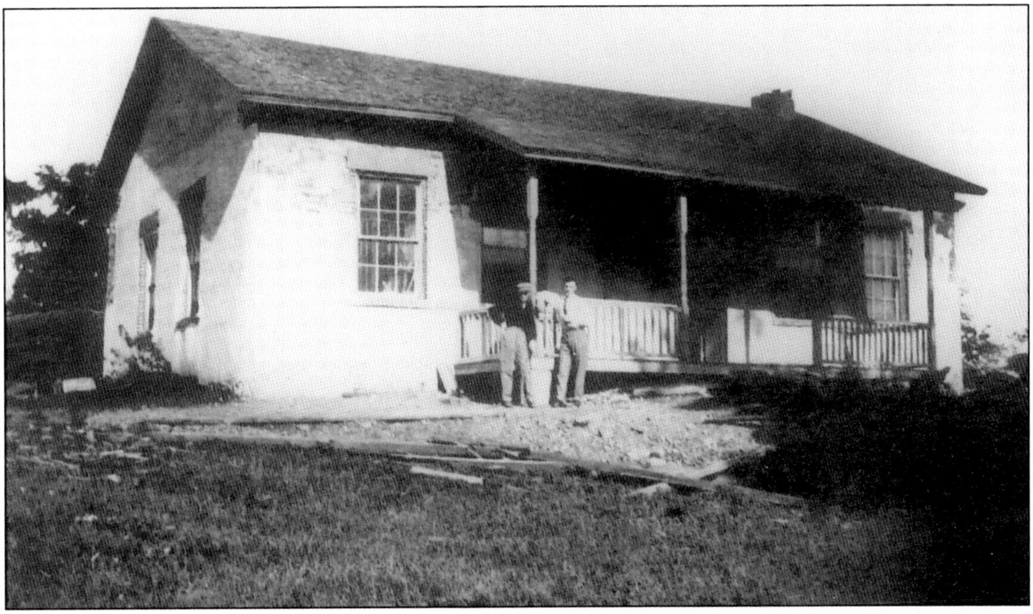

This stone dwelling is located on the south corner of Berea and Coldenham Roads. A close examination reveals that the oldest interior features date from around 1900, but tradition holds that the building was constructed in the 1700s. It is theorized that the structure was rebuilt, utilizing the original exterior walls. The 1862 Montgomery Farm Map lists the property as Whigham Academy, about which little is known.

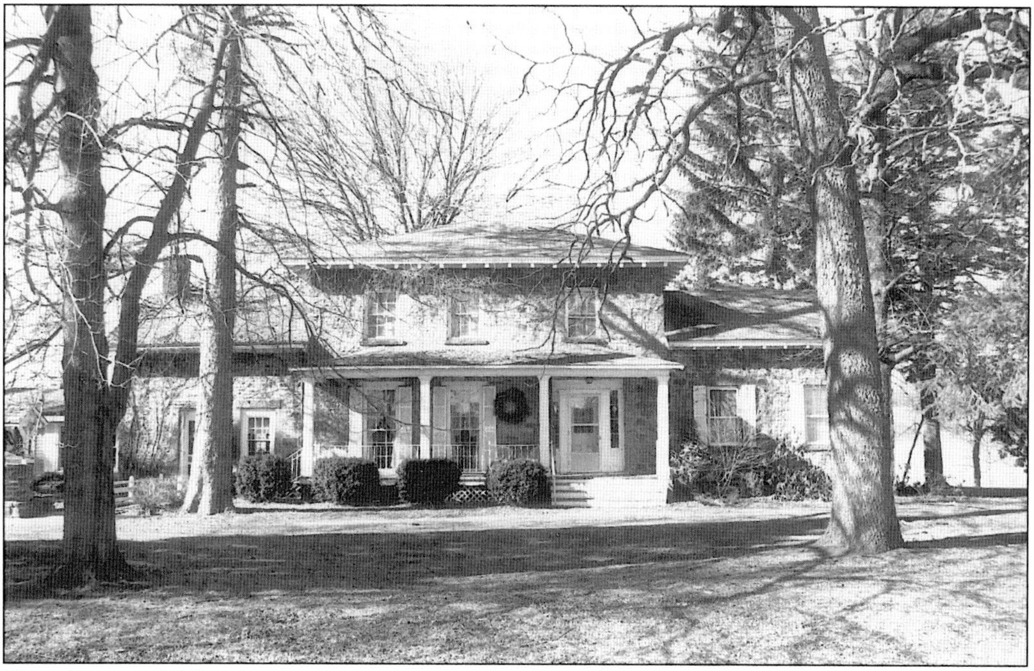

The George Weller house is among the stateliest historical farmhouses in the town of Montgomery. Located off of Coldenham Road, this elegant stone building was constructed in one of the most pleasing settings in town. It is thought that the south (left) wing was the original structure, dating from the 18th century. The remainder of the building was constructed around the middle of the 19th century. Several of the original barns still stand. The property is currently known as the Van Dam Farm.

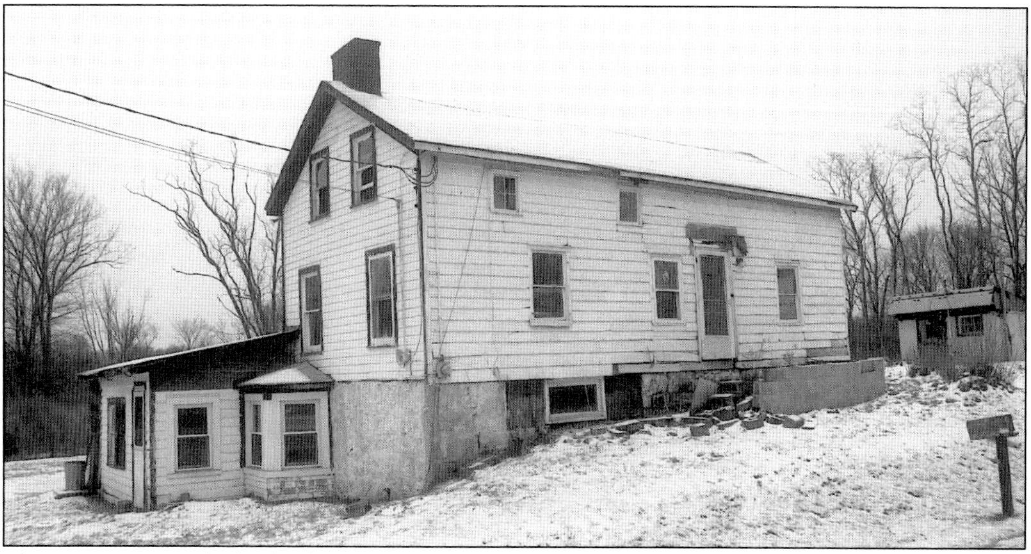

This conspicuous little dwelling is located on the south side of Route 17K, west of Scott's Corners. Labeled as the home of J. Bell in 1850, it is believed that the left half of the house is the older part, possibly dating from the second quarter of the 19th century. The house contains a small basement hearth in what was the original keeping room. A blacksmith shop once stood a short distance to the east.

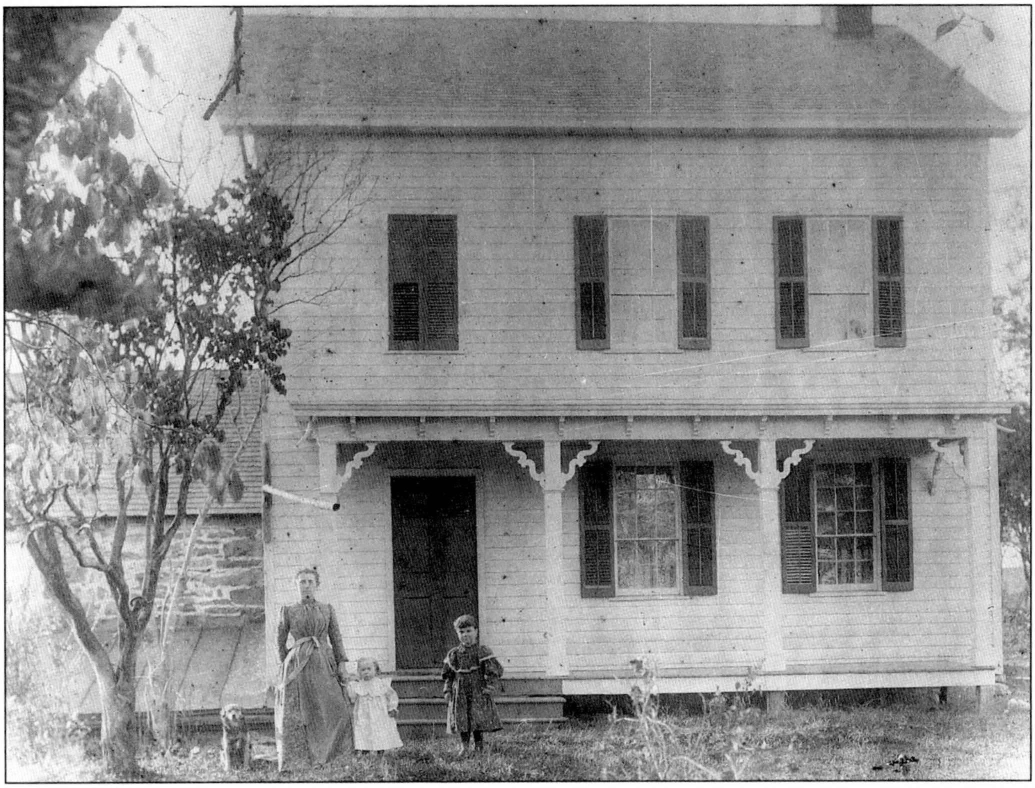

John Milliken, Alexander's Milliken's eldest son, built the stone portion of the Crystal Spring House, located east of Walden on Coldenham Road. His name and the year 1764 are inscribed on a stone in the front wall. The frame wing was added about 1820. The photograph dates from the 1890s. Research indicates that John and his family did not live in the original stone house for long. They built another home nearby and used the old dwelling as a workshop for the itinerant boot maker, tailor, and workers.

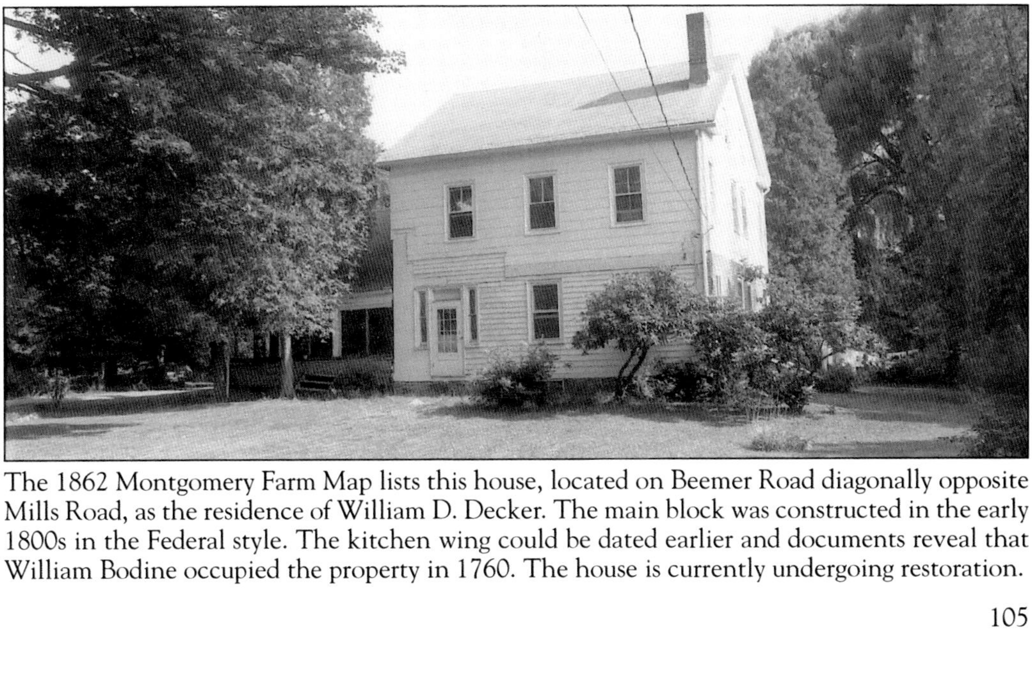

The 1862 Montgomery Farm Map lists this house, located on Beemer Road diagonally opposite Mills Road, as the residence of William D. Decker. The main block was constructed in the early 1800s in the Federal style. The kitchen wing could be dated earlier and documents reveal that William Bodine occupied the property in 1760. The house is currently undergoing restoration.

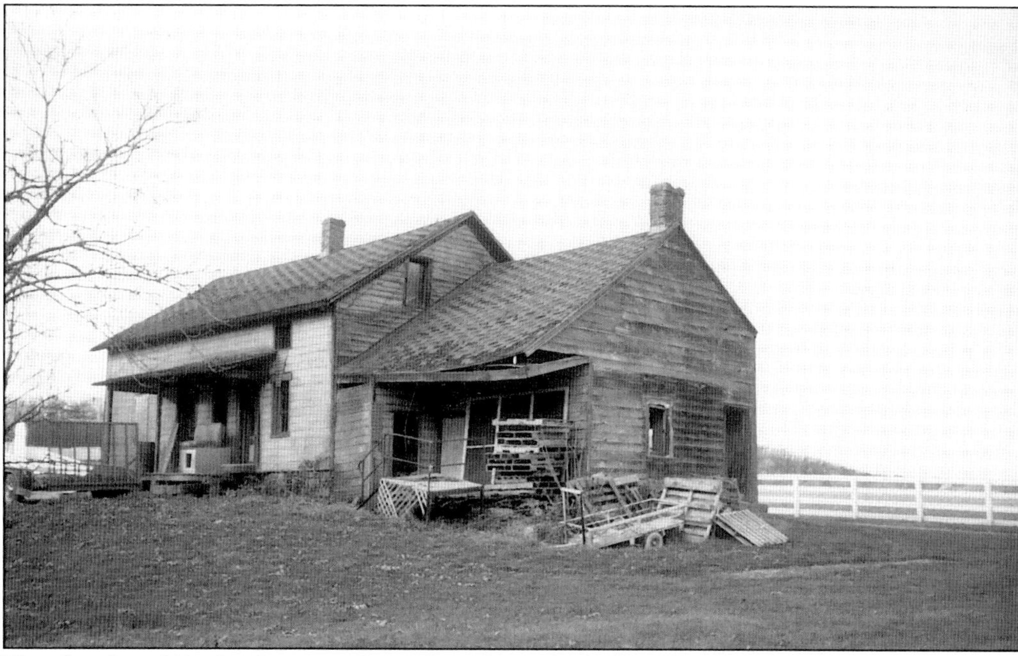

The abandoned Decker homestead stands at the end of a long lane, on the present Alnoff Farm. Records indicate that this farm was settled by Jacob Decker in 1746. The house, which was remodeled several times, had a center chimney containing corner fireplaces within the living area of the main block.

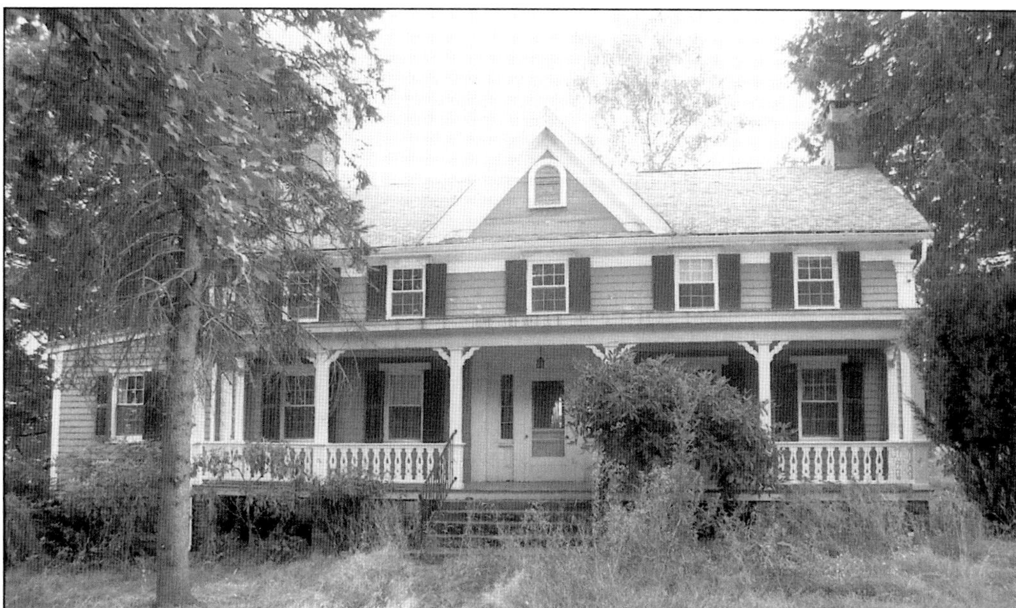

The 1859 map of Orange and Rockland Counties records that this home, located on the corner of Route 17K and Kaisertown Road, was the residence of Moses Mould. Probably built in the 1830s or 1840s, it contains many authentic Greek Revival features. A large hearth is located in the basement in what was the keeping room. In addition to the house, several authentic 19th-century outbuildings stand on the property.

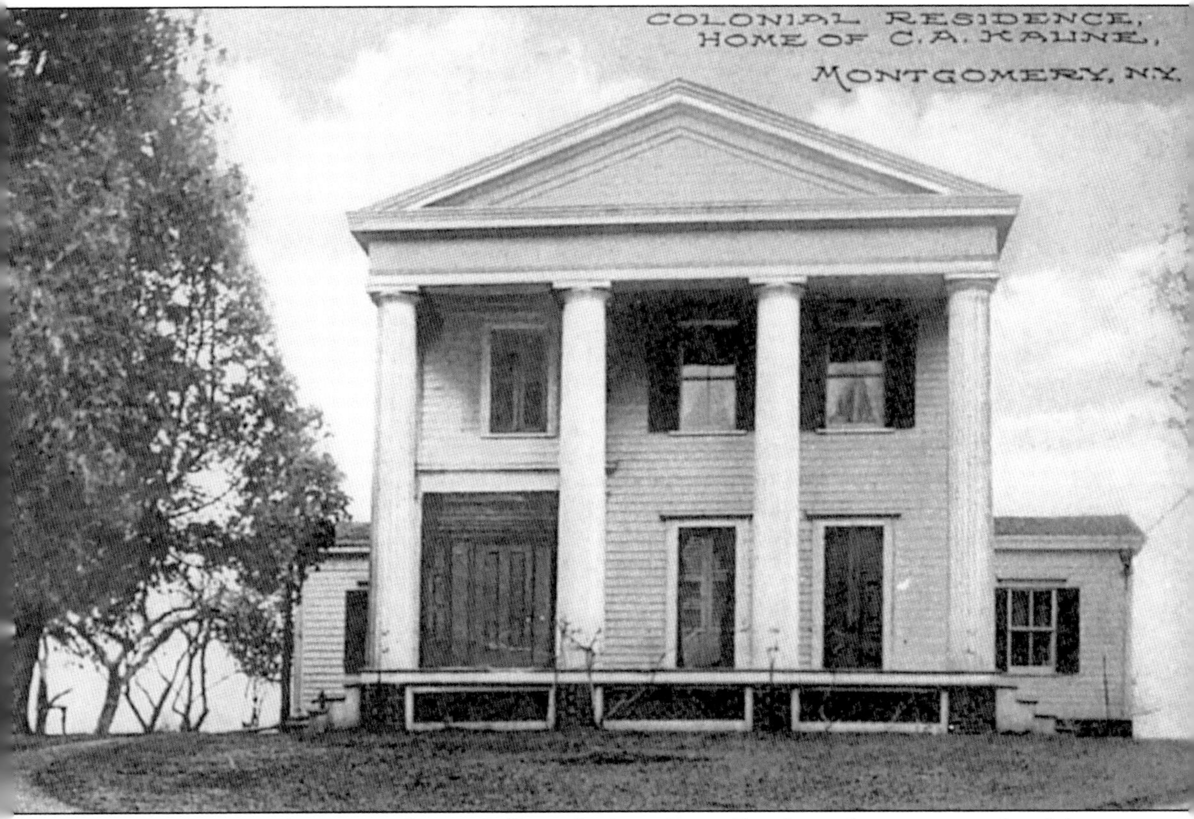

The Daniel Waring house stands on a hill overlooking River Road, on the opposite side of the Wallkill River from the village of Montgomery. Waring, a locally prominent figure, had the main block of the house built in 1844. The rear section may have incorporated the remnants of Jacob Crist's pioneer home. The Daniel Waring house is a remarkable example of Greek Revival architecture and was recently listed on the National Register. It contains four marble mantelpieces in the front block and a cooking hearth with bake oven in the rear wing.

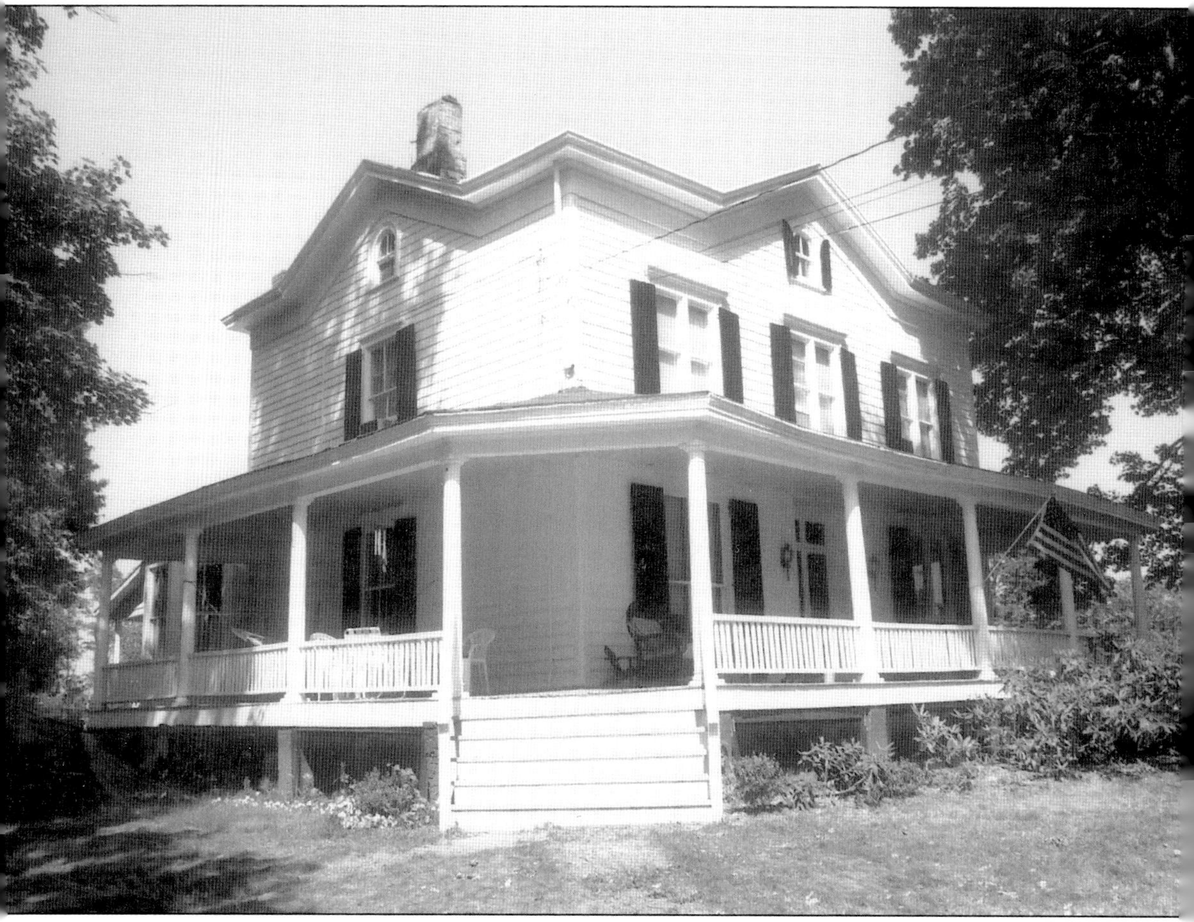

The Devine house, situated on River Road just east of the Daniel Waring house, dates from the 1870s. This wonderful Victorian residence contains a high degree of integrity, including marble mantelpieces, wide woodwork, and ornate plaster cornices. In the rear yard is a period wagon house with horse stables. Labeled as the residence of M. Stager in the 1903 *Atlas of Orange County*, it became the home of the Bevier family in 1914. The Beviers, in turn, sold it to the Devines c. 1923.

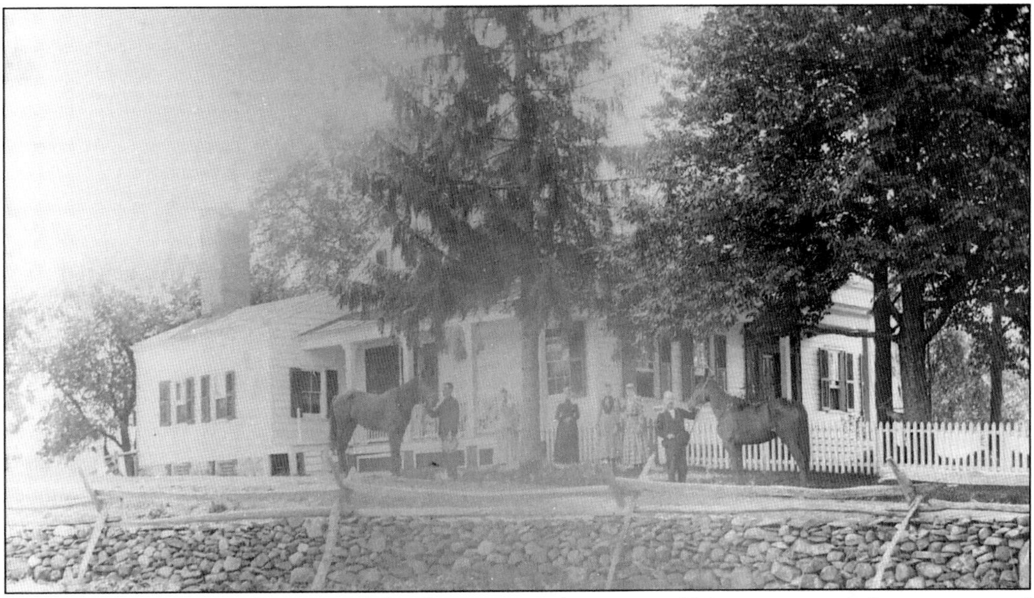

The Tweddle farmstead is one of the few sites in the town of Montgomery to have remained in the same family for over a century. The small rear wing of the house is believed to have originally served as the residence of Bergoon and Jane Van Alst. The large, front Greek Revival block was probably built by George Van Alst in the 1830s. In 1868 the farm was purchased by Thomas Tweddle. These vintage 1890s photographs show the farm in its prime. The barns were destroyed by fire and replaced with the present barn in 1935. Recently, this farmstead was nominated for the National Register.

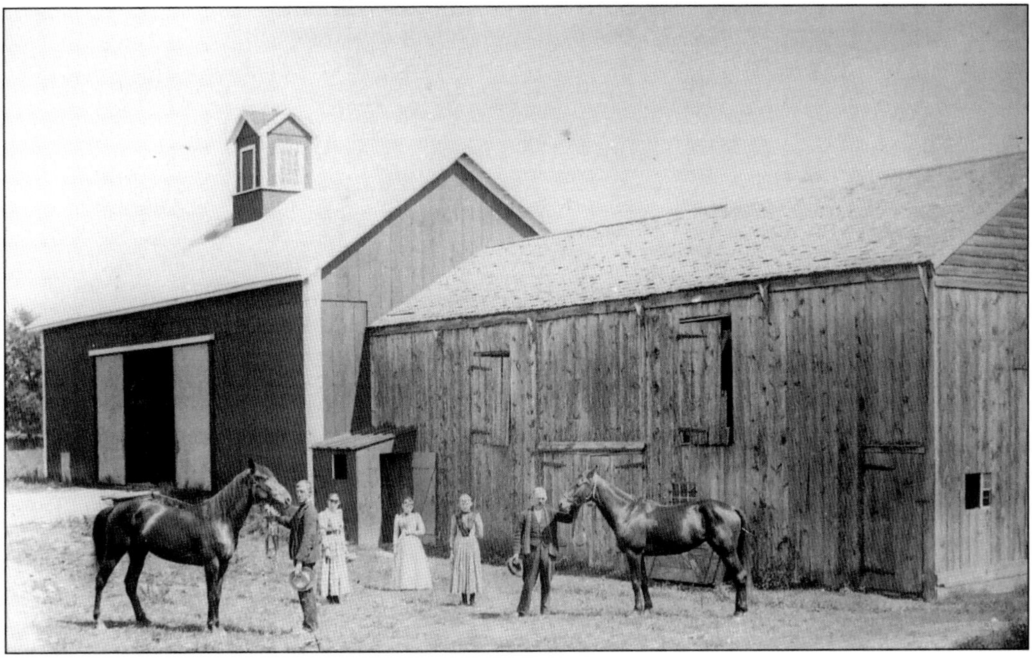

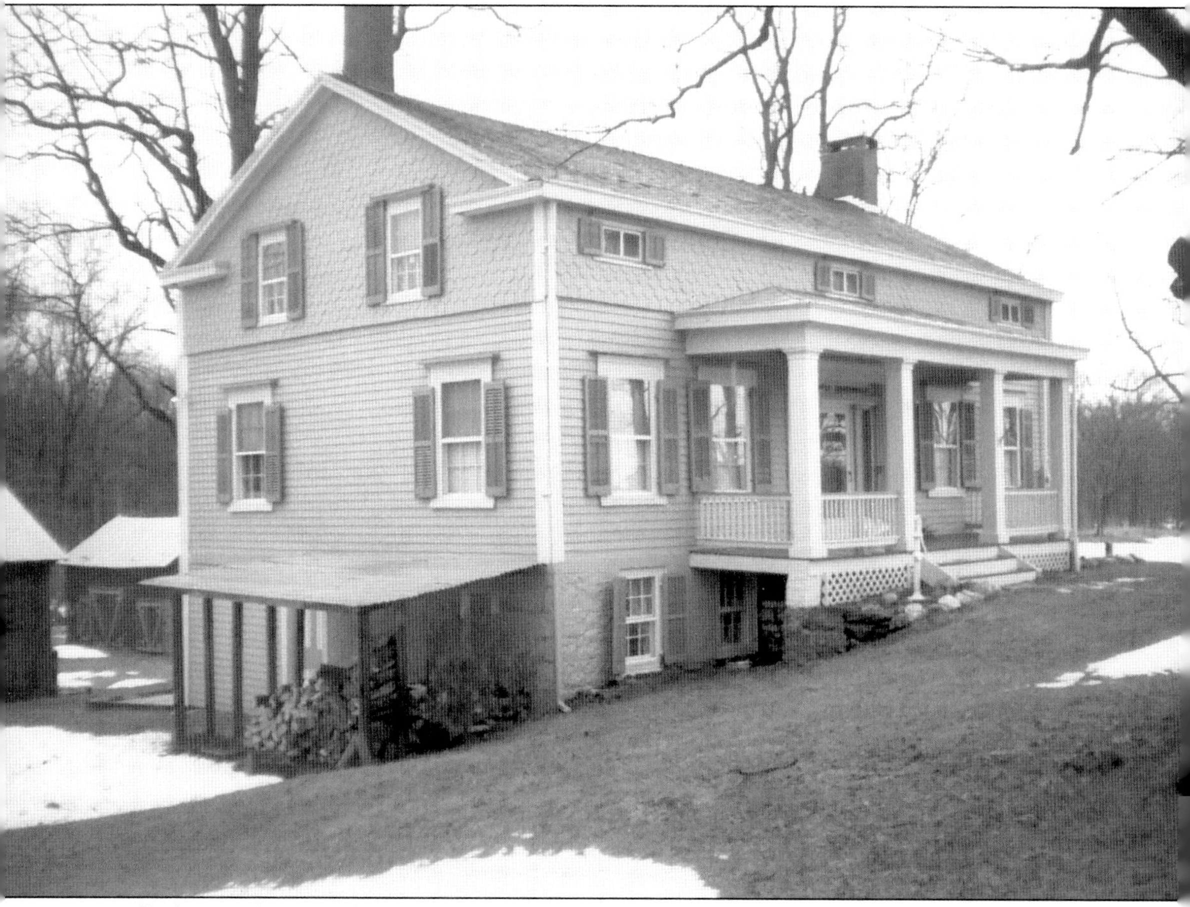

Wilhelm Smidt, one of Montgomery's German settlers and a blacksmith by trade, established himself in a stone farmhouse on a bend in Albany Post Road in 1759. Almost a century later, a descendant (possibly Neil L. Smith) replaced the stone house with the present Greek Revival-era dwelling. Recently listed on the National Register, it contains a great deal of original detailing. During the Victorian era, fish-scale slate siding was attached to the second story of the house and on the entire rear wall. The dwelling also contains some earlier detailing such as doors and hardware that came from the pioneer stone dwelling. Some of the hardware is believed to have been forged by Smidt.

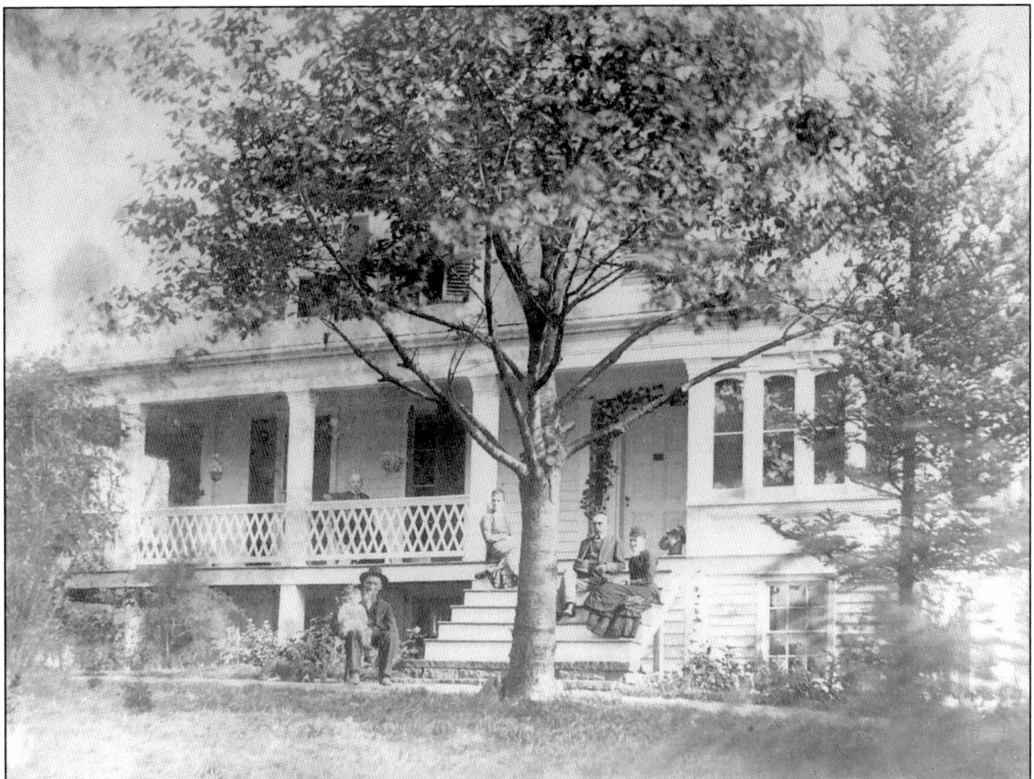

Probably built in the 1840s, the Bull farmstead sets back from the corner of Browns Road and Route 17K. Most of its original outbuildings remain, including a granary, wagon house, and hay and livestock barns. Labeled as the farm of Charles Eager on the 1862 Montgomery Farm Map, the property had passed into the Bull family by 1874. During the 1890s, the house underwent a general remodeling on the first floor. This photo dates from that period.

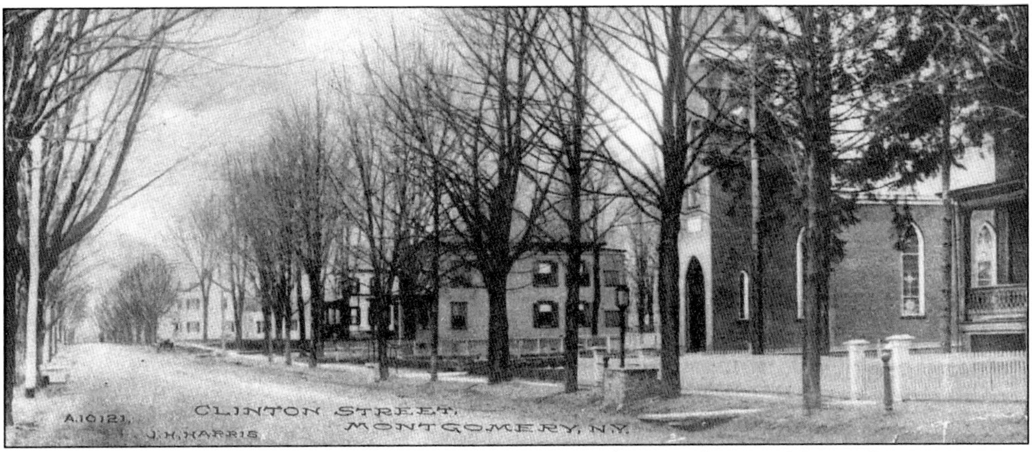

The village of Montgomery is well known for its many historic homes. Union Street contains a wide variety of architecture, ranging from Federal and Greek Revival to Victorian and Edwardian. Older buildings abut on sidewalks and are close together. As with Clinton, a good portion of Union Street is listed on the National Register. This postcard view, *c.* 1915, is facing north from St. Mary's.

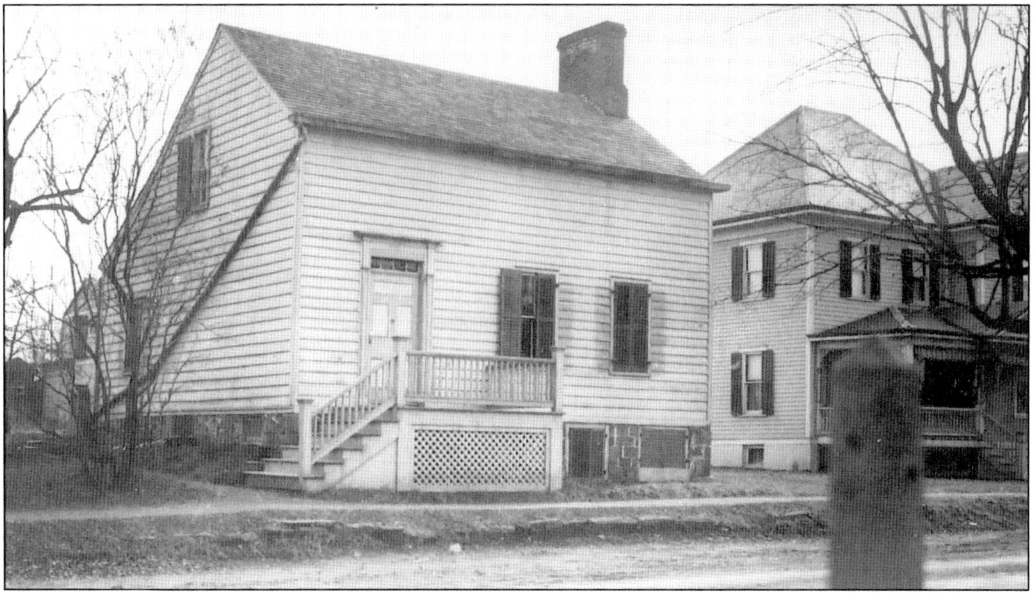

The Daniel Mason house, located at 59 Union Street, dates from the early 1800s. It was built as a typical three-bay box-like dwelling. Around 1920, it was extensively updated by the Senior family. The main entryway contains two carved sunbursts on the pilasters over the transom. Both photographs show the house before remodeling: the front view in 1918, and the rear view c. 1900.

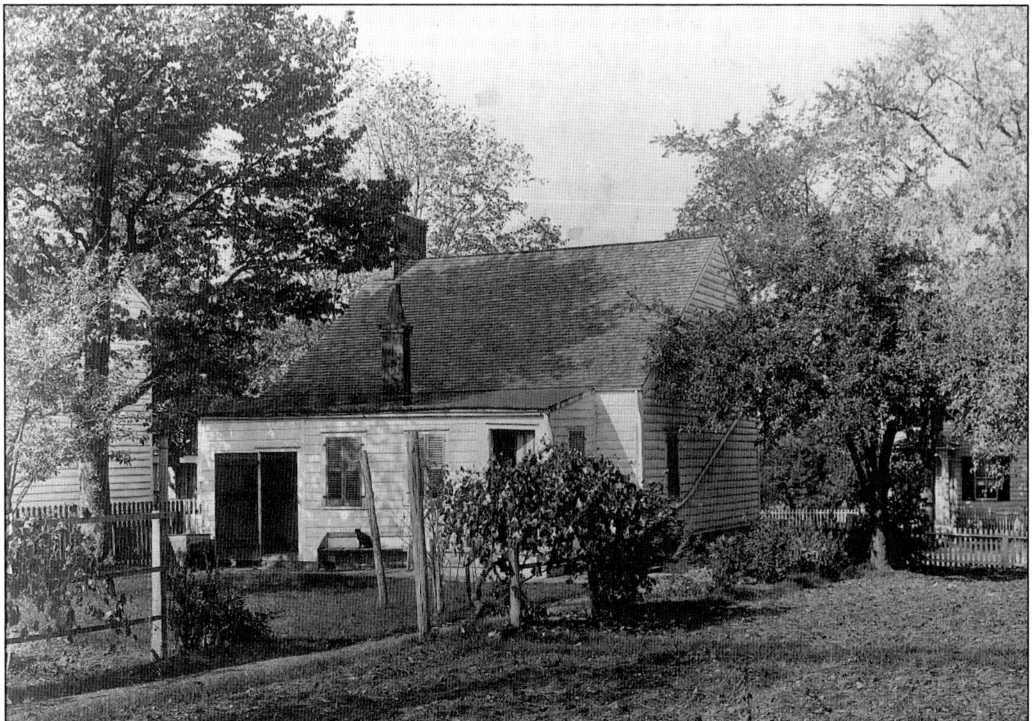

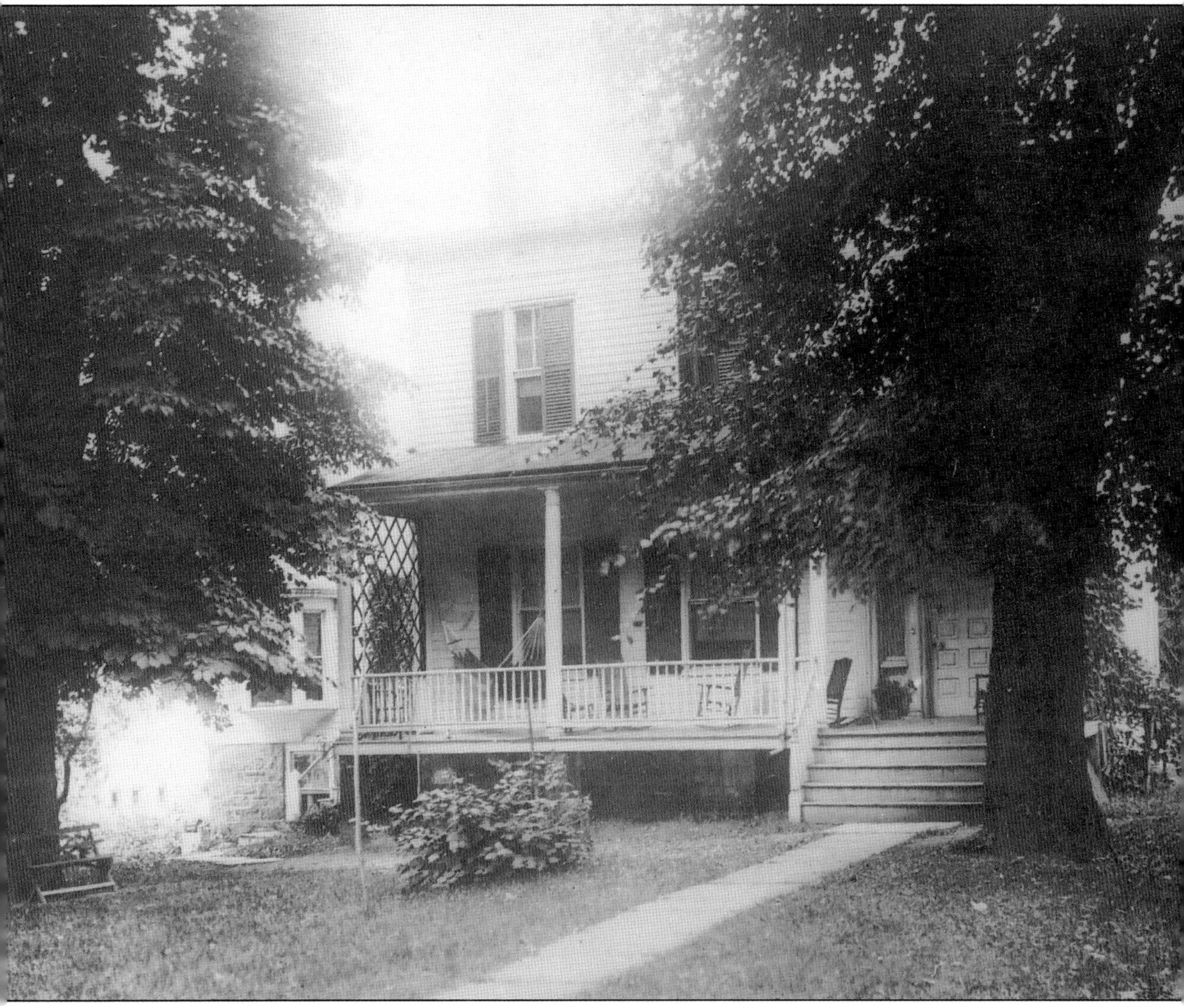

The Charles Borland Jr. house, located on Clinton Street opposite Montgomery Academy, is one of the finest buildings in the village. Built *c.* 1830, it contains high-style Greek Revival-era woodwork and a spacious front hall with a mahogany handrail, newel post, and spindles. In the basement of the utilitarian wing is a large hearth with a beehive oven. A local attorney, Borland was one of the area's most prominent figures of his time. The house is a statement of his importance. It later became the home of William Hanlon, who ran the adjacent harness shop (see p. 53). This photograph was taken about 1910, during the Hanlon ownership.

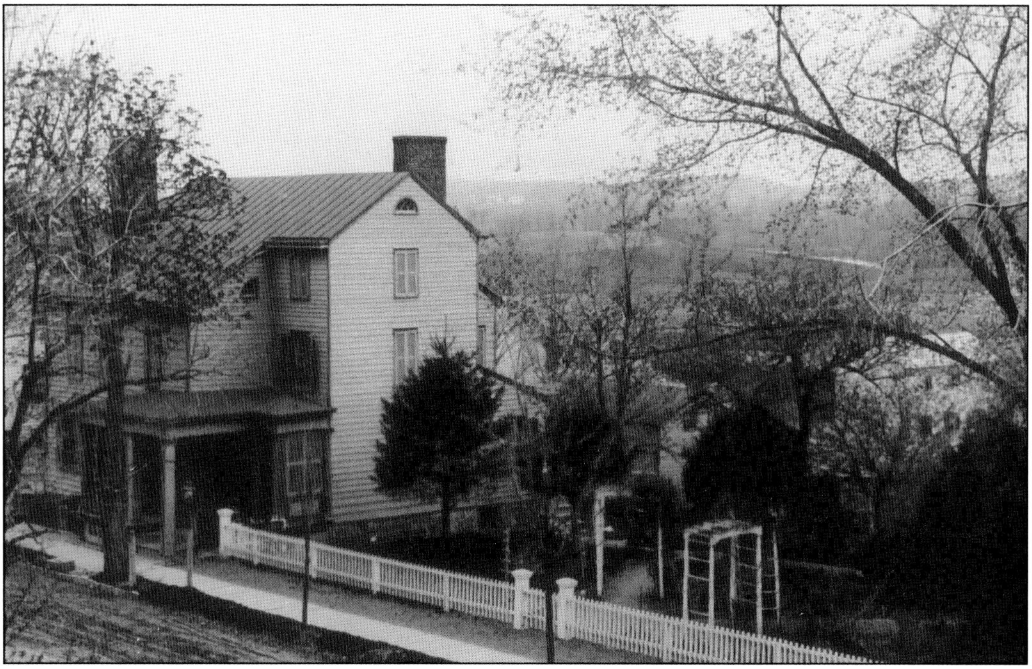

This *c.* 1890 photograph, likely the work of amateur photographer George Eager, shows the Senior residence, located on the corner of Union and Bachelor Streets. The house originally stood closer to Union Street, as shown in the photograph. Around 1900, the Seniors moved the house back from the street and added the large wraparound porch. Previously owned by the Conger family, the house dates from the 1820s.

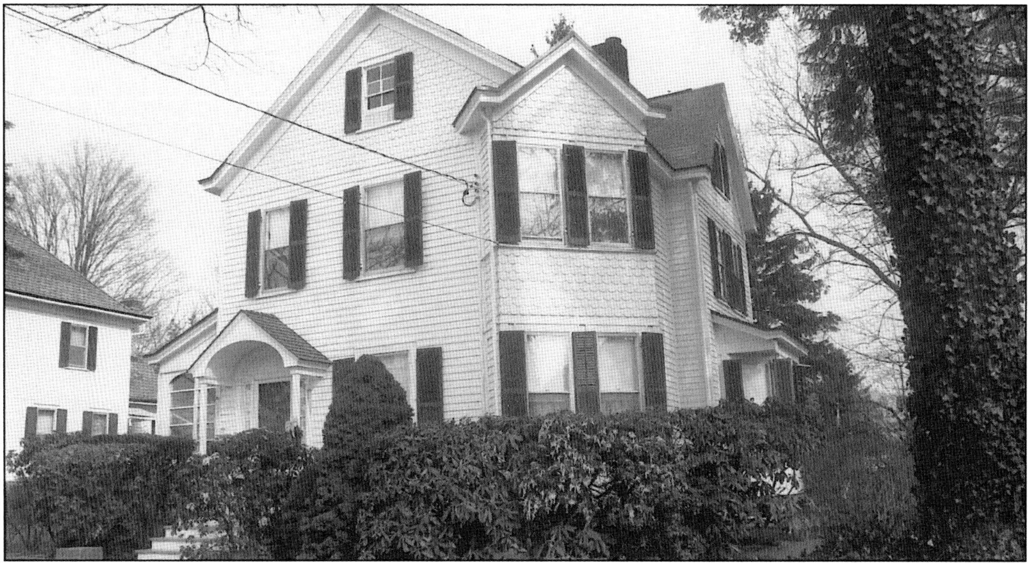

The village of Montgomery experienced a small boom in the 1890s. The Stratton-Hadaway house, located at 67 Union Street, was built in 1895–96 by local builder Chauncey Brooks and his crew for Joseph Stratton. Stratton worked with his brother Thomas, who operated the gristmill on the Wallkill River, opposite the paper mill. In 1911, the house became the property of Frank T. Hadaway. It remained in the Hadaway family until 1989.

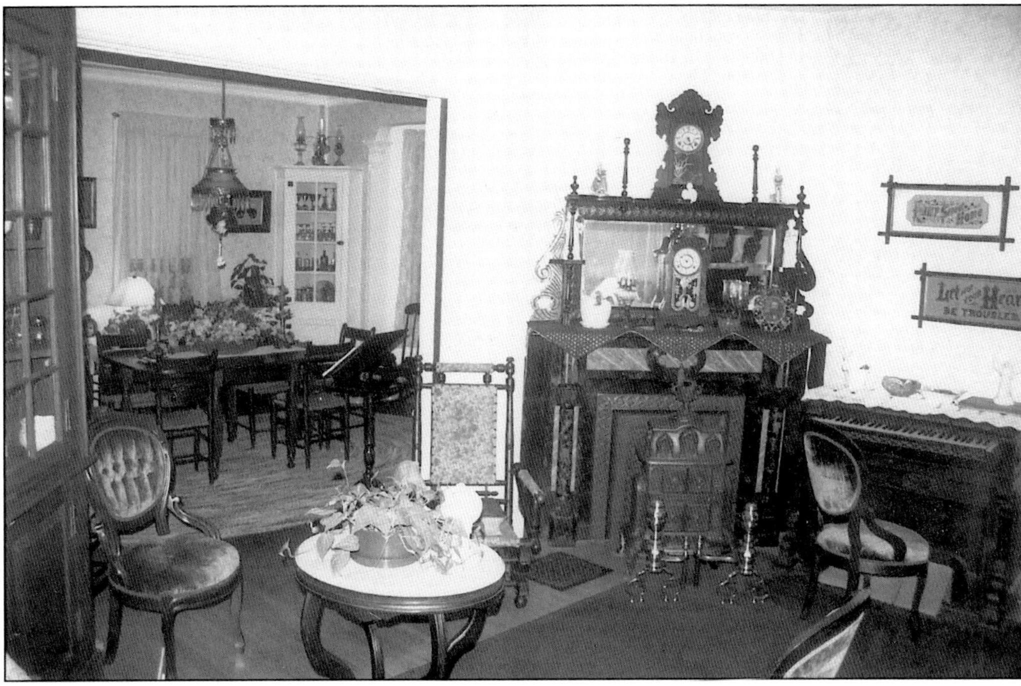

The parlor of the Stratton-Hadaway house, with its marbleized mantel, still appears today much the way it did a century ago. The house was originally heated by coal-burning stoves, but soon after construction a large coal furnace was installed. Like many other village homes, the house was electrified in 1911 with old-style knob-and-tube wiring.

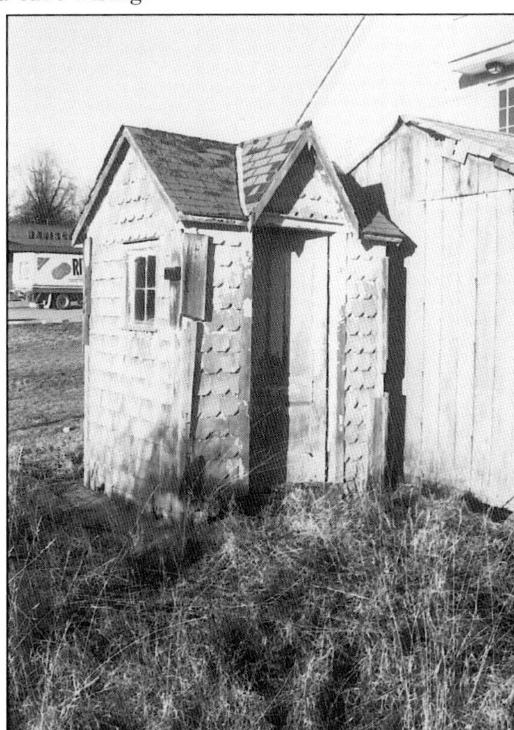

Outbuildings are a vital component of any historical property. This present-day photograph shows the almost forgotten Patchett outhouse, located behind the large brick dwelling on the corner of Ward and Factory Streets. Dating from the 1890s, the outhouse serves as a reminder of what life was like before the convenience of indoor plumbing.

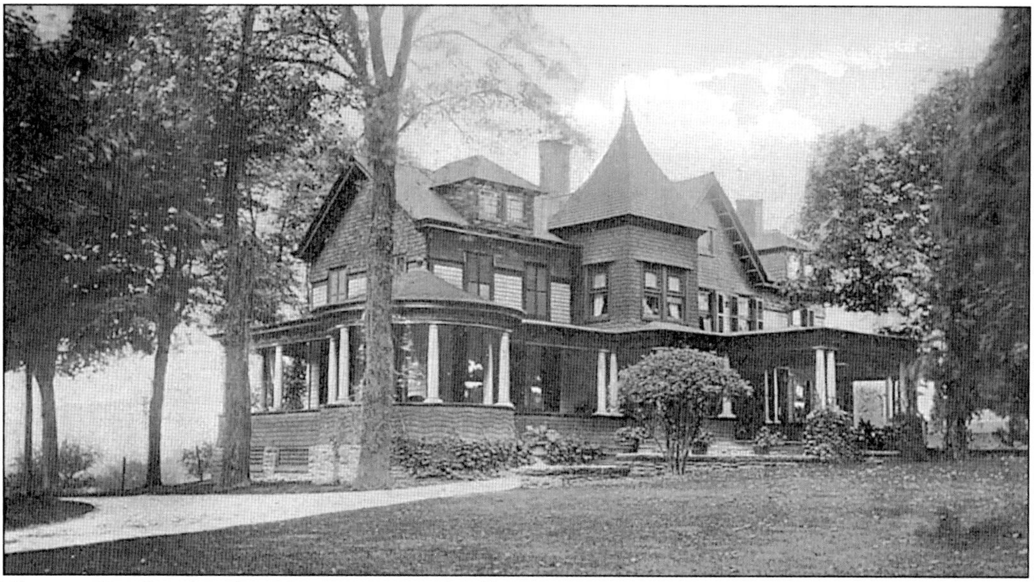

Thomas Bradley lived in this Victorian dwelling on Ulster Avenue. Bradley, whose stepfather was an official in the New York Knife Company, earned distinction during the Civil War. He enlisted as a private in Company H of the 124th Regiment and earned promotions, first to the rank of captain and eventually to brevetted major. He received the Congressional Medal of Honor for heroic service at the Battle of Chancellorsville in 1863. He was among the town's most successful businessmen and was Walden's most notable benefactor.

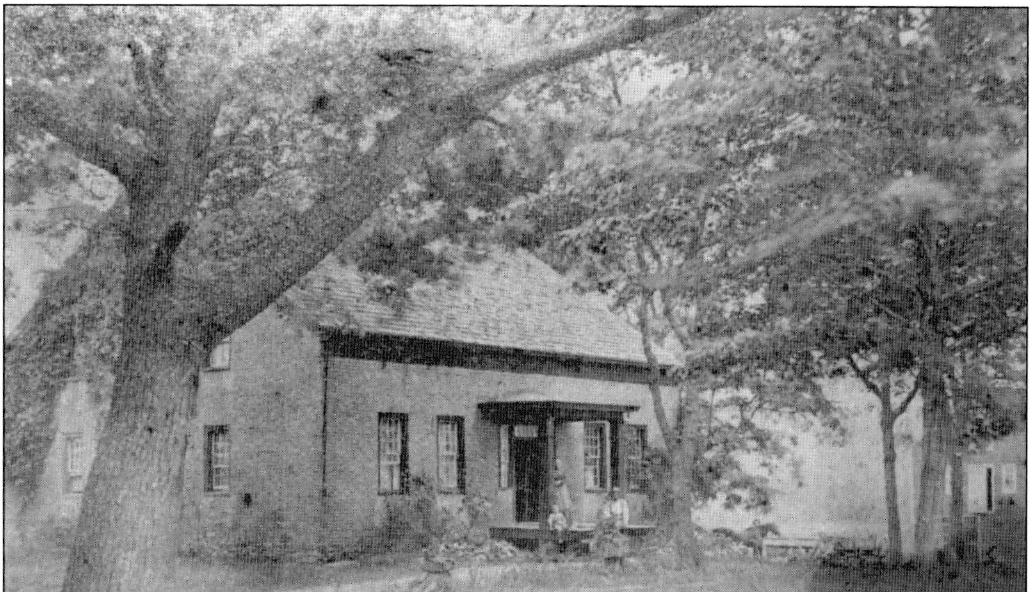

One of the most historic sites in the village of Maybrook is the Blake homestead. The house, built in 1794, has been well preserved and is listed on the National Register. John Blake, who built the house, was a prominent figure. A soldier during the American Revolution, he later served as sheriff of Orange County, a state assemblyman, and a New York Congressional representative. The farmland around the homestead was eventually converted into rail yards (see p. 67) and later taken over by Yellow Freight.

Eight

Vanished Montgomery

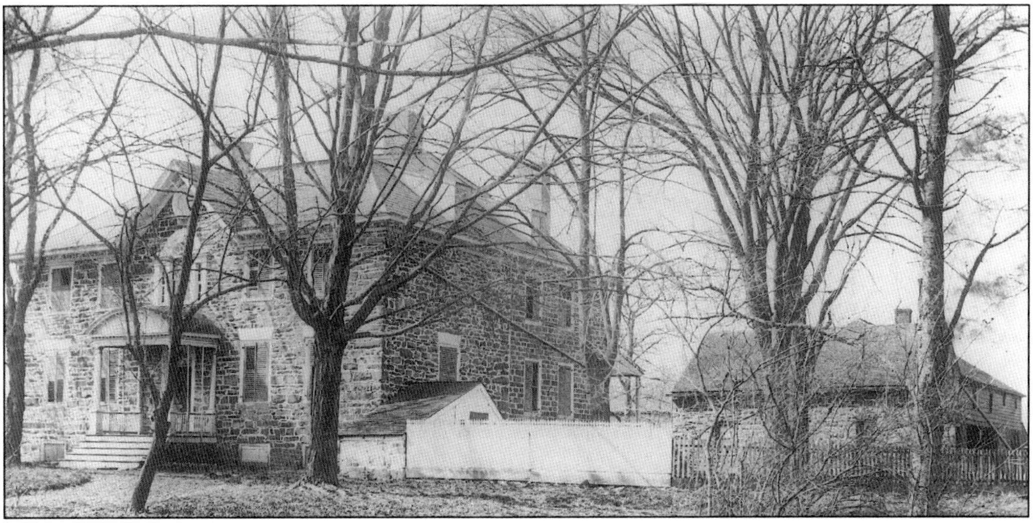

It is unfortunate that, with the passing of time, some of Montgomery's most important landmarks have fallen by the wayside and are now among the lost. One of the finest homes ever built in the town of Montgomery was the Colden Mansion. The site of its massive stone ruins, at the corner of Route 17K and Stone Castle Road, is one of Montgomery's most significant historical treasures and is eligible for inclusion on the National Register. Built in 1767 in the Georgian style, the mansion contained exquisite paneled room ends, one of which is preserved in the American Wing of the Metropolitan Museum of Art in New York City. The Coldens were the most prominent family in the town in their day. Cadwallader Colden Sr., father of Cadwallader Jr. (who had the mansion built), was a noted physician and botanist. He also served as surveyor general and lieutenant governor of the province. This 1880s photograph shows the mansion before its roof was changed to mansard style. The small stone building at the rear served as a cook house.

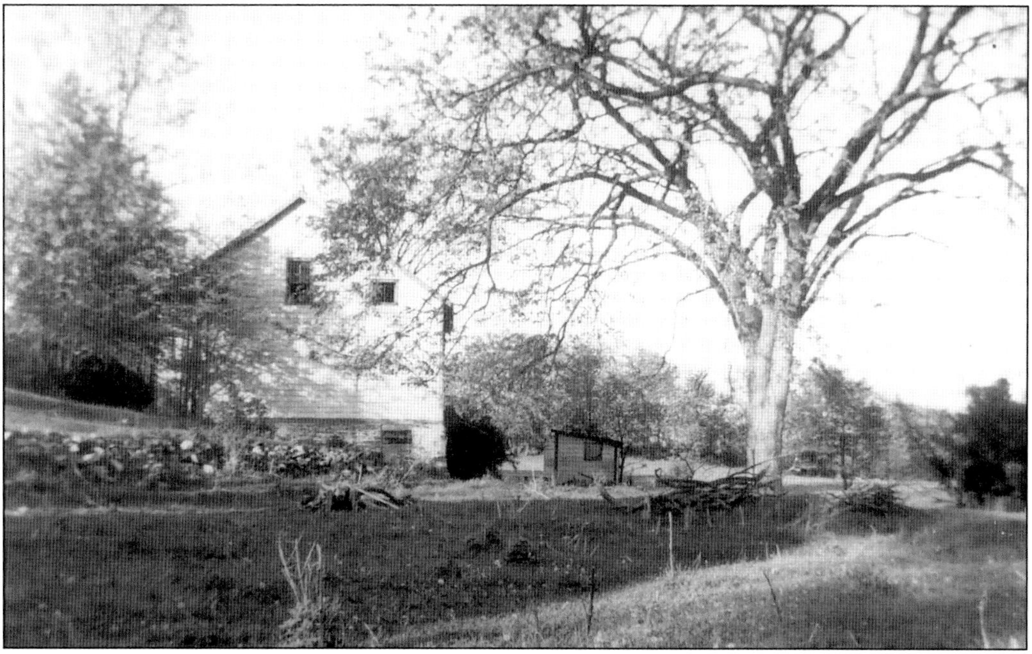

Abandoned since the 1940s, the Miller homestead gradually fell into ruins and became completely entangled in vines. This fascinating structure, built in 1789, contained a basement kitchen with a large hearth and recessed beehive oven. When the surrounding land was developed into the Winding Hills Golf Club, the foundation of the Miller homestead was refurbished and preserved as a part of the golf course.

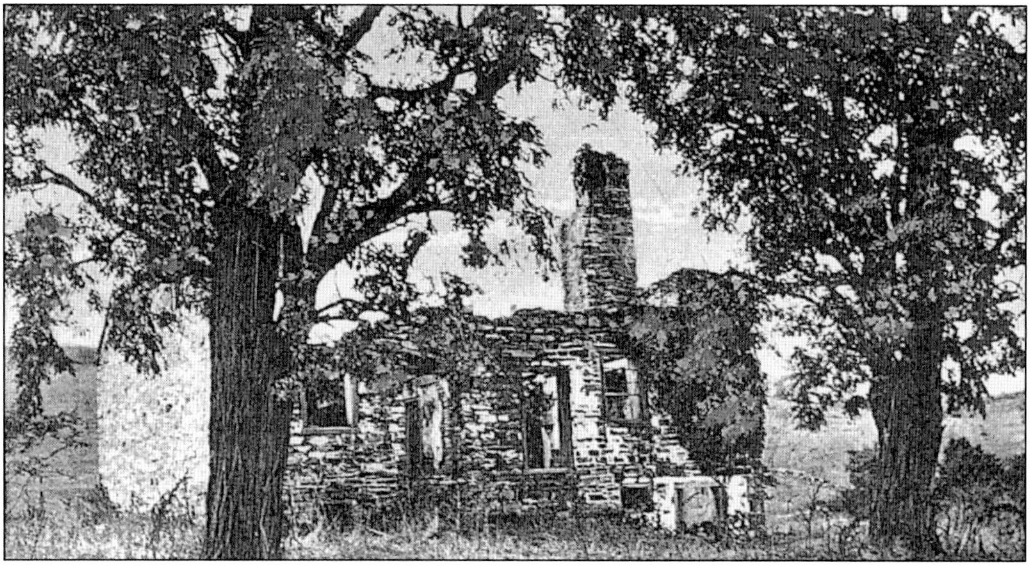

The Newkirk stone house, dating from the 18th century, stood on the east side of Kaisertown Road, south of the Wille Farm. It is said that Revolutionary War soldiers encamped around the house. The dwelling was abandoned in the latter part of the 19th century and eventually fell into ruins. When the nearby Shafer pioneer stone house was undergoing reconstruction in the 1930s, stone was taken from the Newkirk site, leaving only a foundation. In later years, the Chapman residence was built on that foundation.

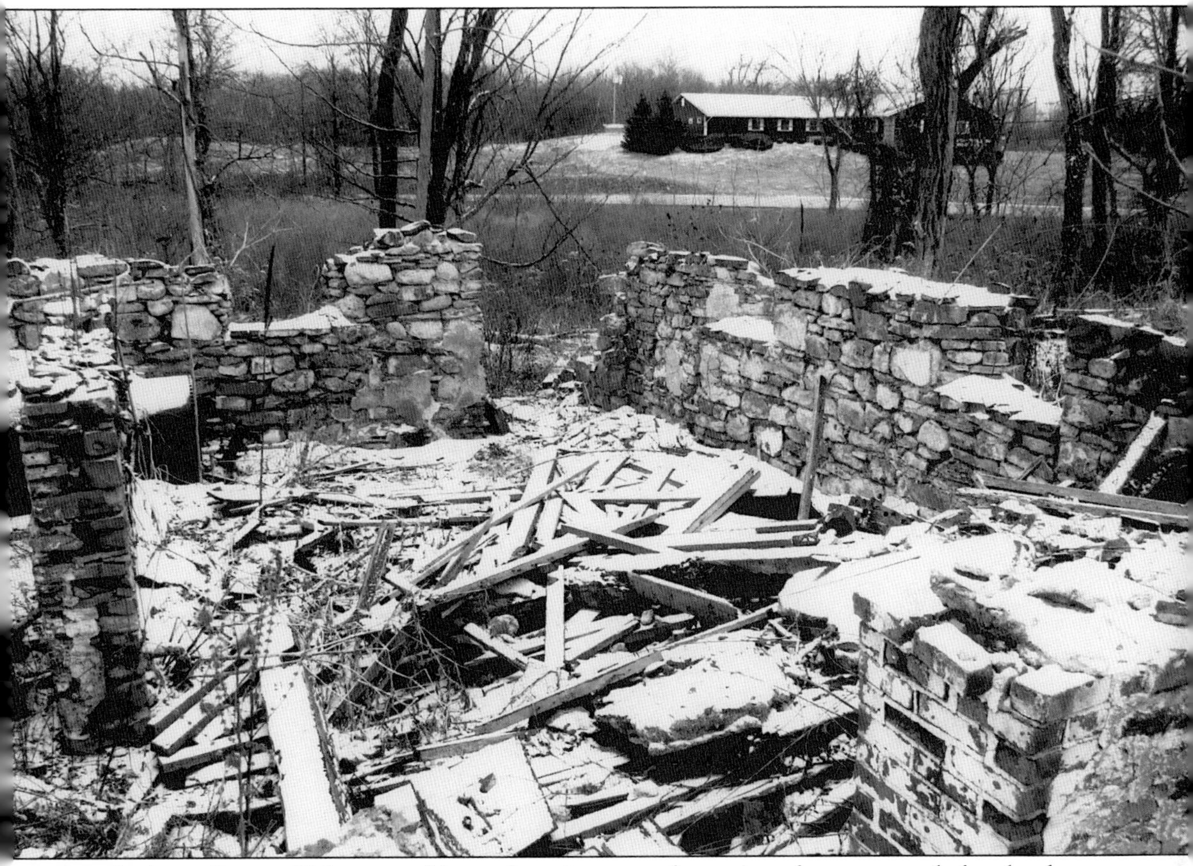

Land along Route 208 is quickly undergoing transformation from pastoral farmland to commercial development. The Graham homestead was located on the west side of Route 208, a short distance north of the Goodwill Church. The Georgian-style house, built *c.* 1766, and surrounding property was purchased by James Graham in 1804 and remained in his family until 1989. A kitchen wing was added in the early 1800s, and the house was extensively remodeled in the 1830s. After the death of the last Graham occupant, the property was sold and the house was dismantled, leaving behind its foundation as a silent memorial of this once great town of Montgomery homestead.

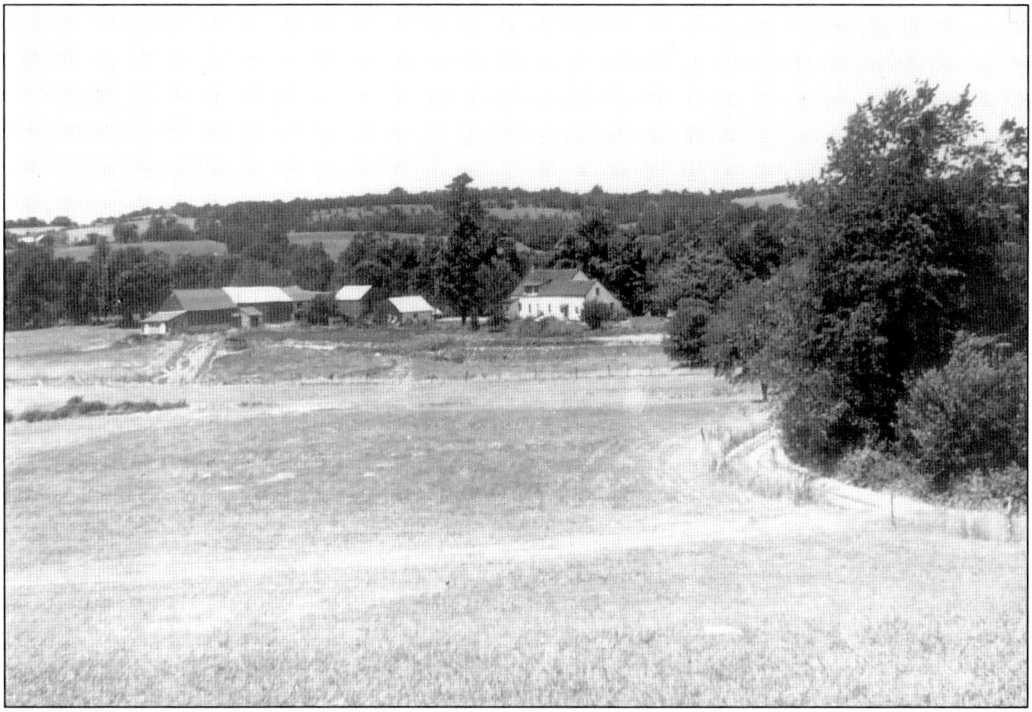

Before Orange County acquired land along the west side of the Wallkill River for the airport, Kaisertown Road extended from Route 211 at Bodine's Tavern to a point near the present K-9 training facility. On this stretch of roadway stood the Joseph Decker farmstead, more commonly referred to as the Zickler Farm.

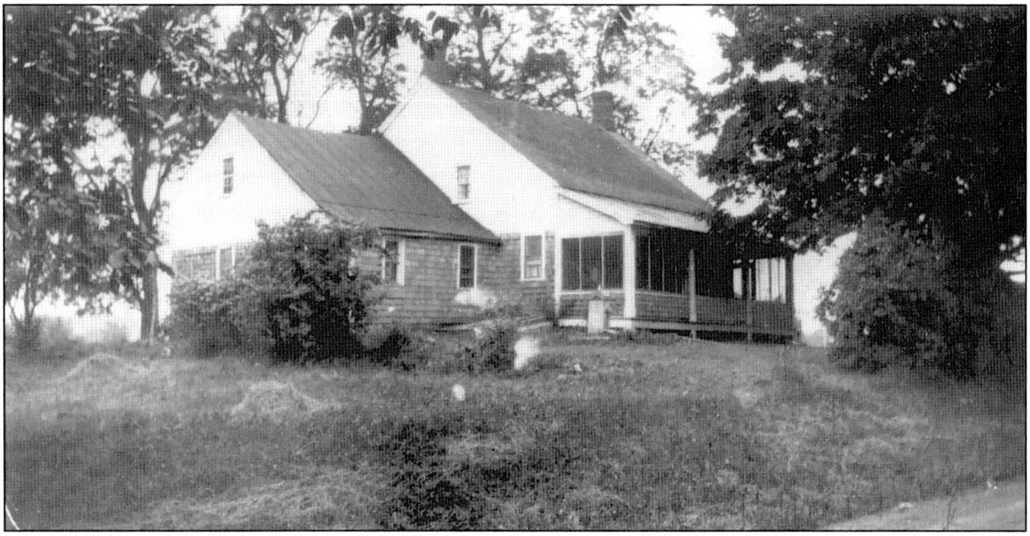

The exact age of the house and the names of the original occupants remains unknown, but the dwelling may have dated from the 18th century. In November of 1909, the farm was purchased by Mr. and Mrs. George Zickler. Over the years, the house was updated by the Zicklers. When Orange County acquired the property, the buildings were demolished. Only a small pile of stones were left to mark the site of this venerable farmstead. This photograph dates from the 1920s.

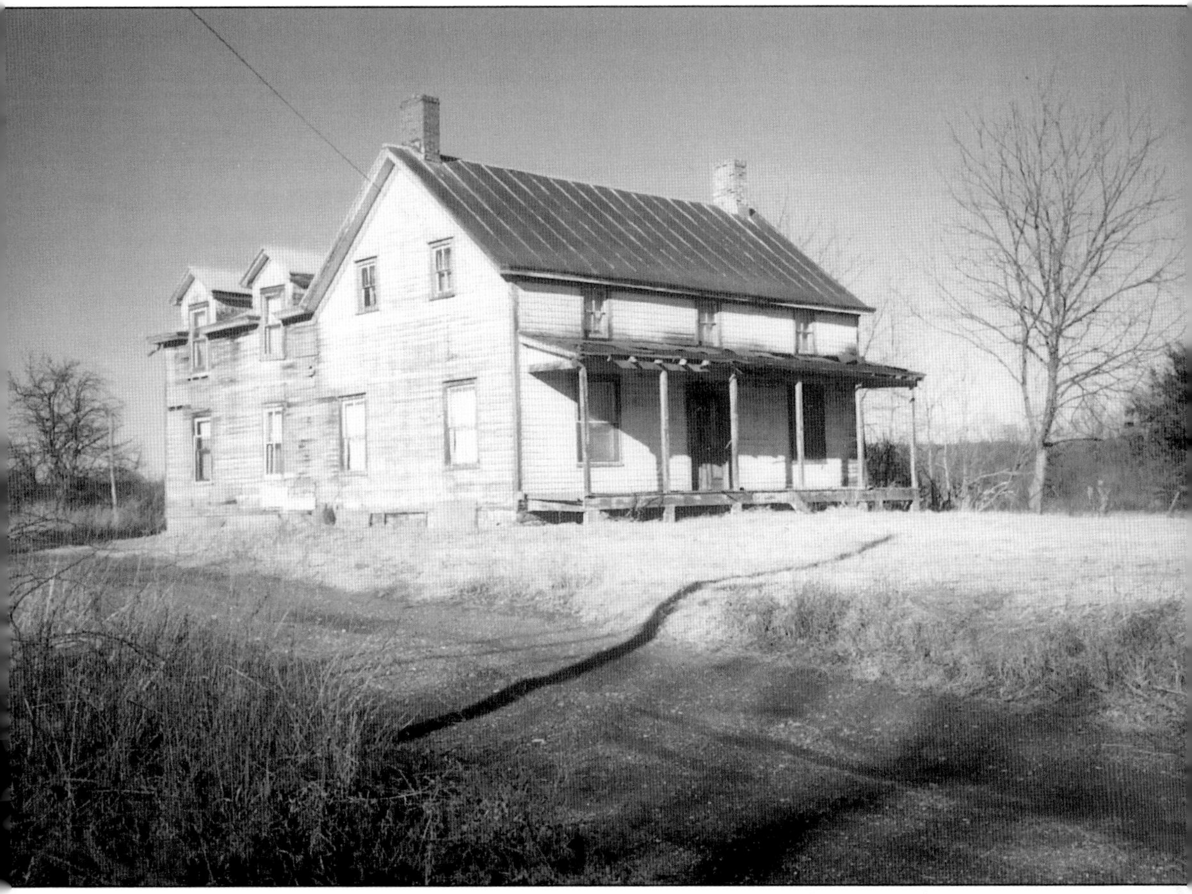

The Bookstaver-McCarthy residence survives today only as a ruin and is situated on Route 17K, diagonally opposite the Brick Church Cemetery. Probably dating to the late 18th century, the house was extensively remodeled during the Victorian era. In the basement lie the remains of large hearths. After the death of the last McCarthy occupant, in the late 1980s, the house and farmland was sold for development. Most of the wide plank flooring and hand-hewn floor joists have been removed. Today, a real estate sign was posted out front, announcing a new 18-lot subdivision named Barley Hill.

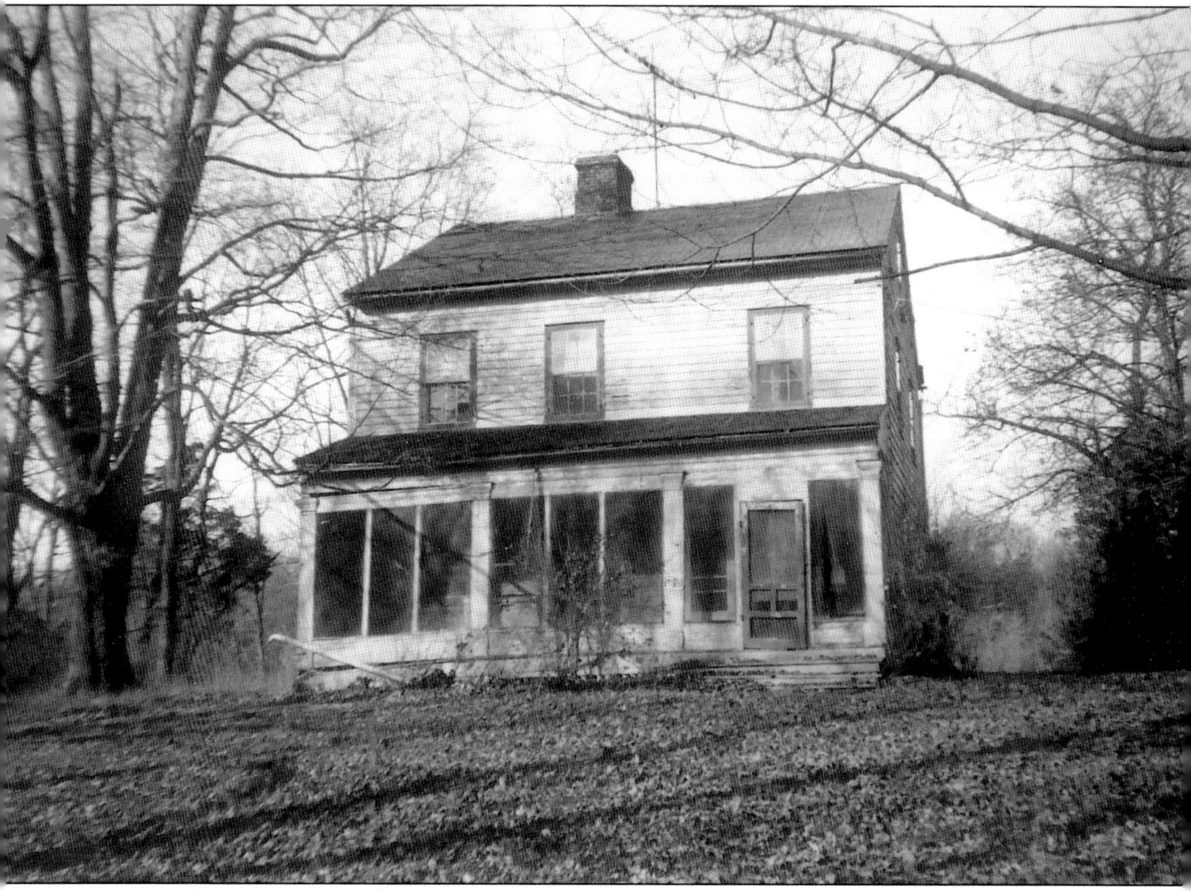

Dating from the early 19th century, the Charles Miller homestead was one of the finest country Federal-era farmhouses ever constructed in the town. It contained a pleasing front doorway that had five carved sunbursts over the transom, and the cornice below the box-line gutter contained a row of sunbursts and quarter fans. The prosperous farm descended to the Denniston family, who operated a successful dairy. A campaign was initiated during the summer of 1993 to relocate this important landmark; however, due to lack of interest, the house was demolished during the winter of 1993–94. The site has been vacant ever since.

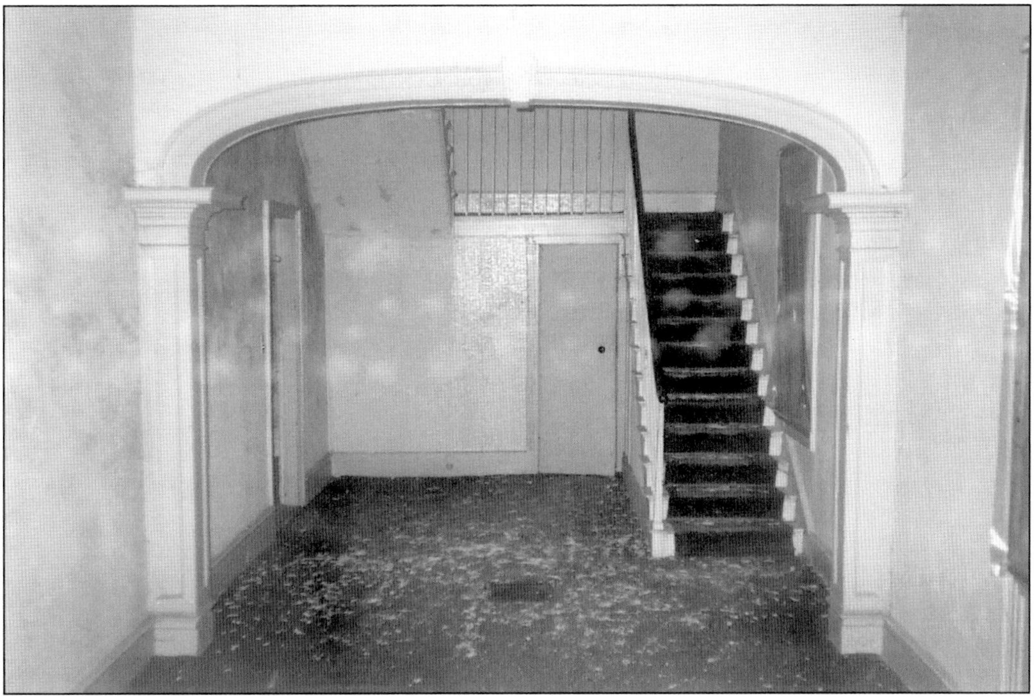

Nearly all of the authentic interior woodwork survived at the Miller homestead. The spacious first-floor hallway was divided by a keystone arch, and a stairway was located in the rear half of the hall. The stairway contained cherry handrails and newel posts that wrapped around from the first floor to the attic. A central chimney provided warmth from its four fireplaces and large hearth with crane and beehive oven, located in the rear wing.

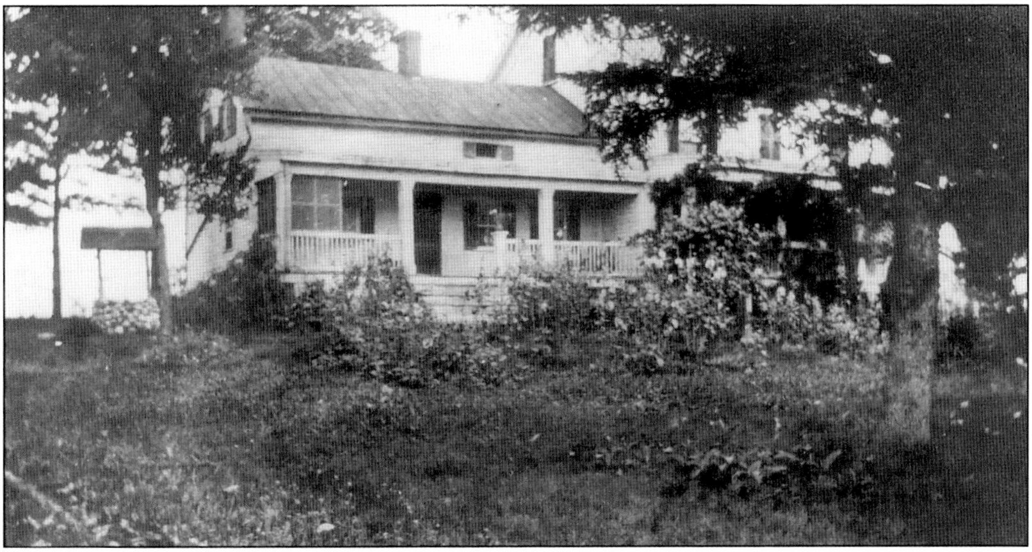

The Van Alst homestead stood on Neelytown Road, opposite Hi-Tech Repair Inc. It may have been built in the mid-19th century for Ebeneazer Van Alst. The house was destroyed by fire some years ago, and only its foundation and chimney survive as a tangible reminder of this once prosperous farmstead. The ruins, somewhat concealed by vines and trees, are visible from the road in the winter months. This photograph dates from 1910, when the house was in its prime.

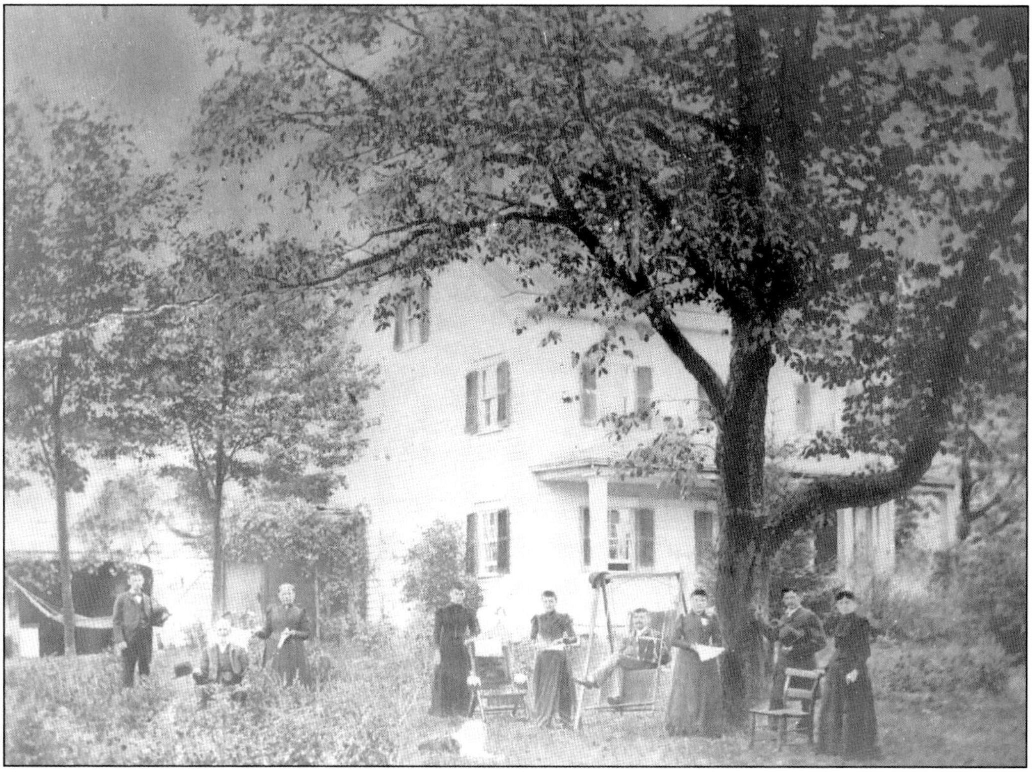

The Warren homestead was located on Neelytown Road between the Van Alst place and the Charles Miller homestead. Identified as the residence of Philip D. Crist on the 1862 map of Montgomery, the house probably dated from the the early 1800s. It vanished long ago, and the site was left a vacant field.

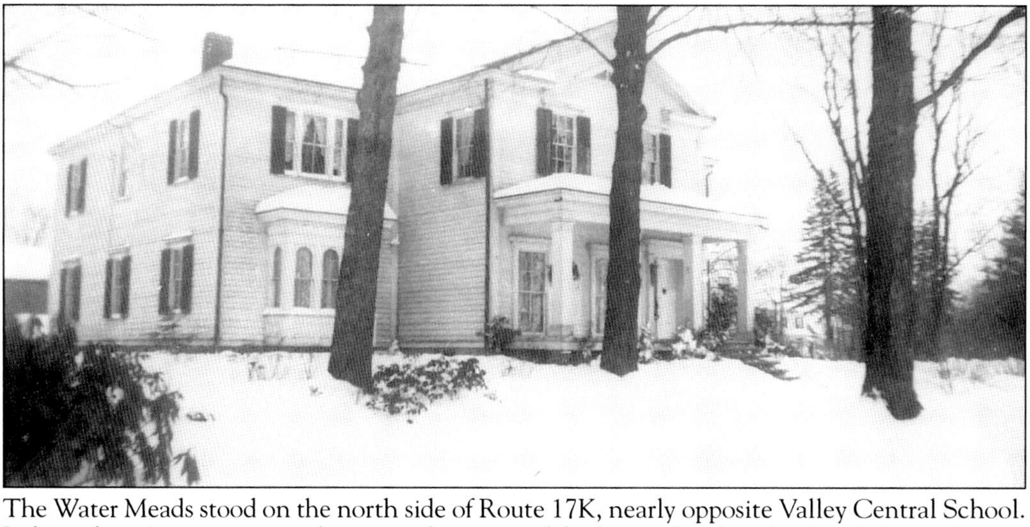

The Water Meads stood on the north side of Route 17K, nearly opposite Valley Central School. Judging from its appearance, the original portion of the house dated to the Greek Revival era—about 1840. The house was apparently updated during the Victorian era. In 1862, Matthew Newkirk, a descendant of one of the early Montgomery families, lived in this stylish residence. The house was destroyed some years later by fire; only the foundation remains.

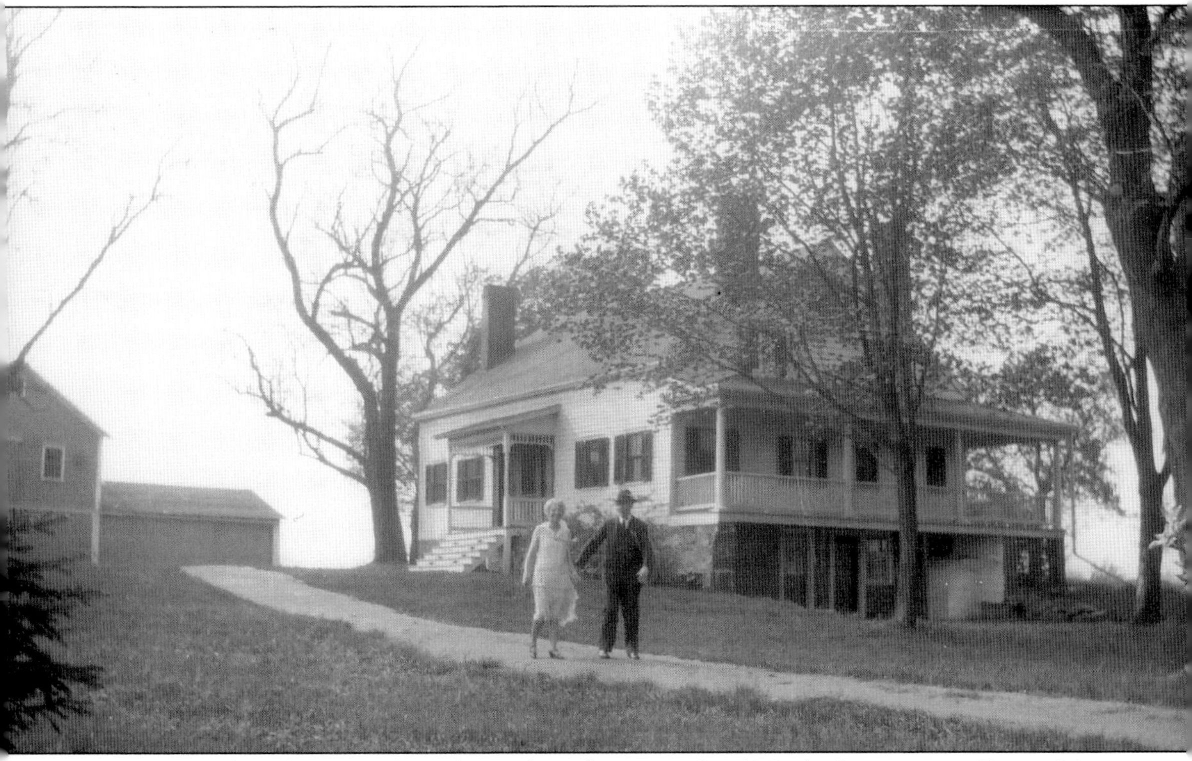

The Lewis Hawkins homestead was located on the west side of Maple Avenue, near Route 84. Family tradition holds that Lewis's father, Jonathan, purchased the farm in 1845 for Lewis and his bride, Mary Blake. Immediately after the purchase, this Greek Revival-era house was built. The farm remained in the family for well over a century. Eventually, the house was destroyed by fire. The foundation and surrounding stone walls have remained well preserved, but are scheduled for demolition. This photograph was taken in the 1920s.

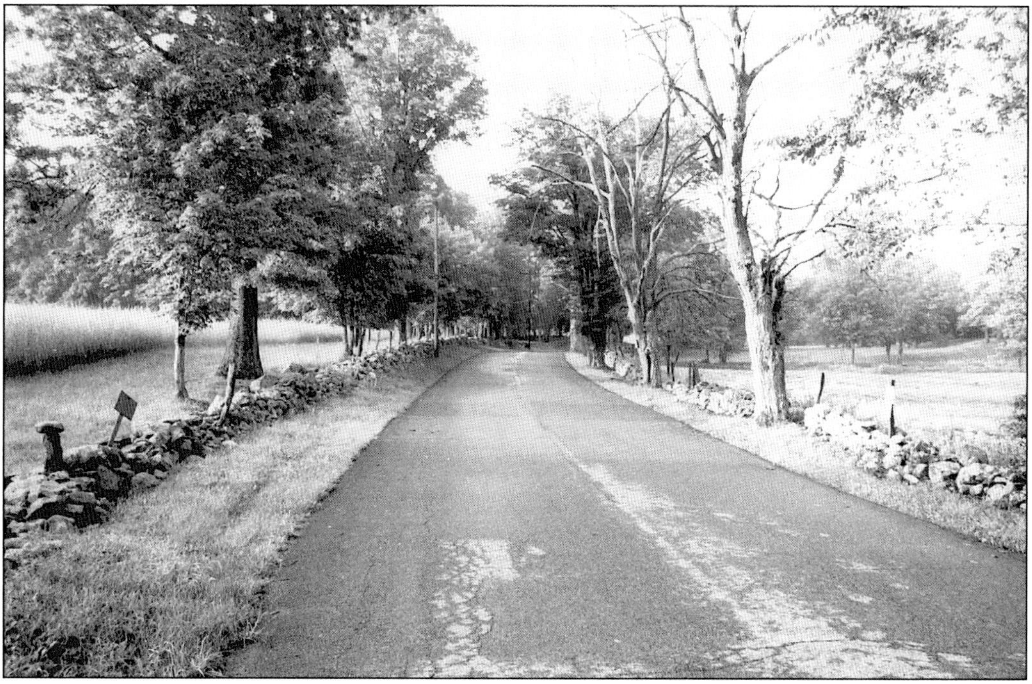

This scenic country lane is the south end of Maple Avenue, as it appeared recently. The whole area, which includes the White Tail Springs Farmhouse, is one of the most historical in the town and was originally part of the Colonial-era Colden Estate. A proposal to clear the entire site and build a warehouse complex was in the planning stages as this book was being written. Plans called for replacing the farmhouse and barns with a parking lot.

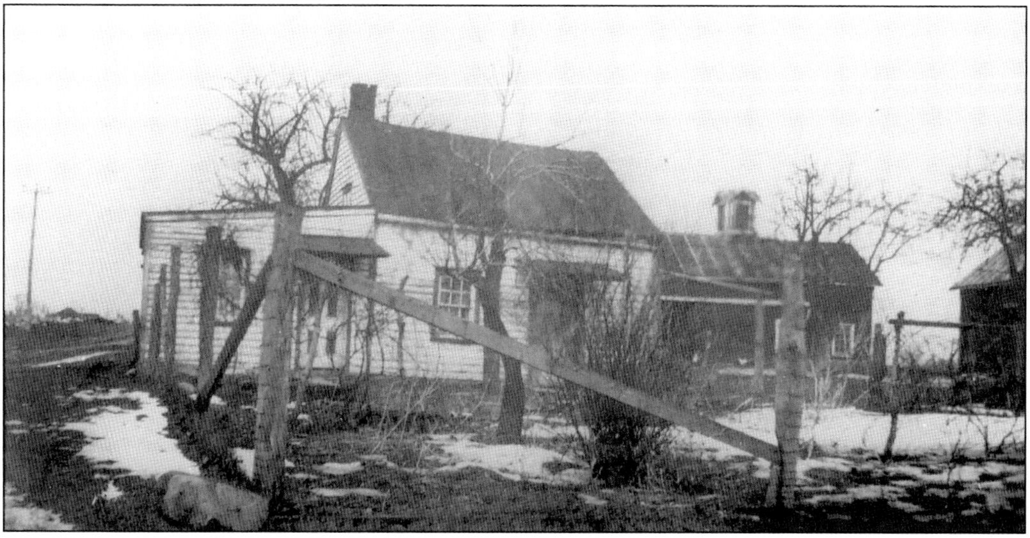

Not everyone was fortunate enough to live in a large house. This tiny dwelling was located on the south corner of Searsville Road and Willow Lane. Its date of construction remains a mystery, but it may date to the mid-19th century. The 1862 map records the name of H.D. Copley as associated with the site. Mueller's 1903 *Atlas of Orange County* shows the house as standing on a 1-acre parcel belonging to S.E. Thompson. A more recent house now stands on the site.

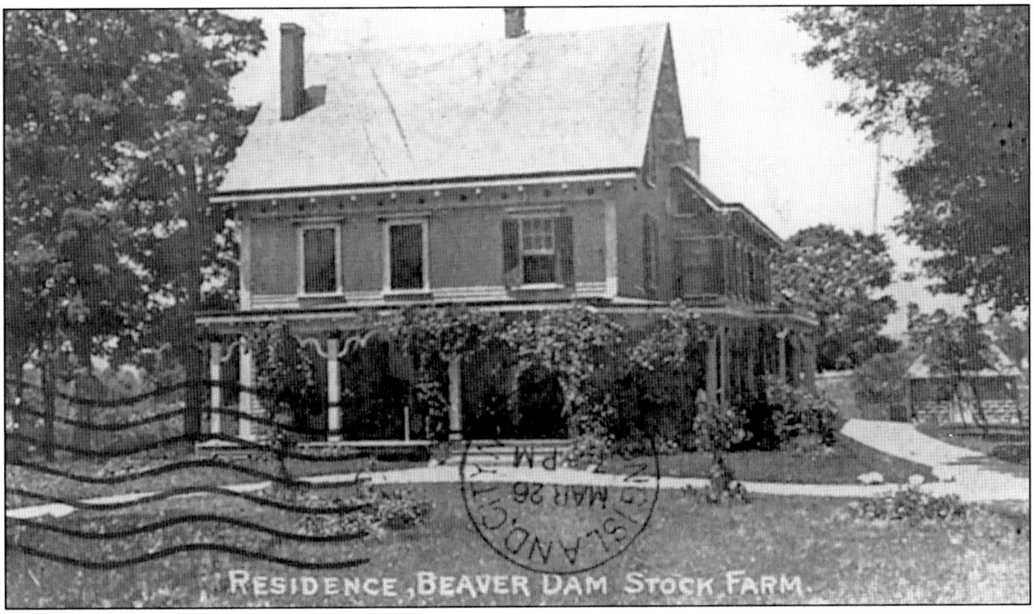

The mansion at Beaver Dam Stock Farm was one of the finest homes ever built in the town of Montgomery. The front block of the house was the oldest, dating from the 1830s. John Quackenbos added the two-story rear wing when he owned the house in the 1860s. John Covert purchased the farm from Quakenbos, and it is thought that he added the square tower, which featured a paneled chestnut staircase extending from basement to attic. Julius Schmid bought the farm shortly after 1900, and under his ownership, the house and farm flourished.

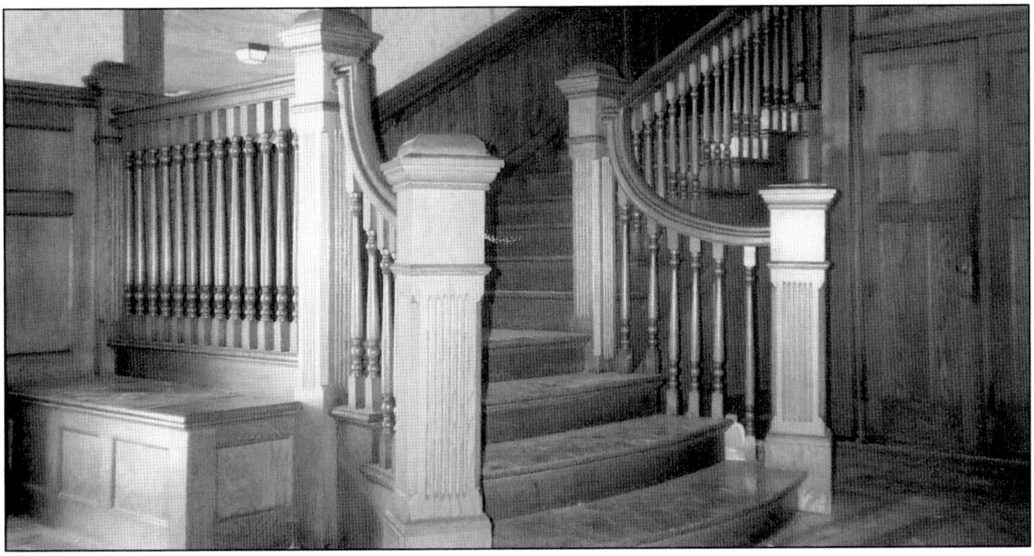

A formal dining room was added during the Schmid ownership. The room featured oak wainscoting, a massive oak mantelpiece with carved lions' heads, stained-glass windows, and, suspended from the ceiling, a Tiffany-style stained-glass chandelier. The upper portion of the walls contained hand-painted wallpaper. A front hall library featured mahogany bookcases and paneled wainscoting. The main stairway was finished in oak, and the surrounding walls contained oak-paneled wainscoting. A bronze statue on the newel post supported a light fixture.

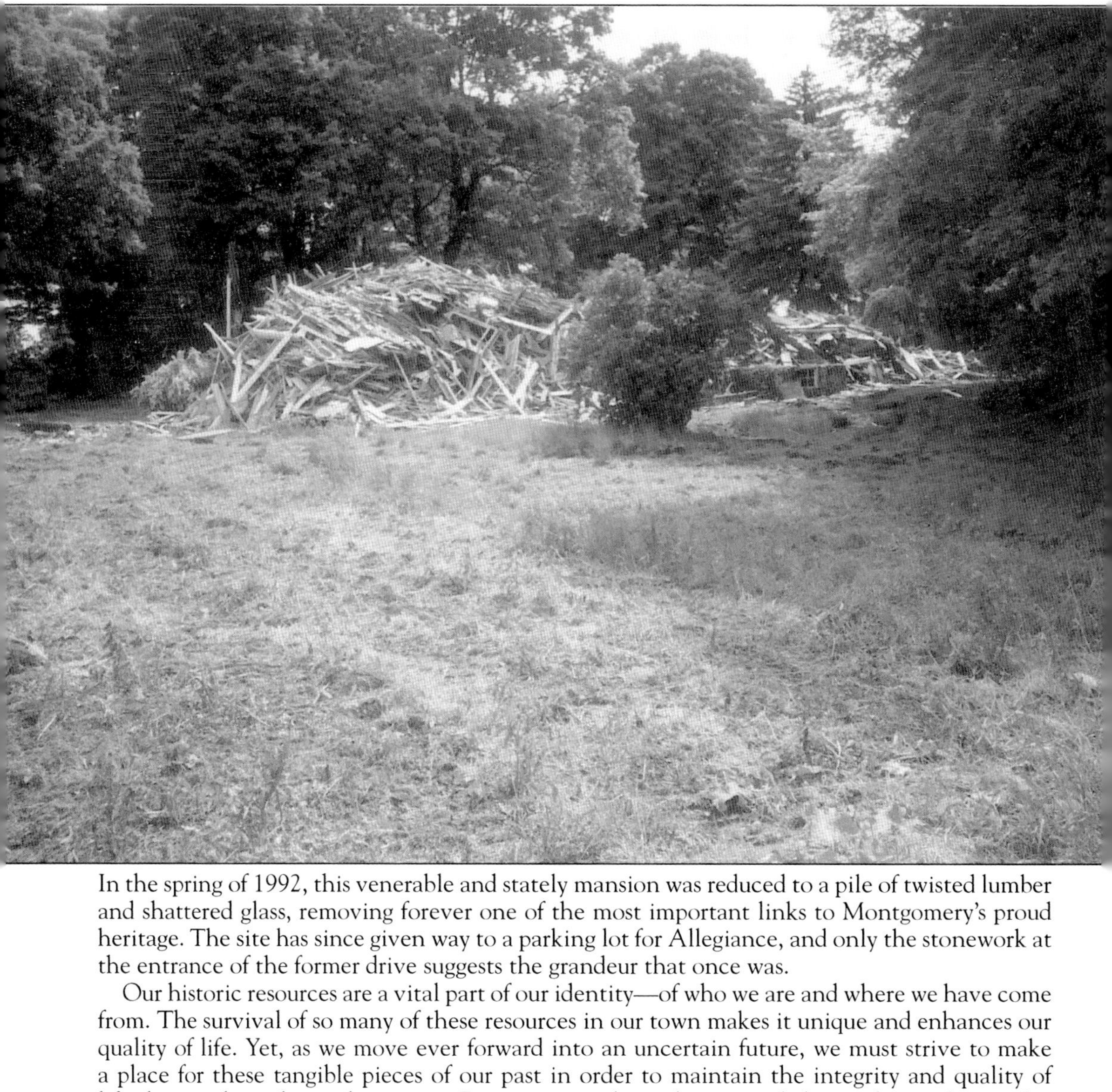

In the spring of 1992, this venerable and stately mansion was reduced to a pile of twisted lumber and shattered glass, removing forever one of the most important links to Montgomery's proud heritage. The site has since given way to a parking lot for Allegiance, and only the stonework at the entrance of the former drive suggests the grandeur that once was.

Our historic resources are a vital part of our identity—of who we are and where we have come from. The survival of so many of these resources in our town makes it unique and enhances our quality of life. Yet, as we move ever forward into an uncertain future, we must strive to make a place for these tangible pieces of our past in order to maintain the integrity and quality of life that we have learned to enjoy. Bigger is not always better, and the seeds we plant today will provide the crops we harvest tomorrow. Making a commitment to preserve what makes us unique will ensure a bright future for the town of Montgomery.